PAX TOKUGAWANA

JAPAN LIBRARY

PAX TOKUGAWANA
The Cultural Flowering of Japan, 1603–1853

Haga Tōru

Translated by
Juliet Winters Carpenter

Japan Publishing Industry Foundation for Culture

Notes to readers

Japanese names are written surname first. Endnotes are by the translator unless marked "AN" (Author's Note). Romanization generally follows the traditional Hepburn system, using "m" before labial consonants (b, p, m), except where established proper nouns follow the modified system. Japanese words that have been naturalized in English, appearing in *Merriam-Webster's Collegiate Dictionary*, are not italicized and do not have macrons to mark long sounds. Plurals of Japanese words, whether naturalized or not, are not marked with an "s."

Pax Tokugawana: The Cultural Flowering of Japan, 1603–1853
Haga Tōru. Translated by Juliet Winters Carpenter.

Published by
Japan Publishing Industry Foundation for Culture (JPIC)
2-2-30 Kanda-Jinbocho, Chiyoda-ku, Tokyo 101-0051, Japan

First English edition: March 2021

This book is a translation of *Bunmei toshite no Tokugawa Nihon: 1603–1853 nen*, which was originally published in Japanese by Chikumashobo Ltd. in 2017. English publishing rights arranged with Chikumashobo Ltd., Tokyo.

Book design: alema Co., Ltd.

Printed in Japan
ISBN 978-4-86658-148-4
https://japanlibrary.jpic.or.jp/

CONTENTS

TOKUGAWA JAPAN AS A MODEL FOR THE WORLD:
The Past as Prologue

Haga Mitsuru*
Professor, Tohoku University

"A Fully Formed, Unique Civilization"

The Pax Tokugawana and the Pax Romana undoubtedly differed in their territorial expanses, food supply, and reliance on slavery, among other things, but in the maturity of their civilizations and the influence of those civilizations on the modern world they were similar. Ancient Roman civilization was the culmination of the Ancient Western Asian world, succeeding the Old Testament Judaism of Ancient Western Asia and Hellenism. Tokugawa Japan was likewise the culmination of civilization in the Japanese archipelago, and more: as "a fully formed, unique civilization," it is a beacon for the world hereafter. This book makes that abundantly clear.

The Position of Japan:
"Girdled by Waves" on the Eastern Edge of the Eurasian Continent

Japan's long, sustained peace is due mainly to its fortuitous position as an island nation protected from foreign invasion by the encircling sea.

> A lightning flash—
> girdled by waves
> the isles of Japan
> —Yosa Buson[1]

---

* Haga Mitsuru is the auther's son.

Japan was also fortunate to be located in the monsoon belt, with plenty of vegetation and an abundance of animals, fish and shellfish, and nuts for nourishment. In another haiku by Yosa Buson (1716–1784), a pot of savory stew is emblematic of the long peace and cultural ripening that took place in Tokugawa Japan (Chapter 12):

> Buried embers—
> finally simmering
> the stew in the pot

In fact, the history of clay stewpots in Japan goes back all the way to the Jōmon period (14,000–300 BCE), when they were used to boil acorns and other nuts that were too hard to eat raw. Japanese culture simmered for a very long time indeed.

Japan's position on the eastern edge of the Eurasian continent was beneficial culturally too. By the late Paleolithic period, around 50,000 years ago, the "races" were settled on four continents in a distribution that was to remain basically constant. Only in Eurasia did two different races occupy the same continent, enabling Caucasoid-Mongoloid interaction. Moreover, the Eurasian continent stretched far across the same latitude, facilitating the transmission of cultivated plants, livestock, and culture. Exchange between the civilization of the West and the civilization of the East took place naturally. Japan, separated by the sea from the eastern edge of the continent, was able to absorb the fruits of that cultural exchange as it wished, while enjoying security and peace.

The Significance of Japan:
An Object Lesson in Relativity and Sustainable Peace

Of what global significance is Japan? In *Gulliver's Travels* by Jonathan Swift (1726), Gulliver finds himself a giant in a land of small people, a tiny person in a land of big people, and a mortal in a land of immortals; in the land of noble, intelligent equines, he resembles the sinister, despicable Yahoos. In other words, the story rejects absolutism in favor of relativity. In the age of imperialism and colonialism, the novel served as a vehicle of self-criticism with its mentions of "remote" foreign lands. (The original title was *Travels into Several Remote Nations of the World, in Four Parts, By Lemuel Gulliver, First a Surgeon, and then a Captain of Several Ships.*) Of all the lands visited by Gulliver, Tokugawa Japan is the only one that actually existed. Located not in the West but the Far East, non-Christian yet civilized, Japan was an object lesson in relativity. This was the significance of Japanese civilization, at least vis-à-vis the West.

What then is the significance of Japanese civilization in the broader context of world history? It is not a particularly ancient civilization, nor does it boast vast territory. Japan has not impacted the world as much as Chinese civilization, the British Magna Carta, the French Revolution, or American Coca-Cola. Rather, the historical significance of Japanese civilization, particularly in the modern world, lies in its long-lasting peace. Japan has never had an out-and-out civil war. The Meiji Restoration was accomplished with virtually no bloodshed. Of the 126 Japanese emperors, not one was ever assassinated by a commoner. No Tokugawa shogun was ever killed. Japan has never had a revolution "decreed by heaven" to unseat an emperor for moral turpitude, as in China, nor anything like the French Revolution, glorified in a truly barbaric national anthem: "*Aux armes, citoyens/Formez vos bataillons/Marchons, marchons!/Qu'un sang impur/abreuve nos sillons!*" (To arms, citizens! Form your battalions. Let's march, let's march! That their impure blood should water our fields!) A dramatic revolution of such bloodthirstiness was never deemed acceptable in Japan or never became necessary there. Rather, peace was maintained through the mild, non-revolutionary will of the Japanese people. The lack of a "French Revolution" in Japanese history is a source of national pride.

As one example, the Shōsōin treasure house and its contents dating back to the year 756 have survived intact despite having no military protection. The Hyakugo Archives, originally housed in Tōji temple in Kyoto, is a collection of nearly twenty-five thousand documents spanning a millennium from the eighth to the eighteenth centuries, perfectly preserved in one hundred lidded wooden boxes. Not only were these cultural assets never seized or burned, they were well maintained even after they had ceased to be of use.

No walls ever surrounded the capital, where the emperor lived. The Japanese learned much from China, including urban planning, and modeled their cities after Chinese ones, but without city walls. Ur and other city-states of ancient Sumer were almost invariably ringed by walls, but Heian-kyō (present-day Kyoto) had none. The closest thing to a wall around the capital was the Odoi mound, an earthwork fortification built by Toyotomi Hideyoshi (1537–1598). Nijō Castle was not a military fort but the Kyoto residence of the Tokugawa shogun and a political stage for his dealings with the court.

Coupled with the dual political structure by which the imperial court possessed authority and the military government wielded power, the lack of a fort in the nation's capital is a point of Japanese pride. The preamble to the UNESCO constitution declares that "since wars begin in the minds of men, it is in the minds of men that the defenses of peace must be constructed," but Japanese authorities had no need of such defenses. Rather, they were gently supported by the Ritsuryō codes, established in the early eighth century, and by the culture that flourished during the Heian period (794–1185), including *waka* poetry, *The Tale of Genji* by Murasaki Shikibu, and *The Pillow Book* by Sei Shōnagon. The vision of the UNESCO constitution was realized long ago in Japan and attained full maturity in the Tokugawa period—a time when samurai government was at its peak. Herein lies the essence and the brilliance of the Pax Tokugawana.

The Anti-Fundamentalism of Japan: Diversity Rooted in the Absence of Absolutes

Japanese history resembles a long springtime on an island nation blessed with gentle natural conditions, lacking the severity of winter or the brutality of summer, conditions leading one to earnestly question the meaning of existence. Accordingly, Japan never created a world religion like the Abrahamic religions or Buddhism, and in a sense never quite attained the maturity of "adulthood" in the manner of the West, the Middle East, India, and China. Tsuji Nobuo, an eminent authority on Japanese art history, maintains that the core elements of Japanese art are *asobi* (playfulness), *kawaii* (cuteness), and *seishunsei* (youthfulness). This helps explain why General Douglas MacArthur likened the Japanese to "a boy of twelve."

Japan does not believe in absolute principles and has none. Japanese people neither expect their universals to apply to the world at large nor suppose that they should. Concerning global political, economic, and cultural systems, Japan borrowed first from China and then, beginning with the Meiji Restoration, the West. Because Japan simply adapts universals to conform to its cultural climate, the country's habits of mind could not be further from the fundamentalism that shakes the modern world.

This lack of fundamentalism is most starkly apparent in Japanese religious beliefs. The 2019 *Religion Almanac* put out by the Agency for Cultural Affairs breaks down the number of believers in various religions as follows:

Shinto	87,219,808
Buddhism	84,336,539
Christianity	1,921,484
Other	7,851,545
Total	181,329,376

The total population of Japan, however, is 126,443,300. In other words, many people believe in more than one religion; few, if any, believe in monotheistic fundamentalism. Are Japanese people extremely impious by nature or unusually pious?

In fact, in the course of a lifetime most Japanese people follow four faiths: for the birth of a child and various annual events, Shinto; for everyday ethics, Confucianism; for weddings, Christianity, as a cool brand of "culture"; and for funerals, Buddhism. The sacred is diverse. The humorous manga series *Saint Young Men* (*Seinto oniisan*) by Nakamura Hikaru follows the madcap adventures of Gautama Buddha and Jesus Christ as they share a vacation apartment in Tachikawa, Tokyo. Japan and perhaps India are the only countries in the world where this sort of playful depiction of the sacred is allowed without someone getting killed. It is fitting that this manga was displayed in the Japanese Department of the British Museum as an introduction to Japanese civilization. This anti-fundamentalism of Japan (Chapter 15) offers a useful suggestion for managing long stretches of peace hereafter.

Tackling the Boredom of Peace: An Urgent Task for Today's World

Lassitude was the prevailing mood in Tokugawa Japan.

> Spring sea—
> all day long the waves
> gently rise and fall

Even the cultural stimulation of Korean embassies slowly disappeared.

> The Korean ship,
> not stopping, passes on
> into the mist

There was a sense of something missing, of things leaking and dissolving.

> Fading spring—
> glasses that don't suit my eyes
> have disappeared

> Washing my feet
> in a leaky tub, the water
> running out like fading spring

> Spring rain—
> someone lives there now, and smoke
> rises over the wall

At the same time, there was a sense of untidy beauty.

> Indifferent and languid
> I burn incense
> this spring evening

Straw sandals
that trampled blossoms—
sleeping late

The mood could be dreamy.

Fading spring—
the lute in my arms
feels heavy

Amid it all was a sweet, pervasive sense of loss...

On a walk
I come to the end
of this last day of spring

...as civilization slowly matured.

Buried embers—
finally simmering
the stew in the pot

Generally speaking, peace and happiness are uninteresting. Languid peace is boring and tedious. War, by contrast, is exciting and fun. Sculptures of dying warriors in the Temple of Aphaia on the island of Aegina wear archaic smiles, radiant with life, because in the moment of death the fulfillment and pleasure of life are felt most strongly.

This being so, the peace-loving, developed nations of the world need to learn above all else how to cope with the boredom of peace. We need to find ways for people to overcome tedium without resorting to the stirring entertainment of war to give meaning to their lives. As this book shows, Tokugawa Japan can teach us how to deal with the tiresome happiness of a long peace.

The German adventurer Heinrich Schliemann (1822–1890) came up with an apt description of the peaceful maturity that Tokugawa Japan attained. A successful businessman in the early stages of his career, Schliemann later became a successful archaeologist, discovering and excavating Troy and other sites. In between, he traveled to the Far East for pleasure and visited late Tokugawa Japan in 1865. Although he stayed only a month, he made this penetrating observation: "Here we see peace, general contentment, abundance, the greatest order, and a nation of more perfect cultivation than in any other country in the world."[2] Schliemann came to understand the reason for the abundance that touched the lives of people in every corner of Tokugawa Japan. Widespread contentment, not happiness for a few, creates the well-cultivated soil that is the foundation of lasting peace. An egalitarian, merit-based system; the ability to find happiness in small things, to "appreciate having enough and be satisfied with one's circumstances," as the saying went: this was the everyday wisdom of Tokugawa Japan.

Egalitarianism: The Modernity of Tokugawa Japan

Both in society and within the home, the Tokugawa period had a strict class system that made inequality acceptable. At the same time, however, there was a merit system. The standard for measuring ability in the cultural sphere—crafts, performing arts, literature, and fine arts— lay outside the class system. Achievements in those fields were highly esteemed even if they lacked direct benefit or utilitarian value, as this book's discussions of Izumo no Okuni, Kōetsu, Sōtatsu, Bashō, Buson, and many other artists and poets make clear. Daimyo from around the country met in Edo Castle to show each other illustrated catalogues of natural history from their respective domains, an interest shared by scholars, artists, and countless ordinary people. Everyone, high and low, freely enjoying the same activities: that is the true meaning of Tokugawa peace. In that environment, no one was arrogant merely because of their social status; social divisions existed, yes, but those above did not despise those below, and those below had little hatred for those above. In that limited sense, there was a modern spirit of egalitarianism in Tokugawa society.

The album *Clean Sweep: Myriad Aspects* (*Issō hyakutai*) consists of sketches of Edo life by Watanabe Kazan (1793–1841), a samurai painter whose criticisms of the government led to his house arrest and eventual suicide (Chapter 17). Kazan, who was well acquainted with the world outside Japan and highly conscious of his elite status, produced vivid sketches of the gestures and expressions of goldfish sellers and other townsfolk. If egalitarianism is too strong a word, we can say he worked with a smile of empathy for all his contemporaries.

"Lingering" in Tokugawa Japan

In Japan's red-light districts, the practice of staying on and enjoying oneself for days on end was known as "lingering" (*itsuzuke*) or the less elegant "soaking in pleasure" (*ibitare asobi*). It is satirically referred to in the poetry anthology *Haifū yanagidaru*,[3] where "early-morning snow" often provides the excuse for lingering. This is another aspect of the peace in Tokugawa Japan, which maintained its policy of cozy seclusion as the rest of the world evolved, "lingering" on a national scale.

By the reign of Iemitsu, the third Tokugawa shogun, European countries had created the 1648 Peace of Westphalia, which established sovereign states guaranteeing freedom of religion and represented a step toward an international community. The tumultuous French Revolution came just five years after Buson's death in 1784. Through such means, Europe formed nation-states possessing sovereignty, a community of citizens identifying as a nation, and clear borders. Meanwhile in Japan, the tenth shogun, Ieharu, pursued amusement, while "Tanuma culture" in the time of Senior Counselor Tanuma Okitsugu produced a rococo beauty of "splendor and uncertainty". Although Matsudaira Sadanobu, the senior counselor under the eleventh shogun, Ienari, sensed the threat from Russia and other countries, the enormous upheaval of the French Revolution kept the Great Powers from attacking Japan. And so for roughly the first quarter of the nineteenth century, Japan was able to "linger" on and on, pleasurably stretching out the last days of halcyon peace in the Pax Tokugawana (Chapter 16).

Secluded though it was, Tokugawa Japan was by no means a "frog in a well." Lively curiosity about things from the West is demonstrated in the way the painter Tani Bunchō, Matsudaira Sadanobu's close attendant, drew the rhinoceros immortalized by Albrecht Dürer, which had wandered from East to West and back again (Chapter 11).

Tokugawa Japan is also important because it did not suddenly end with the demise of the Tokugawa shogunate. Historians generally teach the ways that each new era marks a severance with the past, but it is the continuities that are of pivotal importance. In the Tokugawa period, a nationwide "literary public sphere" was formed through the system of domain schools and the Shogunal National Academy, so that the shogun was surrounded by designated "official authorities." Broadly speaking, those authorities included the artistic and cultural circles involved in producing studies in natural history such as the richly illustrated *Album of Fish* (*Shūrin-zu*).[4] This intellectual network provided a forum for discussion, a practice that was continued in the Meiji era and broadened to "public discussion," as laid down in the first article of the Charter Oath of 1868: "Deliberative assemblies shall be established on an extensive scale, and all governmental matters shall be determined by public discussion." Mori Ōgai's (1862–1922) biographies of Tokugawa-period intellectuals who specialized in Chinese medicine—*Shibue Chūsai, Izawa Ranken*, and *Hōjō Katei*—paint a detailed description of the inner workings of intellectual communities that continued from Tokugawa times into Meiji.

Tokugawa Japan was the beginning of modern Japan. Kaibara Ekiken's *Japanese Herbal* (*Yamato honzō*, 1708) displays the spirit of source criticism found in modern science (Chapter 8), and *Ten Kinds of Collected Antiquities* (*Shūko jisshu*, 1800), a survey of old cultural assets undertaken by Matsudaira Sadanobu and Tani Bunchō, was the beginning of museology and art history in Japan. Museums were a means of colonial domination by the Great Powers, but Japan alone was able to construct them on its own.

In this way, as Fukuzawa Yukichi and Shimazaki Tōson made clear (Chapter 17), the Meiji era grew organically from the Tokugawa period. The transition took place with ideological and cultural continuity. Although the Meiji Restoration did bring enormous change to Japan's political system, the country maintained its identity thereafter thanks to seeds planted in Tokugawa Japan.

Pax Romana and the Peace of Hegemony:
Relativization of the West in the Modern World

From Meiji on, Japan's early modern era was a desperate struggle to acquire Western knowledge and technology in order to guarantee the country's survival. Today, however, at least in principle, countries around the world neither seek identification with the West nor define themselves by their closeness to the West. Certainly the world is overrun with Coca-Cola and McDonald's, but for non-Western countries and cultures, becoming "franchise stores" of the West is no longer the goal.

The Altamira and Lascaux cave paintings, dating from around 15,000–2,000 BCE, have long been regarded as the starting-point of expressions of human creativity, while the professor of paleoanthropology Suwa Gen has shown that Acheulean stone tools produced by *Homo erectus* at Konso in Ethiopia, dating back 1.75 million years, are the oldest to show design: that is, to be shaped to a preconceived form. This is the first known instance of artistic expression in human history. And the recent discovery on the Indonesian island of Sulawesi of a cave painting 43,900 years old shows that the capacity for high-level creative abstract thought did not originate only in the West.[5]

The relativization of Ancient Western Asia, the biblical origin of Western civilization, is also progressing. It is now widely recognized that agriculture did not develop worldwide from the single origin of seed propagation in Western Asia's Fertile Crescent over 10,000 years ago but rather had multiple origins around the world that included vegetative propagation.

Viewing Eurasia as a whole, Europe is merely a peninsula on the western extremity of the continent, and from protohistoric times, civilization, in the East was always the most advanced. Urban civilization arose in Mesopotamia, and in the late Iron Age, the First Babylonian Empire, the Neo-Assyrian Empire, and the Achaemenid (First Persian) Empire flourished as apexes of comprehensive governance systems including multiple peoples, languages, cultures, and faiths. Greek civilization, which finally makes an appearance around this time, was backward, lagging far behind. The relative vitality of East and West only switched places around the Battle of Vienna in 1683, which marked the beginning of the end of Turkish domination in Eastern Europe.

The campaigns of Alexander the Great (334–324 BCE) served to promote further East-West cultural exchange. From the conventional Hellenistic point of view, the diffusion of Greek civilization flowed like water from the heights of the West to the lowlands of the East. However, the East acquired thorough knowledge of Greek mythology and art and absorbed the Greek gods on their own in an exclusive and selective manner, incorporating them into Buddhist art. The power and individuality of the East deserve recognition.

When human "races" settled on the four continents in the late Paleolithic period, Caucasoid Westerners lived only in the western portion of the Eurasian continent. But then they "discovered" a new continent in the New World, incorporated it into the West, and transported Negroid people there as slaves. With production by slave labor on plantations as the driving force, a commercial revolution then took place that resulted in the establishment in modern society of a Western way of life. The "Black Lives Matter" movement represents a recent backlash.

Closeness to the West, or to the authoritarian, modern Western knowledge that might be called an indirect cause of the Fukushima nuclear accident, is no longer a universal standard.

Ancient Western Asia has traditionally been taken as providing the basic pattern for the formation and development of civilization. The onset of agriculture created a stable food supply, which in turn created social surplus and the accumulation of reserves, followed by the emergence of a hierarchical society, cities, and religious institutions. This pattern might be called "Well fed, well bred," in that cultural refinements arose only after basic human needs were met. It is the pattern for the development of Western-style civilizations that culminated in ancient Rome. Byron's "Roman holiday,"[6] supported by slavery, is synonymous with the Pax Romana as the apogee of vertical societies that emerged in urban civilizations in Ancient Western Asia.

Elsewhere in the world, civilization evolved differently. In the ancient

Andes, settlements for raising crops appeared more or less synchronously with ritual buildings. In other words, religious spaces were set aside before agricultural settlements thrived, while people were still struggling to feed themselves. The community lacked earthenware and was of course not yet established as a nation, yet they even held temple renewal festivals. This pattern, where elaborate temples and a wealth of burial properties precede the achievement of economic stability, might be called "Well bred, well fed." It is a non-Western-Asian model of the development of civilization.

Amid the rise in contrasting, diverse models for the formation of civilization, experts point out that modern society is becoming increasingly smaller, denser, and more limited in resources.[7] There is widespread awareness of trends including exponential population growth, revolutionary advances in information technology, the disappearance of the East-West binary, and the rapid development of China and Korea, as well as the fragility of our Earth as seen in global warming and other forms of climate change. Amid these transformations, our view of the Pax Romana also has changed.

Rome's power began in isolation. But after the unification of the Italian Peninsula, Rome destroyed Carthage, which had dominated the western Mediterranean from its base in Africa, and then took over the eastern half of the Mediterranean, consolidating its grip on the Mediterranean with the death of Cleopatra in 30 BCE. The Roman Empire gained its maximum territory during the reign of the emperor Trajan, the second of the Five Good Emperors who ruled when the Pax Romana was in its glory. That peace was won, in short, by military might. The same is true of the Pax Britannica.

The Pax Romana seems irrelevant today, now that imperialism has been repudiated and the world is steadily shrinking. (Even in the field of culture, the age when majestic "central imperial museums" like the British Museum could be constructed in the center of an imperial capital is over; nowadays an online virtual museum would be the best way to display diverse collections in an easily accessible format.) It is rather the Pax Tokugawana, achieved in the laboratory of a small island nation in the Far East, that has universality and can serve as a model for the future world.

From Pax Romana to Pax Tokugawana: The Shape of Civilization to Come

In his essay "In Praise of Shadows" (*In'ei raisan*), novelist Tanizaki Jun'ichirō (1886–1965) wrote:

> I always think how different everything would be if we in the Orient had developed our own science.... [T]his could not but have had profound influence upon the conduct of our everyday lives.... The Orient quite conceivably could have opened up a world of technology entirely its own.[8]

He ends his musing by saying "these are the empty dreams of a novelist."

With conditions today increasingly dire, we naturally consider how our civilization will develop in the future; at such times, Tokugawa Japan becomes a mine of wisdom for the modern world. It has much to teach us about how a civilization can develop "a world...entirely its own." This is of immense significance and not a historian's empty dream.

Thinking of art as a visual philosophy, I would like to follow the lead of this book in drawing attention to the screen painting *Enjoying the Evening Cool under an Evening Glory Trellis* (*Yūgaodana nōryō-zu*) by Kusumi Morikage (cover illustration, Figure 34) as a work that shows a path ahead for civilization. It shows how wonderful a life of modest pleasure can be. The figures in the painting live in a fragile, impermanent home made from vegetation; after bathing, they sit together under a trellis laced with plants, enjoying the evening cool with the moon for company and sharing this earthly happiness with one another (Chapter 11).

The Apadana Palace of Persepolis in the Achaemenid Empire of ancient Persia contained bas-reliefs of messengers bringing tribute from all over the empire, to proclaim and enhance the glory of the emperor. It is said that Alexander the Great, having conquered Babylon, got drunk and let a hetaera set fire to the palace. Centuries later, the destruction of the World Trade Center in New York was likewise a way of destroying the prestige of an enemy empire. Building on the example of the Parthenon, which has symbolized the subjugation of the Achaemenid Empire since the fifth century BCE, the Pantheon, a symbol of imperial rule, has stood since the second century with a rotunda measuring 43.4 meters in diameter.

Kusumi Morikage's painting is the antithesis of the Pax Romana with its accumulation of stone buildings. Nowhere in the painting is there anything like a Roman palace, temple, or grand monument. Tokugawa Japan is the equivalent of living in a small hut, the polar opposite of the Palace of Versailles, say, or China's gorgeous Epang Palace.[9] Nothing in the painting, not even the moon, is unchanging or eternal. And that's fine. The human happiness depicted is not outsized, but human-sized.

While his movements were incomparably smaller in scale than those of Alexander the Great, Bashō too spent his life traveling, but Buson, in contrast, found meaning and beauty in *casanier* or confinement. Buson's poetic world, where there is beauty even in untidiness, lacks a dynamic aesthetic and offers no world religion or system of ethics. It is a lonely world, wide yet dense, of such depth that time seems to waver back and forth.

A pile of glowing coals buried in ashes, inside a small house representing the legendary Peach Blossom Spring, at the end of an alleyway in a corner of the eighteenth-century capital: this is Buson's template for a maturing civilization. His vision has none of the grandeur or the vast territorial reach of a Pax Romana. Pax Tokugawana is indeed quite the opposite of Pax Romana.

> Narrow alleyway
> leading to Peach Blossom Spring—
> winter confinement

> Buried embers—
> my hermitage too
> buried in snow

Inside his hideout at the end of the alleyway, the poet finds a temporary escape from his duties.

Winter confinement—
playing hide-and-seek
from my wife and child too

Time turns back, returning him to childhood and the presence of his mother.

Buried embers—
seeing so clearly
myself at my mother's side

As he is caught up in nostalgia, his very name is buried in the embers.

In buried embers
my name
fades away

Eventually, he finds value in the gradual simmering and mellowing of civilization.

Buried embers—
finally simmering
the stew in the pot

Not an empire, but a hut at the end of an alleyway, and in it the warm glow of buried embers; such a civilization has many lessons to offer the modern world.

None of this is to oppose advancing or evolving into new worlds, nor does it advocate hunkering down in social isolation—*hikikomori,* a word that has gained recent currency in English. *Homo sapiens* was able to replace *Homo neanderthalensis* because our greater power of innovation (continually renewing our "toolbox" of stone implements) gave us such adaptability that during the coldest time of the last ice age, we could advance even into the new world of a high-altitude frigid zone.

I would like to call for renewed focus on the richness of *casanier,* or stay-at-home, introspection. But nowadays people are under pressure to display creativity and uncover new knowledge for the sake of Pax Romana-style aggrandizement and development. This trend reflects the priorities and standards of universities, companies, and society at large. Certainly, it has brought about marvelous advances in science and technology. However, there is too much of a rush to start down new paths, as if waging a foreign campaign. Creativity in modern society has only the current generation in its sights and, far from causing the creator's name to "fade away," asserts rights and ownership while abdicating all responsibility for results. In a risk society in the age of trans-science, such shirking of responsibility imperils humanity's future. The Fukushima nuclear disaster brought this peril home. Surely a vision extending beyond the present generation and a character not seeking personal rewards but instead shouldering responsibility are of greatest importance now.

Not foreign conquest but introspection; not instant upgrades but slow maturation: these things are key. The sense of progress in another Buson haiku is tied to quiet, patient waiting, as sushi in the old *nare-zushi*[10] style slowly and deliciously ferments:

> In loneliness
> I spend the day worrying about
> how my sushi is coming along

With this gentle attitude, rather than anything so clearly defined as intergenerational ethics or a sense of obligation to future generations, one comes to feel that past and present are indistinguishable, that one is beyond the strictures of time and space:

> Slow spring days
> piling up, so far away
> the past

> New Year's kite
> the same place in the sky
> as yesterday

This view of life seeks change that is not reformist or revolutionary but visionary. As one gazes at the sky in a nostalgic mood, rapt and floating freely in time, the future ahead is not, as in the Pax Romana, a Last Judgment; rather, one is moving toward a completely different world, a "world entirely. . .its own," where the air at dawn is filled with the delicate scent and the faint white glow of blossoms.

> White plum blossoms
> emerging from the night
> at daybreak

Until that time, may the stew go on slowly simmering in the pot.

---

1 All haiku in the Foreword are by Buson.

2 AN: *La Chine et le Japon au temps présent* [Present-day China and Japan] (Paris: Librairie centrale, 1867), 141. (Translated from the French by JWC.)

3 Published in 165 volumes between 1765 and 1841. The title, meaning "Haikai-style willow tub," is taken from the compiler's pen name, Senryū ("river willow"), which became the name of this genre of short satirical verse.

4 The project, ordered by Lord Matsudaira Yoritaka of Takamatsu in Shikoku, was directed and organized by Hiraga Gennai (1728–1780). The final edition was produced in 1760–1762.

5 AN: Maxime Aubert et al., "Pleistocene Cave Art from Sulawesi, Indonesia," *Nature*, Oct. 8, 2014, 223–227. Ewen Callaway, "Is This Cave Painting Humanity's Oldest Story?" *Nature*, Dec. 11, 2019. https://www.nature.com/articles/d41586-019-03826-4

6 In his 1818 poem "Childe Harold's Pilgrimage," Lord Byron wrote of a gladiator who was "butcher'd to make a Roman holiday," referring to the practice of having gladiators fight to the death for the amusement of spectators.

7 AN: Johan Rockström et al., "A Safe Operating Space for Humanity," *Nature*, Sept. 23, 2009, 472–475.

8 Tanizaki Jun'ichirō, *In Praise of Shadows*, Thomas J. Harper and Edward G. Seidensticker, trans. (New Haven: Leete's Island Books, 1977).

9 A majestic palace in western Xi'an, Shaanxi province, built for Emperor Qin Shi Huang. Construction began in 212 BCE, but due to the emperor's death, only the front hall was completed. The palace was burned in 207 BCE.

10 An old-fashioned form of sushi, dating back to the eighth century. Fish were stuffed with salt and pickled in wooden barrels, then repacked with cooked rice to ferment in a process taking weeks or months.

AUTHOR'S INTRODUCTION:
The Changing Image of the Tokugawa Period

The nearly three centuries of Tokugawa rule are generally known in Japan as the "Edo period," since Edo was then the nation's capital; I, however, prefer "Tokugawa period." In English, the phrase "Edo Japan" is confusing, consisting as it does of consecutive place names. Perhaps for that reason, Japanologists in the English-speaking world were quick to adopt the term "Tokugawa Japan." Using the same terminology in Japanese as well would allow a more universal approach to the history of that period and have broader scope and freshness—or so it seems to me. "Tokugawa Japan" is concise and has a fine ring to it. Adopting that expression would also enable us to do away with a couple of unfortunate habits.

First is the habit of exaggerating the "Edo flavor" in speaking of the period; that is, giving Edo too much importance. All too often, the age has been narrowly defined by things like the tricolor kabuki curtain (vertical stripes of deep green, persimmon, and black); ukiyo-e and netsuke; spirited sons of Edo like the stock character, fishmonger Isshin Tasuke; and "*arinsu*," a word used by *oiran*, high-ranking courtesans in Edo's red-light district. As a consequence, the richness and surprising universality of broader Tokugawa culture are overlooked. Of course, the Edo leitmotivs mentioned are beautiful and fascinating in their own right. Overemphasizing them, however, is misguided. Partiality to Edo is apt to leave the rest of Tokugawa Japan confined to the dark. I am pleased to note that what I call "Edo gourmets," the connoisseurs of Edo flavor, have unquestionable love and respect for the old capital, but for better or worse their numbers are dwindling and their voices are fading.

The second habit is far more pernicious and deeply established. I refer to the tendency to look down on Tokugawa Japan as a dark, warped, and stunted "feudal society." This dismissive view of the Tokugawa period is what I call the "dark ages" or "before-the-dawn" historical perspective. It's not fair to blame author Shimazaki Tōson (1872–1943), but the title of his historical novel *Before the Dawn* (*Yoake mae*, 1929–1935) was just too good. The title took on a life of its own, creating the widespread and deep-seated impression that dawn came to Japan with the arrival of United States Commodore Perry's Black Ships in 1853 and the Meiji Restoration in 1868, preceded by dark and stifling night.

This misperception was of course not the fault of Tōson's novel alone, for the problem existed before and after Tōson. Beginning with the "civilization and enlightenment" view of history at the start of the Meiji era (1868–1911), followed by the Marxist view of history before and after the war in the Shōwa era (1926–1989), and on to postwar views of modernization, Tokugawa name-calling continued without letup in Japanese academic circles and the press. Accounts in middle- and high-school textbooks were tainted by such views. These accounts and the pervasive image created by Tōson's book amplified one another, painting Tokugawa history in yet darker, gloomier tones. This led to the conclusion that, unlike the shining histories of popular revolution and democracy in Britain, France, and the United States, the modernization of Japan suffered severe delays, distortions, and setbacks because of the heavy residue of feudalism and the emperor system. From prewar days until just recently, Japanese historians debated in all seriousness whether the Meiji Restoration, having failed to purge Japan of those undesirable remnants of its past, was an "absolutist revolution" or a "bourgeois revolution" after all. By arguing peevishly about such concepts, these Japanese scholars struggled to fit Japan's experience into a Western framework. It seems strange that even today those debates still echo in my ears.

The Japanese history books by Japanese historians that I encountered in college and graduate school all took the position that the Western route to modernity was the ideal. They disparaged the modernization of Japan, charging it with "setbacks" and "limitations." Japanese scholars ignored their own limited approaches and looked down at the nation's history from a lofty vantage point indeed. I completely sympathized with Tokugawa Japan, the victim of their denunciations, and with the people of that time, whom populist Japanese history treated like animals crawling in the dust, lifelong strangers to laughter. Forgive my odd comparison, but in such accounts, Tokugawa Japan became something like the yawning communal grave at the end of the film *Amadeus*. Like Mozart's mortal remains, the "evils" of Japanese modernity were bagged and dumped into the pit in freezing rain.

And so when, half a century ago, my research took me from the Meiji era through Western studies back into the Tokugawa period, I felt vaguely guilty, as if I were stumbling into a dim, dark world or some kind of swamp. The discoveries I made were all the more thrilling, all the more fascinating to me as a result. Whether because of the Japanese historians' political ideology or because of their complex regarding the West, the "before-the-dawn" historical perspective was entirely too narrow-minded. Such an approach lacked the human tolerance, the human magnanimity to place all of Tokugawa Japan, its isolationist policy and its shogunate-domain system included, in the wide expanse of world history; for this reason, those historians' approach could not provide context and perspective on the happiness and misery, the brightness and shadows of that time. While claiming to examine Tokugawa Japan in the light of "basic laws of world history," which had been provided by the West, Japanese scholars resented the failure of the history of an island nation in the Far East to follow those laws. They looked on the Tokugawa period as an aberration, and so after filling in local details, they accorded Tokugawa history special treatment because it did not fit into Western models. But why not reexamine the history of modern Japan as definitely a special case and use it to amend the supposed universality of the vaunted "basic laws"? Why forever compare Japan to other countries and never other countries to Japan? Albert M. Craig, an American scholar of Japanese history, once presented me with this challenge.

Looking back now, I have to say that liberal Japanese historians writing in the Taishō era (1911–1925), government-sponsored and otherwise, did a far better job of equating the Edo period with Tokugawa civilization; they were able to evaluate that period empathetically and with a more balanced approach, finally seeing that time as the "early modern" phase of Japanese history, not a time cut off from everything else. I am thinking of Uchida Ginzō, Tsuji Zennosuke, Tsuda Sōkichi, Muraoka Tsunetsugu, Kōda Shigetomo, Naitō Konan, Tokutomi Sohō, and Mori Senzō. Their immensely learned books continue to make fascinating reading, full of intellectual stimulation and suggestion as well as literary appeal. The historical biographies of Mori Ōgai (1862–1922) should of course be added to the list as well. Free in their approach, rich in their ideas, broad in their cultivation and outlook, and supple in their prose, such works are far superior to the atrocious writing of the later Marxist camp, which is rubbish.

Those Japanese scholars of the humanities stood fast against the increasingly dominant view that the Tokugawa period was Japan's dark ages. Then in the 1960s, *Studies in the Modernization of Japan* (1965–1971), a series of books by mainly American scholars, shook that negative view to the core. This composite work of leading scholars of Japanese history in the United States and Europe, including luminaries such as Edwin O. Reischauer, John Hall, Ronald Dore, Marius Jansen, and Donald Keene, took as its framework the broad comparative historical concept of "modernization," dragging Edo-period Japan into the light of world history and reconfiguring it as "Tokugawa Japan." That provocative series sent shock waves through academic circles in Japan. From that point on, both in Japan and abroad, the word "Tokugawa" began to carry an entirely different tone.

Looking back, however, I would say that the American-led research on the modernization of Japan, my own contribution included, placed value on or chiefly emphasized only those aspects of Tokugawa culture and society that enabled the "successes" of Meiji and beyond: the high level of education, for example, or the development of practical, rational thought, or the nurturing of a pool of able samurai bureaucrats. It seems to me that a single-track way of thinking was at work, a kind of utilitarianism that looked down from the heights of modernity and bestowed approval on whatever was close to being "modern."

Now that the 1960s have receded into the past, and we are in post-industrial, post-modern times, the early-modern age of Tokugawa Japan has taken on much greater depth and intimacy and seems also laden with much greater significance. Perhaps now for the first time we can approach Tokugawa Japan as a whole, including cultural products that may be totally unrelated to Japan's later highs and lows, as well as the tidbits beloved of the "Edo gourmets"—placing all in the context of world history.

Tokugawa history covers precisely 265 years, from 1603, when Ieyasu established a new government in Edo as the first Tokugawa shogun, until 1868, when under the fifteenth shogun, Yoshinobu, that government collapsed and the era name was changed to Meiji. It is unusual in world history for any political system to have such a clearly shaped beginning and end—"like a grilled fish served with head and tail intact," as the historian Ōishi Shinzaburō (1923–2004) humorously put it. During that long time span, Tokugawa civilization developed at a leisurely pace, ripening and eventually collapsing, all within the confines of the Japanese archipelago. Tokugawa Japan was a fully formed, unique civilization.

In the period between the Shimabara Rebellion of 1637–1638 all the way to the Boshin War of 1868, there was neither civil strife nor war with a foreign power—not even an insurgency or a religious conflict. The archipelago was full to the brim with peace and tranquility.

Perhaps these haiku by the Kyoto poet Yosa Buson, among others, can be seen as showing an awareness of the enduring peace of the Pax Tokugawana and illuminating the cultural maturation that took place during that halcyon time.

> Spring sea—
> all day long the waves
> gently rise and fall

> Mustard flowers—
> not even a whale comes by

as the sea darkens
Buried embers—
finally simmering
the stew in the pot

Our attention must focus less on the many individual products of Tokugawa civilization and more on historical processes. The entire Tokugawa period allows us to observe the interaction between culture and society and the process of absorbing foreign cultures; it is a vehicle for meditation on the philosophy of history and a suitable laboratory in which to study cultural dynamics. Furthermore, the Tokugawa period is a treasure house of data, a rich source of knowledge on enormous issues affecting world history, such as connections between the maintenance of long-term peace and the transformation of a nation's culture. Perhaps from now on that is where scholars will see Tokugawa Japan's significance in world history.

A Note from the Translator

These essays appeared separately in various publications over a span of nearly half a century. Professor Haga revised them for inclusion in this book, but they still retain the flavor of distinct essays, some covering the same topics from different perspectives; they always reflect his newest approach to his study of the Tokugawa period. This volume represents the culmination of Haga's Tokugawa research, but sadly, he died while it was being translated. I am honored to be able to carry out his wishes and introduce his final work to English-speaking readers.

Professor Haga, rejecting outright "the standard left-wing dismissal of the Tokugawa period as the dark ages," set out to show the creative benefits of those long centuries when Japan was isolated from the rest of the world. Here, with wide-ranging scholarship and immense enthusiasm, he highlights stunning achievements in painting, poetry, natural history, and other fields during that time—achievements made possible, he believes, by Japan's peaceful seclusion. He marvels at the never-ending curiosity of the artists and scholars he writes about, for they longed for knowledge and embraced innovation despite, or indeed because of, their limited resources.

Everyone will have a favorite topic here, but I especially recommend Haga's essay on the seventeenth-century hand scroll *Anthology with Crane Design*, a collaborative work by Tawaraya Sōtatsu and Hon'ami Kōetsu (Chapter 3). I feel sure that readers will never look at cranes in the same way again.

—JWC

Part

I

1 | *RAKUCHŪ RAKUGAI-ZU*:
PAINTINGS OF SCENES IN AND AROUND KYOTO

Multiple Versions of *Rakuchū Rakugai-zu*

Of the various painted folding screens in the genre *rakuchū rakugai-zu* (scenes in and around Kyoto), the oldest, dating from the first half of the sixteenth century, was handed down within the Machida family and is now in the National Museum of Japanese History in Sakura, Chiba. Many more screens were painted from that time until the end of the Tokugawa period in the mid-nineteenth century. Over eighty survive. The total number must have been enormous.

Among the surviving works is a famous pair of six-fold screens by Kanō Eitoku (1543–1590), the favorite painter of Oda Nobunaga (1534–1582). In 1574, shortly before building and moving into Azuchi Castle, Nobunaga presented the screens to Uesugi Kenshin, his rival for supremacy over the land. The involvement of the eminent trio of Nobunaga, Eitoku, and Uesugi in the paintings' creation is in itself remarkable. The Uesugi family, former rulers of the northern Yonezawa domain, kept the screens carefully stowed away, and today they are designated a National Treasure, periodically on display in the Yonezawa City Uesugi Museum. That this masterpiece survived the ups and downs of 450 years of history seems mysterious and wonderful.

Another famous example of the genre, known among specialists as the "Funaki version," is in the collection of the Tokyo National Museum. It, too, consists of a pair of six-fold screens painted in color on gold leaf paper. The screens are large, each one 163 × 343 centimeters, for a combined width of nearly 7 meters. Just after World War II, they were purchased in Hikone by a physician named Funaki who lived in Nagahama in Shiga prefecture. In 1949, the art historian Minamoto Toyomune happened to visit the area and stayed in Dr. Funaki's home. Dumbstruck with admiration on seeing the screens, he arranged for them to be displayed in the Kyoto National Museum and introduced to the world. The Funaki version, too, went through various vicissitudes but later was designated an Important Cultural Property.

The process of dating *rakuchū rakugai-zu* screen paintings is difficult, relying as it does on records of the construction and repair of buildings depicted in the panels, but Tsuji Nobuo, a specialist in early-modern Japanese art history, estimates that the Funaki version was painted in 1616 or 1617. That would be right about the time the retired shogun Tokugawa Ieyasu died at seventy-three in Sumpu Castle, in present-day Shizuoka City, roughly a year after he had eliminated his last rival in the siege of Osaka and brought peace to Japan.

Another example of the genre from roughly the same era, estimated to date from 1613 or later, is the Kōzu version in the collection of the Kōzu Kobunka Museum in Kyoto. Its bold composition has a wide Kamo River flowing vertically across the center of the right screen, with a panoramic view of the bridges at Sanjō, Shijō, and Gojō, and the bustling east-west streets. The painting's composition differs from other versions in a way that I find delightful.

The vast majority of *rakuchū rakugai-zu* screen paintings are painted on a pair of screens roughly 150–160 centimeters high and 6–7 meters wide in total. The screen surfaces are nearly covered with horizontal cloud formations of gold leaf, and peeping through rifts in the clouds are the hills and rivers, temples and shrines, palaces and mansions, bridges and streets of the city and its surrounding area, along with detailed images of shops, houses, and townspeople of all social strata. There is so much detail that on the rare occasions when a museum puts a *rakuchū rakugai-zu* on special display, an hour is nowhere near enough to take it all in. The sheer scale of the work, the resplendent beauty of

Figure 1. Uesugi version, *Scenes in and around Kyoto* (*Rakuchū rakugai-zu byōbu*).
Left-hand screen. Yonezawa City Uesugi Museum.

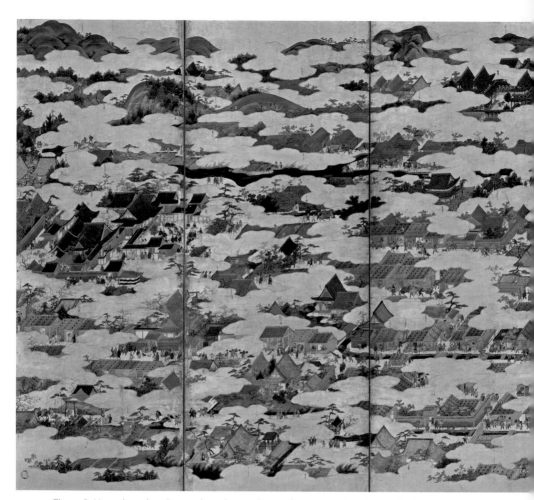

Figure 2. Uesugi version, *Scenes in and around Kyoto* (*Rakuchū rakugai-zu byōbu*). Right-hand screen. Yonezawa City Uesugi Museum.

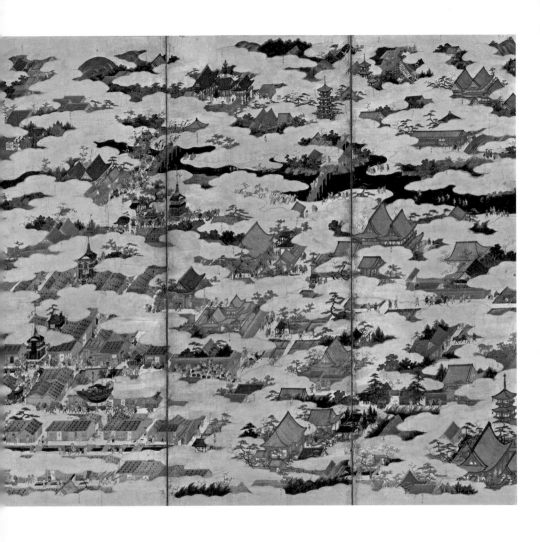

Figure 3. Parade of decorated floats in the Gion Festival. Uesugi version, *Scenes in and around Kyoto* (*Rakuchū rakugai-zu byōbu*), detail. Yonezawa City Uesugi Museum. (Next page)

the golden clouds, and the liveliness of the city scenes in between are so breathtaking that one comes home having barely begun to examine the details. Amateur viewers, myself included, inevitably respond in this way.

To get a really good look at the paintings, one should either take along a small pair of binoculars suitable for museum-going and set out resolved to spend an entire day parked in front of the screens, or else lug home a big, heavy book from the library and spend the evening poring over enlarged plates with a magnifying glass. Viewing a painting of "scenes in and around Kyoto" isn't like sitting on tatami mats in Nijō Castle or a minor temple of the Daitokuji and gazing at landscape paintings or flowers and birds painted on sliding-door panels, nor is it like standing before a Rubens in the Louvre or a Botticelli in the Uffizi Gallery. These particular Japanese works require an entirely different way of looking.

The Uesugi Version

Anyone who takes the time and trouble to look carefully at a *rakuchū rakugai-zu* screen will be fascinated. It is hard to pull oneself away from the mesmerizing sight of vibrant scenes of capital life four and a half centuries ago.

The viewer is first drawn to major landmarks: temples with big, ultramarine-colored tiled roofs, shrines with brown thatched roofs, and splendid buildings scattered everywhere, each a famous spot that is the pride of Kyoto residents. In the Uesugi version, the eye moves from the Tōji Pagoda on the lower right edge of the right screen upward and eastward to the deep ultramarine blue of the Kamo River, crossing over it via the bridge at Gojō to reach the temples Sanjūsangendō, Tōfukuji, and Kiyomizudera with its famous balcony—these stand out sharply amid the trailing clouds. Continuing left, or north, along the Higashi-yama hills at the top of the screen, the eye comes to far-off yet distinct images of the Yasaka Pagoda, Gion-sha (today's Yasaka Shrine), and Nanzenji temple in turn, finally reaching, at the top of the sixth and final panel, Mt. Hiei and Ginkakuji temple. Then the eye circles west, back across the Kamo River and down to a panoramic view of some ten

Figure 4. A lively street in Kyoto. Uesugi version, *Scenes in and around Kyoto* (*Rakuchū rakugai-zu byōbu*), detail. Yonezawa City Uesugi Museum.

roofs of residences in the Imperial Palace and the white sands of the garden by the Hall for State Ceremonies, where a performance of *bugaku* court music and dance is underway as part of New Year's Day ceremonies. Surrounded by these famous and scenic spots to the south, east, and north, the bustle of life in the Shimogyō (lower) area of the capital is meticulously depicted in the center of the right-hand screen.

While the right-hand screen of the Uesugi version thus offers a bird's-eye view of the Shimogyō area from the west, extending beyond the Kamo River to the Higashiyama hills on the city outskirts, the six left-hand panels offer a bird's-eye view of the Kamigyō (upper) area, beginning with Midorogaike Pond, Kamigamo Shrine, and Mt. Kuramayama north of the city, then showing in the upper part of the screen the western hills, dotted with Mt. Takao, Mt. Atago, Saga, and Arashiyama, and below that, streets lined with the magnificent residences of court nobles and daimyo and the mansion of the Muromachi shogun, making a leisurely progression from right to left, or north to south, to the vicinity of Imadegawa.

In the Funaki version, dated over forty years later, the layout has changed considerably. Distant views of the hills to the east, north, and west are largely eliminated, and most of the six right-hand panels abound with the energy of the area around the Kamo River and Rakutō, the area east of the river from the Great Buddha Hall of Hōkōji temple down to Gion-sha and Gojō Bridge. On panels one and two of the left-hand screen, warriors in helmet capes parade down Teramachi Street, west of Sanjō Bridge and smaller bridges, and on panels five and six the Imperial Palace and Nijō Castle vie in splendor. Throughout, the focus zooms in on architectural structures with far more detail than in the Uesugi version. City streets connect horizontally across the two screens, and the overall composition is novel, with the thriving Shimogyō and Rakutō areas shown looking north from somewhere above the Tōji Pagoda.

The layout and depiction of shrines and temples, palaces and private houses are certainly interesting and matters of great concern. Viewers today, however, are most drawn by far to the countless townsfolk seen everywhere on these great screen paintings, both inside and outside the various buildings. Countless though they seem, these people have in fact been counted: the Uesugi version contains 2,485 different figures, and the Funaki version even more—fully 2,728 people are shown going about their business. Except for the emperor and the shogun, every class and occupation is represented, from aristocrats and warriors to Buddhist and Shinto priests, artisans, merchants, peasants, fishmongers, pilgrims, saints, actors, prostitutes, lowly people, and beggars, each figure vividly drawn with the clothing, gestures, and facial expression appropriate to each one's station in life. The paintings' strong vitality comes above all from the depictions of these townsfolk.

Most *rakuchū rakugai-zu* paintings have the summer Gion Festival as their central focus. In the Uesugi version, the procession of decorated floats makes a great show of its movement along Shijō Street, across the third panel of the right-hand screen. Portable shrines have left Gion-sha and have just crossed, or are about to cross, a bridge at Shijō set up for the occasion. They are watched over from the front and rear by a crowd of people, including Shinto priests. Leading the procession of floats are the Naginata float, named for the long-handled halberd jutting from its top, and the Tōrōyama float, featuring a massive mantis atop an imperial bullock cart. Float after float comes after them, including the Niwatori float with its precious Gobelin tapestry and the Iwatōyama float with its statue of the sun goddess. Bringing up the rear is the Fune float, a representation of the ship in which Empress Jingū traveled to the kingdom of Silla in ancient times; this float heads north on Shimmachi Street in front of Zenchōji temple and is about to turn onto Shijō.

Men clad in *yukata* or naked to the waist pull the *yama* and *hoko* floats, their heads turned back to watch as they strain mightily, while men in armor and helmets lead the way. Others stoop over to change the direction of a float as it rounds a corner, their bodies inclined as they lever the great wheels with long sticks. Men in travel garb alongside women in sedge hats rush forward excitedly beside the canal on Muromachi Street, shouting as if to say, "There it is! The parade!" Across the street are monks craning their necks to see the enormous height of the floats and women in hats with trailing veils, accompanied by children. Shouts of admiration and joy from 450 years ago seem to rise from the painting. Kanō Eitoku must have been intimately acquainted with the liveliness of the Gion Festival, and he surely shared the townsfolk's joy in the festival's revival following the devastation of the Ōnin War (1467–1477).

The Funaki Version

The left-hand screen of the Funaki version portrays Part II of the Gion Festival with still greater boisterousness and vividness. In front of the portable shrine just turning south from Sanjō onto Teramachi, more than fifty men dance wildly, their bodies at all angles, while further ahead are three men dressed as warriors wearing mammoth hoods that tower three times their height in the air. In front and in back of them are men wearing big demon masks or sporting long black haori coats and hats marked with a white disk on a black background. Shouts and foot-stomping seem to arise from that section of the painting.

Meanwhile, the Misuji-machi red-light district, comprised of three

Figure 5. Funaki version, *Scenes in and around Kyoto* (*Rakuchū rakugai-zu byōbu*).
Right-hand screen. Tokyo National Museum.

Figure 6. Parade of warriors in helmet capes. Funaki version, *Scenes in and around Kyoto* (*Rakuchū rakugai-zu byōbu*), detail. Tokyo National Museum.

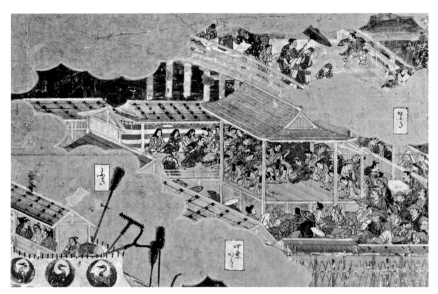

Figure 7. Kabuki in the riverbed at Shijō. Funaki version, *Scenes in and around Kyoto* (*Rakuchū rakugai-zu byōbu*), detail. Tokyo National Museum.

streets (Ue no machi, Naka no machi, and Shita no machi), extends from the bottom of the sixth panel on the right-hand screen to the bottom of the first panel on the left; there sinuous young women perform a circle dance (*furyū odori*) while men apparently of the warrior class appraise these goings-on, their faces concealed by their sleeves or open fans. One street down, various scenes of unconventional, indecent behavior are taking place in broad daylight: a woman takes a *kabukimono* (person of unconventional dress and demeanor) invitingly by the hand; a middle-aged man embraces a woman from behind, groping her breast; a man and woman are locked in an embrace in the middle of the street.

At Shijō Kawara, just between Gojō Bridge on the right-hand screen and Sanjō Bridge on the left, playhouses on both sides of the river, offering performances of *yūjo kabuki* (courtesan kabuki) as well as puppet plays and noh drama. On a stage surrounded by curtains with a crane crest, a performance is underway in the style of the shrine maiden Okuni of Izumo, the progenitor of modern kabuki. Each playhouse is packed with men and women of all ages.

Figure 8. Circle dancing (*furyū odori*). Funaki version, *Scenes in and around Kyoto* (*Rakuchū rakugai-zu byōbu*), detail. Tokyo National Museum.

On the fourth right panel of the Uesugi version, a mother has alighted from a palanquin on a narrow street just east of Muromachi to have her child urinate against the mud wall surrounding the house of the court physician Takeda Hōin. I was surprised and delighted to come across this scene; then I learned from art historians that similar scenes were often put in *rakuchū rakugai-zu* paintings to lend interest, along with scenes of playing children, performing monkeys, and quarreling *kabukimono*.

One such art historian, Tsuji Nobuo, points out that in the Funaki version, four Westerners are walking with a police escort just before the procession of the warriors with their mammoth hoods. He believes the one in the middle, a tall bearded man in a black hat and cape accompanied by a Black man shading him with a parasol, is most likely Richard Cocks (1566–1624), the head of the British East India Company trading post in Hirado. According to Cocks' diary, on November 2, 1616, his interpreter, Tom, took him sightseeing in Kyoto, starting with the Great Buddha Hall of the Hōkōji and Sanjūsangendō. Traders with the East

Figure 9. A Westerner walking a dog. Funaki version, *Scenes in and around Kyoto* (*Rakuchū rakugai-zu byōbu*), detail. Tokyo National Museum.

India Company often went to the capital on business, so this theory, which allows Tsuji to pinpoint the date of the Funaki version as late 1616 or 1617, may well be correct.

Another attendant is leading a large black Western dog on a red leash, and a young man in a hat beside Cocks is also walking a small brown dog. Tsuji points out that the black dog is panting, its red tongue hanging out as if to say, "Summer in Kyoto sure is hot!" Ahead of the party of foreigners, a cluster of men and women of the samurai and merchant class stare in wonder by a temple gate, and inside the temple grounds two black-robed monks come running, as if telling each other, "Don't miss it!"

The Composition of Portraits of Urban Life

When one takes a magnifying glass in hand to look at these screen paintings, the details prove fascinating. The question then arises: what is the origin of the distinctive compositional format of these outstanding portraits of urban life? Surely such works didn't spring out of nowhere.

There are various theories, ably summed up by Takeda Tsuneo, a

Figure 10. A roadside hamlet portrayed in *Illustrated Biography of the Monk Ippen* (*Ippen shōnin hijiri-e*), detail. Tokyo National Museum. Image: TNM Image Archive.

specialist in early-modern Japanese art history. Takeda concludes that the themes and techniques of *yamato-e* (Japanese painting), an indigenous style of painting going back to the Heian period, form the background of these paintings of scenes in and around Kyoto. Unlike *kara-e* (Chinese painting), which developed from the early fourteenth century under the influence of Sung and Yuan painting, *yamato-e* depict Japanese scenery, manners, and customs, using light colors. Those strongly associated with poetry depict scenery and customs connected with the four seasons (*shiki-e*) or the twelve months (*tsukinami-e*); another type focuses on famous scenic spots in the capital or elsewhere (*meisho-e*). Such paintings are known collectively as "partition paintings" (*shōhei-ga*) as they were executed on sliding-door panels and folding screens.

Those two streams of *yamato-e* came together early on, so that a painter might depict the same famous spot in different seasons, often drawing on *utamakura*—place names with strong poetic associations. Limiting the scenes depicted in such paintings to the capital would have led to the emergence of the *rakuchū rakugai-zu* genre. As Takeda explains in copious detail, with reference to an album of six replica paintings by Tosa Mitsunobu (ca. 1434–1525), the Machida version and other early examples combine a right-left spatial composition (from south and east to north and west) with a time element, showing seasonal changes in nature and seasonal events.

Later, with the long-awaited advent of prosperity and stability following the destructive Ōnin War, painters were increasingly drawn to actual scenes in and around the capital, as well as the manners and occupations of residents, rather than set combinations of famous sights and seasonal attractions. This trend is noticeable in the latter half of the sixteenth century with the Uesugi version; by the time of the Funaki version in the early seventeenth century, the earlier practice had all but vanished, apart from the inclusion of the second half of the Gion festivities and a few other events. The creation of the Uesugi version was fueled by Nobunaga's ambition and the conviction that he who ruled the capital ruled the land, a sense that no doubt was understood by Kanō Eitoku; seen from those heady heights, peaceful scenes of idyllic life in the capital must have inspired pride and affection. In the Funaki version, completed after the summer siege of Osaka, when the last threat to Tokugawa rule had ended, perhaps a mix of different emotions was on display: tension and anxiety that sprang up in the old capital after the locus of government shifted to Edo; hope for continued prosperity nonetheless; and a savoring of the decadent flair of eccentric *kabukimono*, who appeared during this period of change.

In portraying a major city and the lives of its inhabitants from a certain height, painters must have developed a new awareness of cities or a new way of thinking about them. Though this was a time of classical revival in Japan, the traditional combination of seasonal attractions and famous places associated with *waka* poetry no longer satisfied painters' psyches.

Still, how did Kanō Eitoku and his successors learn how to depict the area in and around the capital as it might look from a helicopter 100 meters (the Uesugi version) or 50 meters (the Funaki version) in the air, not "carpet bombing" but "carpet depicting"? As Takeda Tsuneo points out, they did not unite the various elements but rather assembled them, presenting each one as a separate entity. Painting a city section or a roadside village as part of an unfolding story was skillfully done in hand scroll paintings such as *The Legends of Mt. Shigi* (*Shigisan engi emaki*) and *The Tale of Great Minister Ban* (*Ban dainagon ekotoba*), both from the late twelfth century, as well as in the 1299 *Illustrated Biography of the Monk Ippen* (*Ippen hijiri-e*). In those works, however, the scenery was never more than background or incidental detail. What inspired painters to fill pairs of large six-fold screens with a bird's-eye view of scenery and scenes of life in and around the city, portrayed continuously from top to bottom and right to left from a uniform height and in minute detail? To borrow from Takeda Tsuneo once again, this style is a kind of "collective space achieved through [the art of] miniature painting."

The source of the painters' inspiration is unknown. As one possibility, Naitō Akira, an authority on the history of urban Japan, cites a letter dated New Year's 1584 from the Portuguese missionary Luís Frois to the father general of the Society of Jesus commenting that paintings of

Figure 11. *Along the River during the Qingming Festival* (*Qingming shanghe tu*), detail. The Palace Museum, Beijing.

Rome, as well as of the papal mass and procession, were effective props in conveying to daimyo the splendor and solemnity of the Roman Catholic Church. Naitō also mentions that the *Theatrum Orbis Terrarum*, a 1570 atlas by Flemish cartographer Abraham Ortelius (1527–1598), was brought to Japan during the "Christian century," 1549–1639, and copied onto a pair of eight-fold screens showing twenty-eight cities on a map of the world. However, those copies were made several years, or several dozen years, after the Machida and Uesugi versions.

Perhaps Eitoku did see some sort of painting of a Western city that had been brought to Japan by a Christian missionary. Even so, late Renaissance renderings of cities, whether oil paintings or copperplate prints, all use perspective, the technique invented in Renaissance Italy and copied in the "twenty-eight cities" screen painting, offering a bird's-eye view from a fixed vantage point. In Vermeer's *View of Delft* (1660–1662), Hobbema's *The Haarlem Lock, Amsterdam* (1663–1665), and Canaletto's

and Guardi's views of Venice, as well as in the urban landscapes of Turner and the French Impressionists, the restrictive technique of focusing on a single point in the distance imposes severe restraints on the entire canvas.

Portraying an urban panorama in what may be called a "worm's-eye" view, with all of the interesting details laid out with equal focus, may be a uniquely Japanese invention. The technique is perhaps an expression of the attention to detail that characterizes Japanese culture in general and of the egalitarianism seen for example in haiku, which pays no regard to social standing or wealth. Or it could be the expression of a new urban consciousness in painters, extending from the Machida version to the Funaki version.

A possible precedent is the late Northern Song dynasty scroll painting *Along the River during the Qingming Festival* (*Qingming shanghe tu*, 24.8 × 528.7 centimeters) by Zhang Zeduan (1085–1145). A supreme masterpiece of Chinese art, the panoramic painting employs a diffuse perspective to capture the prosperity and festivity along the banks of the Bian River during the Qingming Festival, held in the capital Bianjing (present-day Kaifeng) on the fifteenth day after the spring equinox. I have long thought that Japanese artists could have been influenced by a reproduction or replica of that work, or by similar paintings of famous Chinese cities well known in Japan. Other possible influences include the Ming dynasty painting *The Prosperous Southern Capital* (*Nandu fanhui tu*), showing Nanjing and Beijing, and the much later scroll painting *Prosperous Suzhou* (*Gusu fanhua tu*; originally titled *Burgeoning Life In a Resplendent Age* [*Shengshi zusheng tu*]) by the court painter Xu Yang, dated 1759, midway through the reign of the Qing emperor Qianlong.

In the early Meiji era, Edo townspeople contemplating the transformation of their city into a capital on a par with Kyoto felt eagerness and anxiety, impatience and empathy—emotions reflected in a brilliant pair of eight-fold screens in the Idemitsu Museum of Arts entitled *Guide to Famous Edo Sites* (*Edo meisho-zu byōbu*; 107.2 × 488.8 centimeters). Clearly those screens were created with the Kyoto genre in mind and a determination to emulate it by offering a bird's-eye view of Edo containing multiple worm's-eye views. A comparison of that work and paintings of scenes in and around Kyoto will have to wait for another time.

2 | "COME, LET US BE CRAZY": IZUMO NO OKUNI AND *RYŪTATSU KOUTA*

Rakuchū rakugai-zu often depict a circle of men and women dancing at an intersection or elsewhere to the lively music of hand drums and flutes. Such group dancing, known as *furyū odori* (literally, "drifting on the wind" dance), stemmed from the late Heian practice of enlivening festival performing arts with the music of flutes, large drums, and bells or singing. In the fifteenth and sixteenth centuries, such festival music and dancing (*hayashimono*) fused with the ancient *nembutsu odori*, a Buddhist ritual dance, to form *furyū odori*. As the genre of "scenes in and around Kyoto" became established and more and more such works appeared, the new form of dancing, especially popular in the capital, naturally figured in the paintings.

In the oldest extant example, the Machida version (ca. 1525), which I touched on briefly in the previous chapter, the sixth or far-left panel of the left-hand screen shows ten men dancing in a circle at an intersection on Ichijō Street. Wearing woven hats and gray kimono with dark blue aprons, they are bent low at the waist with the right hand outstretched, as if planting rice seedlings. In the center of the circle, another four or five men in different attire are playing drums and flutes. A well-dressed man striding into the circle, followed by three attendants, seems to be a samurai or an aristocrat complaining that the dance is obstructing traffic.

The early seventeenth-century Kōzu version, roughly a hundred years later, has a bold composition with the Kamo River flowing vertically on the right screen and streets zigzagging alongside it. Here too, a lively *furyū odori* dance is underway at an intersection on Ichijō or Nijō, with some sixty people joining in. Men wearing woven hats and long robes form a tight circle, dancing to the music of bells and large drums played by three men in the center. Here and there is a hatless man with top-knot, though it isn't clear whether such men are spectators or whether, drawn in by the music, they are starting to join the fun.

Dancing was particularly popular among Kyotoites from the late Azuchi-Momoyama period (1573–1603) through the early Tokugawa period, and it shows up frequently in other kinds of screen paintings as well. A six-panel screen owned by the British Museum called *Outdoor Amusements* (*Yagai yūraku-zu byōbu*) shows roughly sixty people gathered in the front garden of a nobleman's residence, each one dressed in a showy hat and robe, dancing *furyū odori* in a circle three deep. The family and followers of the owner of the residence, men and women alike, are looking on with enjoyment, some indoors and others outdoors on rugs.

What appears still more enjoyable is the portrayal of Gion-sha on a pair of six-fold screens (153.3 × 362 centimeters each) entitled *Amusements of the Kitano Gion-sha* (*Kitano Gion-sha yūraku-zu*) in the possession of Chōenji temple. In a pine grove with a red *torii* gate in the middle is a group of men and women who have brought with them sake and food in elegant gold-lacquered boxes. Perhaps feeling the effects of the sake, they are starting to get up and dance to shamisen accompaniment. One group above the *torii* is already dancing in a circle, with a palanquin and palanquin-bearers nearby, while farther down, another ten people are just starting to dance and have yet to form a circle. Picnic boxes overflowing with delicacies lie open, but the picnickers are calling to one another and singing, unable to resist the urge to dance. A young man in a bright kimono with a sword at his side is dancing with his arms spread wide, holding a fan decorated with the rising sun.

Yet more amazing are the large screen paintings of a special Hōkoku Festival held in the eighth month of 1604 to commemorate the sixth anniversary of Toyotomi Hideyoshi's death. One pair of six-fold screens in the possession of Hōkoku Shrine, completed soon after the festivities, is by Kanō Naizen (1570–1616), the official painter for the Toyotomi family. The other is an anonymous work in the possession of the Tokugawa Art Museum. On the left screen of each pair is a vivid rendering of the festival centerpiece, a "Hōkoku dance" performed on the fifteenth day of the eighth month by large circles of dancers.

In the Funaki version, the first panel of the right-hand screen has a large, detailed painting of dozens of people from every district in Kami-gyō and Shimogyō gathered in the wide space in front of the Great Buddha Hall of Hōkōji temple. Representatives of each district wear a distinct style of kimono and a black-lacquered hat marked with a crest, each of them holding a long-handled war fan (*gumbaidan uchiwa*) as they dance together. In the Kanō Naizen work, which was commissioned by Hideyoshi's son Hideyori (1593–ca. 1615), people from each district are dancing in three fairly orderly concentric circles around a large hat (*furyūgasa*) that serves as divine abode (*yorishiro*); the circles move in different directions, clockwise alternating with counterclockwise.

In the anonymous work in the Tokugawa Art Museum, however, the dancing is a collection of mad swirls. Some of the dancers maintain distinct circles, but those in the Kawanishi district of Shimogyō, in the center of the painting, have fallen out of sync; people are leaning to the left or right as they please, nearly bumping into one another as they feverishly wave their hands and stamp their feet. Outside the circles, flutists and drummers are playing with verve, spurring on the wild dancing. Moreover, here the viewer's vantage point is much lower than in the Hōkoku Shrine screen; the painting's "carpet depiction" is in the style of the Funaki version and allows the expressions of the male danc-ers to show clearly beneath their hat brims. You can almost hear their breathing, shouts, and stomps.

All these paintings, up to the painted screens of the Hōkoku Festi-val, indicate that from the late sixteenth century to nearly the middle of the seventeenth century, the citizens of Kyoto were gripped by dancing fever. Of course, scenes in paintings do not constitute historical reality. Though the screen paintings may all portray city streets and customs in general, they naturally differ by theme, perspective, and composition,

Figure 12. Iwasa Matabei, *The Ritual Celebration Memorializing Toyotomi Hideyoshi* (*Hōkoku sairei-zu byōbu*). Left-hand screen, detail. The Tokugawa Art Museum. The Tokugawa Art Museum Image Archives / DNPartcom.

as well as the elements that each painter chose to emphasize or exaggerate. However, the paintings are not pure fabrications. They portray the changing atmosphere in the ancient capital, the center of radical political change, as the age of Oda Nobunaga and Toyotomi Hideyoshi gave way to the age of the Tokugawa. The screen paintings reflect fluctuations in the psychology and sentiments of Kyoto residents of all walks of life, including the observers as well as the observed. The insights they provide are indirect but real.

Okuni Kabuki

Amid the craze for *furyū odori* in Kyoto came the "kabuki dance" of Okuni from Izumo. Said to have been an attendant at the Grand Shrine of Izumo, Okuni first made a name for herself in Nara and Kyoto performing *yayako odori*, also known as *musume odori* (girls' dance). Then in the spring of 1603—the year before the great mass dance held at the Hōkoku Festival by the Great Buddha Hall of Hōkōji temple—she borrowed the noh stage in Kitano Temmangu Shrine and acted out contemporary tales of the pleasure quarters, dressed in splendid male costumes. Her performances were a smash hit; overnight, she was the talk of the town.

Some such development was perhaps only natural, given the dance craze sweeping the capital. But while the rise of "Okuni Kabuki" was certainly prompted by the craze, Okuni's contribution bears the marks of her own originality. Hattori Yukio, an authority on the history of Japanese performing arts, explains her contribution in this way: "[Okuni] transformed *kouta odori*, a form of dance in the vein of *furyū odori*, from *an art form of mass participation into art for viewing*; and she *performed it on stage*."[1]

People like the riotous dancers in the screen paintings we have examined must have nodded to themselves as Okuni danced in the shrine and on the dry bed of the Kamo River at Shijō Kawara, musing, "Yes, very interesting!" and "She's shown us up," and becoming all the more inspired to be crazy, uninhibited *kabukimono*.

According to *Kabuki Stories* (*Kabukizōshi*), a somewhat later record in the form of a fictional tale, the sight of Okuni dancing onstage in male attire had powerful allure:

> With her obi slung low around her hips and a long sword strapped at her side, you might look at her expecting to see a woman, but you'd find a man, and if you expected her to be a man, you would find she is female after all. Tapping the hilt of her long sword, she performs all manner of stories of love, for all the world like the reincarnation of Narihira[2] of old.

Even now, such a figure might have the power to captivate.

Images of Okuni dancing at Kitano Temmangu Shrine are to be found in many screen paintings of Kyoto and its environs, including the set in the collection of the Myōhōji temple on Sado Island, the set belonging to the Yamaoka family, and those in the Idemitsu Museum of Arts and the Suntory Museum of Art. In the style of Oda Nobunaga (the first Japanese in recorded history to wear European clothes), she is dressed in bright, exotic "southern barbarian" (European) style men's attire of black, green, and red, yet retains an air of sinuous grace as she sings a love song to a man in female attire playing the role of a teahouse madam. In the Myōhōji version, displayed prominently alongside the stage are titles the emperor bestowed on Okuni in admiration of her dancing: "First under Heaven" (*tenka-ichi*) and "Lord of Tsushima" (*Tsushima-no-kami*).

Okuni's actual lover on stage was Nagoya Sanza, a dandy who went all-out to dress in eye-catching ways, a flamboyant eccentric and a true *kabukimono*. Sanza meets an untimely stage death in the 1600 Battle of Sekigahara but, summoned by Okuni's recital of the *nembutsu* prayer, he returns to her as a ghost and utters this line: "Very well, let us cast all to the winds, sing a song of bygone days, and be crazy! (*Yoshi, nanigotomo uchisutete, arishi mukashi no hitofushi o utaite, izaya kabukan*)."

The phrase "*Izaya kabukan*" (Come, let us be crazy!) is marvelous. The underlying meaning of *kabuku* is "to slant"; the word then took on the meaning of being deviant or eccentric, saying and doing outlandish things—being liberated from convention, daring to act with freedom

Figure 13. *Kabuki Picture Scroll* (*Kabuki zukan*), detail. The Tokugawa Art Museum.
The Tokugawa Art Museum Image Archives / DNPartcom.

from restraint. No mere dancer, Okuni of Izumo was a "slanted" (*kabuita*) man, behaving like one while retaining the appearance of a woman: the very symbol of a *kabukimono*.

According to Kawatake Toshio, the late authority on comparative theater, the essence of Okuni's art through all its later permutations, from women's kabuki, young men's kabuki, and men's kabuki, up to and including the present day, can be summed up in three words: deviance, excess, and sensuality. Kawatake also said that those same words define Baroque art of the era, encompassing the art of Okuni and of her contemporary, William Shakespeare. Okuni did indeed make kabuki the Baroque theater of the people—*kabukimono*—in contrast to noh, the classical theater of the aristocracy. All sorts of early Tokugawa-period paintings feature *kabukimono* who are kin to Okuni: the exhibitionistic men sporting enormous hoods in the Funaki version; the enraptured dancing men and women in the Hōkoku Festival painting; the swaggering figures of dissolute young men and women sporting bold colors and designs in *Cherry Blossom Viewing Picnic*, a four-panel screen in the Brooklyn Museum; the wanton young women eyeing each other in a painting of six *yuna* (public bathhouse workers) in the MOA Museum of Art. These figures all embody deviance, excess, and sensuality, and in concert with Okuni of Izumo and Nagoya Sanza, they fairly shout out the catchword of their time: *Izaya kabukan!* Come, let's be crazy!

Cherry Blossom Viewing and Falconry

Another screen painting of this era that I like very much also shows the popularity of *furyū odori*. This masterpiece, probably my favorite among all the early modern genre paintings, is *Cherry Blossom Viewing and Falconry* (*Hanami takagari-zu byōbu*), a pair of six-fold screens (142 × 347 centimeters each) in the MOA Museum of Art in Atami, attributed to Unkoku Tōgan (1547–1618) or someone from his school. I have to wonder, though—how could Tōgan, a painter employed by the Mōri family of the Chōshū domain and a specialist in monochrome ink painting in the manner of Sesshū (1420–1506), have produced a work of such brilliant color and charm? I cannot account for it.

Figure 14. *Service Women in Bathhouse (Yuna-zu)*. MOA Museum of Art.

Figure 15. *Hikone Screen* (*Hikone byōbu*). Hikone Castle Museum / DNPartcom.

Figure 16. Kanō Naganobu, *Merrymaking under the Cherry Blossoms* (*Kaka yūraku-zu byōbu*), detail. Tokyo National Museum.

Figure 17. Attributed to Unkoku Tōgan, *Cherry Blossom Viewing and Falconry* (*Hanami takagari-zu byōbu*). Right-hand screen. MOA Museum of Art.

Figure 18. Attributed to Unkoku Tōgan, *Cherry Blossom Viewing and Falconry* (*Hanami takagari-zu byōbu*). Right-hand screen, detail. MOA Museum of Art. (next page)

2 "COME, LET US BE CRAZY": IZUMO NO OKUNI AND *RYŪTATSU KOUTA*   73

The left screen shows some thirty men running around a brown landscape sparsely dotted with pine trees, engaged in falconry. In contrast to that rather stark scene, the right screen vividly represents a bright and beautiful spring. On the far right, next to a hilltop spreading out flat like a stage, several large cherry trees are in full bloom. Some seventy women and girls gathered nearby are starting to dance in a circle. A girl who has just arrived is leaning over to join the others, her foot half raised. Some of the women wear hats of black and gold lined with vermilion, while pretty scarves of various colors cover the head and the lower half of the face of others. Holding large and small branches of cherry blossoms in their hands or across their shoulders, they dance.

One woman has attached a fan and colored strips of paper to a large branch of weeping cherry blossoms adorning her decorative umbrella. Another woman's umbrella is decorated with a phoenix. The colors and patterns of the *kosode* kimono are all charmingly different, according to each woman's taste. Some dancers have slipped out of the sleeves of the *uchikake* robes worn on top and tied them around their waist; others are wearing aprons in front. The boldness of the color combinations rivals that of their contemporaries, the *kabukimono*, but these are women and girls of classical beauty and refinement, undoubtedly wives and daughters from proper homes. As proof, over on the left edge of the third panel, at the base of a spreading pine tree, are the palanquins that brought them to this spot. The palanquin bearers are crouched over, smoking long pipes and chatting to pass the time.

In front of the large house and cherry trees on the right hangs a curtain marked with a family crest, either a twelve-spoked wheel or the Kinoshita wheel,[3] alongside which a band of six beautifully attired women including a little girl are enthusiastically performing on drums, both large and small, and flutes. The circles of dancers also include a woman beating a drum on her shoulder and another woman with a spray of cherry blossoms at her waist playing the flute. The inner circle of dancers is moving clockwise in time to the music, the outer circle counterclockwise, with stunning grace and vitality.

Wafted by the spring breeze and the music, the women's sleeves and hems, as well as their long red sashes worn slantwise from shoulder to waist or tied around the waist, form alluring curves, no less than the figures of the women themselves. Their lithe arms and legs are the essence of dance, beautiful to the tips of their fingers and toes.

Words like "elegance" and "grace" do not apply only to women of the Bourbon aristocracy. I would venture to say that those words perfectly describe these Kyoto women dancing under cherry blossoms in the early seventeenth century. In this corner of the capital, an elegant and graceful form of the ubiquitous *furyū odori* took place—one utterly different from the dancing in screen paintings of Kyoto and its environs or the boisterous dancing in the Hōkoku Festival paintings.

The question then arises, what corner of the capital is this? The answer is far from clear. Across the second panel on the right, behind the deep green of a grove of evergreens or cedars are two overlapping shingled roofs with large gables. Wondering if this detail, along with the family crest on the curtain, might not be enough to identify the location, I inquired of several experts but met with little success. Designer Hisatani Masaki, a former colleague from my Kyoto days, suggested that it could be Imamiya Shrine in the Murasakino district of northern Kyoto, where from the Heian period on, every year on the tenth day of the third month by the lunar calendar, just as the cherry blossoms begin to scatter, a *hanashizume* (pacifying the blossoms) festival has been held to banish sickness and ill fortune. Because women sang "*Yasurae hana yo*" ("Flowers, be at peace") while dancing, in time this became known as Yasurai Festival. I have come to think that the painting probably represents that festival.

What songs did those lovelies dancing under cherry blossoms know and sing at other times, besides those occasions when they did the *furyū odori*? I wonder about this whenever I look at the painting. It gives me pleasure to know that they must have sung *ryūtatsu kouta*, songs that were all the rage in the late sixteenth and early seventeenth centuries. Takasabu Ryūtatsu (1527–1611), the gifted son of a wealthy merchant family in the city of Sakai, set to music lyrics composed by himself and others. They are short love songs, flirtatious and pleasing to the ear, more stylish than Parisian *chansons*. In reference to the establishment of Okuni Kabuki, Hattori Yukio has said that Okuni performed *kouta odori*, love-song dances "in the vein of *furyū odori*," on stage. *Ryūtatsu kouta* in particular seem to me fitting not only for Okuni but for the women in this painting.

> Lovely to look at
> with an air so fine
> like a blossom
> perfectly graced with scent
>
> Ah, won't someone
> let it blossom anew—
> this body between dreams
> frail as dew
>
> This spring you're here
> lovelier than blossoms
> tangling my feelings
> like green willow threads
>
> As I try to make out
> your receding figure
> mist rises
> morning mist
>
> Out of the way, let me go!
> My sash will come undone!
> This isn't the only chance, you know
> We'll surely meet again
>
> Hand in hand, bound tight
> as the cords on a drum—

Am I a hand drum
for you to tap?

Deep down you've opened up to me
Your pretense of indifference
is only more endearing

Let the storm rage
scattering the blossoms
as long as your heart
never flits away from me

We're far apart but
dreams bring us together
Across mountains and seas
I see you night upon night[4]

Like the verses in *Secret Selection of Rafter Dust* (*Ryōjin hisho*), a late twelfth-century anthology of popular songs compiled by the retired emperor Go-Shirakawa (1127–1192), and *Songs Sung in Tranquility* (*Kanginshū*), a 1518 collection of *kouta*, these verses are infused with a sense of life's impermanence and *mono no aware* (awareness of the ephemerality of all things); at the same time they are more free-spirited, alert to the give-and-take of love, filled with sprightliness and verve and temptation. Perhaps Okuni of Izumo sang some such song to Nagoya Sanza. Any man would surely be transported if he sang "lovely to look at, with an air so fine" to one of the young women in *Cherry Blossom Viewing and Falconry* who was swaying her hips and artfully moving her arms in time to the music, or if he had her croon those words to him.

"This spring you are here, lovelier than blossoms." This line is well worth reciting aloud. The words could just as well be said by a woman to a man as the other way around. In the springtime, as I walk along Kawabata Street by the Kamo River admiring the slender willow branches just sprouting the buds of green leaves between the blossoming cherry trees along the riverbank, I always think of the line "tangling my feelings like green willow threads." If only women of today would now and then hold up a spray of cherry blossoms and sing like that, even if they didn't mean it . . .

---

1 AN: Hattori Yukio, *Kabuki seiritsu no kenkyū* [Studies in the origins of kabuki] (Kazama shobō, 1968). Emphasis added.

2 Ariwara no Narihira (825–880) was a famous *waka* poet, many of whose poems are included in *The Tales of Ise* (*Ise monogatari*), a mid-tenth-century poem-tale that portrays his various love adventures.

3 Crests of noble families, derived from the wheels of the oxcarts they used as conveyances.

4 AN: "*Ryūtatsu shoka*" [Ryūtatsu songs], *Chūsei kinsei kayōshū* [Medieval and early modern popular songs], *Nihon koten bungaku taikei* [Compendium of Japanese classical literature], vol. 44 (Iwanami shoten, 1959), 320–330.

3 | KŌETSU, SŌTATSU, AND THE CLASSICAL REVIVAL

Dancing to Shake Heaven and Earth:
Tawaraya Sōtatsu's *Wind God and Thunder God*

When the emblem for the 2020 Tokyo Olympic and Paralympic Games had to be jettisoned and new entries were solicited, I immediately had an idea. I thought it was such a good idea that I tried to persuade a graphic designer acquaintance to submit it. Rather than the stylish geometric design of the scrapped logo, my idea would be far stronger and more dynamic, at once suitable for a celebration of sports and instantly identifiable as Japanese. I was sure that it would eclipse even the famous logo that Kamakura Yūsaku designed for the 1964 Tokyo Olympics.

My thought was to use the images in the screen painting *Wind God and Thunder God* (*Fūjin raijin-zu*) by Tawaraya Sōtatsu (ca. 1570–1640), a National Treasure in the Kenninji temple collection in Kyoto. I wanted to place the two gods unchanged or with minimal trimming on the right and left sides of a poster. Whether contest guidelines would allow the use of such classic images, I didn't know, but a close-up look at Sōtatsu's masterpiece in the special exhibition *Rinpa: The Aesthetics of the Capital* at Kyoto National Museum in 2015 only strengthened my conviction.

On a pair of wide two-fold screens (each 154.5 × 169.8 centimeters) covered in gold leaf, the two gods ride on light clouds painted in the *tarashikomi* (dropping ink) technique. They set heaven and earth aroar as they rush along, the green wind god on the right and the pale thunder god on the left. Where else in Japanese art is the beauty of physical vigor and vitality expressed with such humor and exuberance?

The gods' burly limbs are planted firmly in space and their mouths are opened wide in toothy grins. They roar to each other from the far edges of their respective screens, so high they all but burst out the top as, both facing left, they go bounding through the sky. Their strength is concentrated in their limbs, which are bent in impossible ways, legs curved backward or toes curled up in strikingly dynamic shapes against the gold background. They kick aside the mottled clouds at their feet, making one wonder what gives them purchase to obtain such height and speed. In Sōtatsu's rendering, they have the flight accuracy and speed of a pair of jets. The gods that Ogata Korin (1658–1716) painted a century later in homage to these two are more like propeller planes emitting thick black smoke as they putter low in the sky.

Sōtatsu's gods are sparsely dressed, the god of wind in black drawers and red sash, the god of thunder in green drawers and gold sash; they are shirtless, showing off muscular torsos. The long curving lines of the ribbons winding aloft by the gods' shoulders, front and back, add a touch of breathtaking elegance to the dynamic scene. Each god has a pair of horns on his head, around which the hair, depicted in marvelous lines of gold (the wind god) and brown (the thunder god), blows to the right. The round swelling of the white windbag that the wind god is gripping, one end in each hand, and the circle of the thunder god's drums, partially hidden by clouds, give the intervening space a fitting dignity and also a sense of lightness and calm. In the paintings of these same gods by Kōrin, and by Kōrin's devoted admirer, Sakai Hōitsu (1761–1829), the circular outlines of the props are too geometrically precise and do not capture the surprising suppleness of the gods' energy or the vibrant space of seemingly unlimited depth and width we see in Sōtatsu's painting.

Works of art East and West are connected in unexpected ways. Expert opinion[1] says that Sōtatsu's wind god came to Japan across the vast distance of time and space separating Tokugawa Kyoto from Mt. Olympus, the home of the Greek gods. Boreas, the god of the north wind, followed Alexander the Great on his Asian expedition over the Silk Road, and by the time they arrived in Gandhara, Boreas' cape had become a wind-swollen bag that he carried about his shoulders, gripping one end in each hand. An early sixth-century ceiling painting in the Dunhuang caves portrays him that way, paired with a thunder god. The motion and humor in that painting mark it as a precursor of Sōtatsu's work. In the mid-twelfth century, a similar image was transmitted on the endpaper of a sutra in the collection of the Kongōbuji temple on Mt. Kōya in Wakayama prefecture and recreated in a standing *yosegi-zukuri* statue (one whose individual parts are carved separately from wood, then joined and coated with lacquer) among the thousand Kannon statues in Kyoto's Sanjūsangendō.

Another Greek wind god, Zephyros, went through various permutations before appearing in that exquisite masterpiece of the Italian Renaissance, Botticelli's *The Birth of Venus* (ca. 1482). The god of the west wind, Zephyros, bringer of love, blows forcefully at the newly-born, voluptuous goddess Venus as she stands nude in a giant scallop shell afloat on the sea, moving her steadily toward shore, where Hora, a goddess of the seasons, waits holding out a red cloak. This brilliant, sensuous tempera painting suggests that while the significance of images of the wind god and thunder god in statuary and painting may vary from culture to culture, a certain universal mythological imagination is always at work.

Sōtatsu's painting is a free working of that imagination laced with humor, a rare masterpiece. That it appeared in Kyoto not long after the shogunate was established in Edo seems significant. *Flowering Plants of Summer and Autumn* (*Natsu aki kusa-zu byōbu*), a pair of two-fold screen paintings by the Edo Rimpa painter Sakai Hōitsu, shed light on that synchronicity for me. Hōitsu's work is painted on the back of Kōrin's *Wind God and Thunder God* screens. Behind the wind god on the left are autumn grasses being tossed by a fierce wind, and behind the thunder god on the right, getting soaked in a shower, are lilies, bindweed, *kaya* and other grasses, amid pools of water. This, too, is a masterpiece, overflowing with the spirit of a man of refined taste brought up in Edo.

As I reexamined the Sōtatsu screens with Hōitsu's work in mind, a new interpretation suggested itself: perhaps the wind god is blowing away the last traces of the dust of the long Warring States period, and the rain brought by the thunder god is putting out the smoldering fires of war. These paintings, relaxed yet forceful and exhilarating, convey the deep longing of Kyoto townsfolk, and indeed of all Japanese people, for a return of peace.

(Let me add that the association of Sōtatsu's wind god and thunder god with a desire for peace would make the images all the more appropriate as emblems of the Olympics, that celebration of peace among nations. The gods' figures suggest a variety of sports, from marathons and footraces to shot-put, gymnastics, and even, through the fluttering ribbons, rhythmic gymnastics.)

In the recent Kyoto National Museum exhibition, Sōtatsu's screens occupied the entire center wall at the back of the room, flanked by Kōrin's screens on the right and Hōitsu's on the left. The arrangement was similar to one seven years earlier in a special 2008 exhibition at Tokyo National Museum entitled *Treasures by Rinpa Masters: Inheritance and Innovation*, but the room was a bit smaller. Kōrin's work in particular suffered as a result. It seemed to me that while the facial expressions of his gods and the movements of their arms and legs were virtually identical to Sōtatsu's painting, the gold-leaf space between them wasn't quite big enough (even though Kōrin's screens are each 12 centimeters higher and 13 centimeters wider than Sōtatsu's) and the composition felt cramped. As I mentioned before, in Sōtatsu's work the gods' possessions—the bag of wind and the circle of drums—are slightly hidden and far apart, on the right and left edges of their respective screens, and the gods themselves are near the top edge, yet the tension and close interplay between the two figures comes across vividly. Kōrin, however, may have failed to grasp that interplay; his gods are each enveloped in a big, dense, black cloud, looking out at each other but not communicating. Also, to me their expressions are less skillful than those of Hōitsu's wind god and thunder god, descending to the realm of manga.

A Flock of Cranes in Flight over the Sea:
Anthology with Crane Design by Kōetsu and Sōtatsu

Almost nothing is known of the life of Tawaraya Sōtatsu, including his birth and death dates. His life is one of the great mysteries in Japanese cultural history. In every genre that he took up, whether folding or sliding screen paintings, ink painting on hanging scrolls, underpainting on hand scrolls, or fan decoration, his art shows such stupendous originality in composition, coloration, and line drawing that the mystery of his life looms all the larger and adds all the more to his appeal.

Despite the lack of biographical details, Sōtatsu's art and life clearly took on even greater luster under the influence of Hon'ami Kōetsu (1558–1637), a fellow artistic genius in Kyoto with whom he developed a long, close working relationship. An early collaborative work by Sōtatsu and his circle of painters consists of paintings of the moon, vines, azaleas, Chinese bellflowers, and the like, with Kōetsu's calligraphic overlay of autumn and winter poems from the *New Collection of Poems Old and Modern* (*Shinkokinshū*, 1439); this work bears a poem-card (*shikishi*) that is inscribed, unusually, with the date: the eleventh day of the eleventh month, 1606. Another collaboration, an album of poem-cards with paintings of flowering grasses and poems, also from the *Shinkokinshū*, dates from around the same time. In both works, the collaborators give full play to their respective geniuses, working not in rivalry but in perfect harmony to vividly recreate the sumptuousness of classical works of art.

I'd like to take a close, appreciative look at the largest and greatest of their surviving collaborations, *Anthology with Crane Design* (*Tsuru shita-e sanjūrokkasen wakakan*). Of the nearly ten other works combining Sōtatsu's underpaintings with Kōetsu's calligraphy and classical poetry, the majority were cut up before or after World War II and scattered among various collectors and museums. The crane hand scroll alone was safely hidden, emerging in 1964 in its full proportions (34 centimeters in height and an astonishing 13.56 meters long) with the silver and gold paint scarcely changed from when Sōtatsu applied it. Arakawa Toyozō, the Shino ware potter who witnessed this miraculous discovery and became the first owner of the masterpiece, and Yamane Yūzō, the foremost authority on Rimpa painting and aesthetic design and the first to verify the scroll's authenticity, wrote about their astonishment and joy in the December 1964 issue of the visual arts magazine *New Currents in Art* (*Geijutsu Shinchō*).

The year the crane hand scroll was completed is unknown, but Yamane estimates that it dates from around 1610, when the two artists were working the most closely together. That would have been five years before Kōetsu had an audience with Ieyasu in Kyoto's Nijō Castle and was granted a tract of land in Takagamine, northwest of Kyoto. Sōtatsu had already painted flocks of cranes in flight on poem-cards and *utaibon* (books of words and musical notation for noh plays), also in color with silver and gold, as well as in woodblock prints. But in *Anthology with Crane Design*, the cranes fly the length of the nearly 14-meter-long scroll in a flock, as if chased by the surf, soaring now high, now low before finally coming to rest at the water's edge. The design is simply stunning.

Having purchased a smaller copy of the scroll in Kyoto, I spread it out on the floor and counted the cranes. I could have miscounted, but I came up with a total of 133—seven of them represented merely by bills pointing down from the top of the scroll. Rather than 133 individual cranes, it may be that the scroll shows the same flock of twenty or thirty over and over as they fly toward shore.

Enthralled, I examined the brilliant, fascinating painting again from the far right starting-point and decided that the gold oval stretching below a flock of a dozen or so cranes must be the rising tide, about to flood the tidal flat. Seven of the birds have realized what's happening and are turned facing left, their bills open as they cry out. Another four or five remain unaware that the tide is coming in and are engrossed in hunting for grubs on the shoal, heads down.

At last, spurred by the incoming tide, the flock takes to the air. Most of them face left, in the direction of the scroll's progression, as they fly high and low over the surface of the water, their wings beating hastily. One crane is for some reason turned the other way, its bill open as it calls toward the sea, perhaps realizing its mate lags behind.

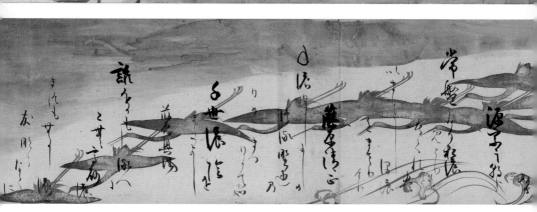

Figure 19. Calligraphy by Hon'ami Kōetsu, painting by Tawaraya Sōtatsu. *Anthology with Crane Design* (*Tsuru-zu shita-e sanjūrokkasen wakakan*), detail. Kyoto National Museum.

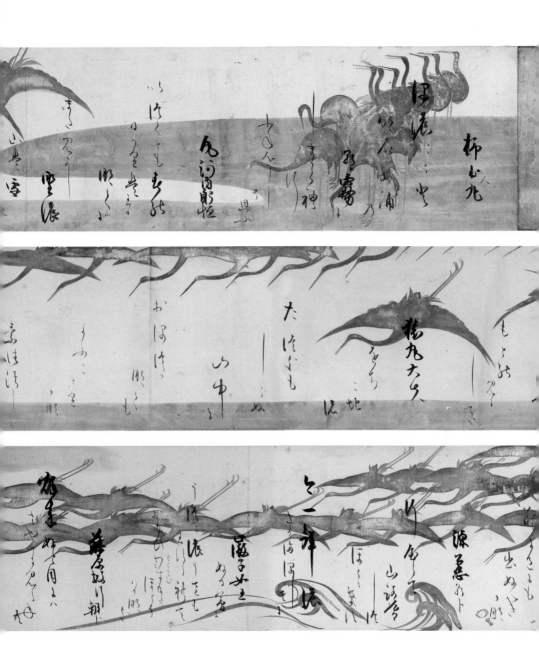

The cranes' bills, tail feathers, and legs, the latter stretched out in straight lines behind them, are painted in gold, and their long necks, chests, and fully extended wings are rendered in a bit of gold paint and spots of silver paint mixed with *gofun* (white pigment made from pulverized clamshells), with no outlining. But the birds are not uniform in shape, as if created from the same pattern; rather, the wingspread, the curve of the neck, the degree of openness of the bill, and the extension of the legs all differ slightly for each one. Sōtatsu must have often observed cranes and been deeply familiar with their ways.

That said, this is by no means a realistic rendering of cranes in flight. The silver-and-gold birds soar high above the surface of the water, then swoop down and skim the waves, only to mount high again by the dozens. Within the flock, some glide in a straight line and others veer upward in overlapping groups of a few or dozens, creating an easy rhythm and motion. About two thirds of the way through the painting, approximately 10 meters from the beginning, the cranes abruptly change direction and, now facing right, finally alight in the shallows near the beach where the waves roll ashore. Then they stand still, bills closed in apparent relief. The silver paint and thin black ink with which their figures are drawn are also somewhat fainter.

The more I study the painting, the more I am struck by the lightness and grace of the outspread wings, the long, slightly rising necks, and the slender legs, all rendered distinctively in silver and gold for each bird. As the scroll unfolds from right to left, the flock of cranes flies up and down in a vivid pattern, undulating like a beautiful melody. The effect is breathtaking. This painting cannot be summed up by an epithet like "decorative." It is music. Below and sometimes above the flying cranes, the swell of the rising tide is suggested by a gold that is now deeper, now paler, while the cresting waves, large and small, are drawn in silver. Along with the beating of wings and the cries of cranes calling back and forth, the painting echoes with the sound of waves.

What further elevates and enhances the melody formed by the rise and fall of cranes and sea is of course the overlay of classical poems in Koetsu's superb calligraphy. Known as one of the "Three Brushes of the

Kanei Era" (*Kanei no sampitsu*; the others are the nobleman Konoe Nobutada and the monk Shōkadō Shōjō), Kōetsu has a style that is easy and flowing, elegant yet bold, and above all, perfectly free. The subtle shading of ink, the variation in size between *kanji* and *kana*, and the spacing of the lines form a visual counterpoint to the variations in Sōtatsu's rendering of the flock of cranes. The inimitable grace and suppleness of Kōetsu's brushwork is maintained tirelessly to the end.

The very first poem on the scroll, attributed to Kakinomoto no Hitomaro (fl. ca. 686–697), gives the poet's second name mistakenly as "Maru," and the character "*hito*" has been added unobtrusively on the side. This detail serves only to underscore the serene self-confidence of the great Kōetsu.

These are the first four poems:

> Dimly in the morning mist
> of Akashi Bay
> my thoughts follow a boat
> disappearing behind an island
> —Kakinomoto no Hitomaro

> Though all around
> the light of spring
> floods the land
> yet on fair Yoshino mountains
> again the snow comes down
> —Ōshikōchi no Mitsune

> When I see the whiteness
> of frost on Magpie's Bridge
> then do I know
> the night has deepened
> —Chūnagon (Ōtomo no) Yakamochi

> Is this not the moon?
> Is this spring not
> the spring of old?

Only I myself alone
remain the same as ever
　　—Ariwara no Narihira

The poems are by the Thirty-Six Immortals of Poetry, a grouping established in the early eleventh century during the reign of Emperor Ichijō (r. 986–1011) by the court noble Fujiwara no Kintō (906–1041), who served with distinction during this golden era that also saw the creation of Sei Shōnagon's *Pillow Book* (*Makura no sōshi*) and Lady Murasaki's *Tale of Genji* (*Genji monogatari*). Joined with the poems six hundred years later are the underpainting of Sōtatsu and the calligraphy of Kōetsu. Art historians frequently refer to the *Anthology with Crane Design* as a calligraphy and painting "duet," but they are wrong. This masterwork is a trio of calligraphy, painting, and poetry.

Reading through this anthology, one cannot help but be overwhelmed by the richness and power of the revival of the Heian classical tradition. Kōetsu and Sōtatsu, along with other artists, created calligraphy and painting ensembles with underpaintings not only of cranes but also of flowers and grasses of the four seasons, deer, lotuses, and butterflies, with calligraphic renderings of poems from *Poems Old and New* (*Kokinshū*, 905); *New Collection of Poems Old and New*; *One Hundred Poets, One Poem Each* (*Hyakunin isshu*, twelfth century*); Japanese and Chinese Poems for Recitation* (*Wakan rōeishū*, ca. 1013); and other collections. Many such hand scrolls and poem-cards were produced. Kōetsu and Sōtatsu also collaborated with their friend Suminokura Soan (1571–1632) to design and publish *sagabon*, gorgeous illustrated books that include noh plays and selections from *The Tales of Ise* (*Ise monogatari*, ca. 980) and other works of classical Japanese literature.

With the restoration of peace, culture in the capital underwent a steady rebirth, escaping the dominating influence of the continent. Emperor Go-Mizunoo (1596–1680), who after abdicating would build the simple and elegant Shūgakuin Detached Palace, was exceedingly cultured; he and all his courtiers were well versed in Japanese and Chinese classics as well as the tea ceremony and flower arranging. Wishing to control and use that energy, the first three Tokugawa shogun sought compromise with the court. Elsewhere in Kyoto, upper-class townspeople made wealthy by intermediary trade with the Dutch and Chinese had the freedom to enjoy vigorous intellectual and artistic activities. That environment allowed the geniuses of Sōtatsu and Kōetsu to burst into full flower, earning the admiration and support of the townspeople.

One question intrigues me. Where did Sōtatsu get the unusual idea of portraying a flock of over a hundred cranes in flight? Hardly any art historians have managed to shed light on this issue. Tamamushi Satoko, an eminent scholar of Rimpa art, has suggested that Sōtatsu's inspiration may have come in part from the ink painting *The Hundred Geese* (*Bai yan tu*), traditionally attributed to the Northern Song (960–1127) painter Ma Fen, in the collection of the Honolulu Museum of Art.[2] After learning of her theory from someone close to me, I searched in Tamamushi's book with eager anticipation, but as far as I could tell from photographic evidence, there is too great a difference in the fundamental gracefulness of cranes and geese for such a painting to have exerted much influence. Moreover, Ma Fen's portrayal of geese in flight lacks the melodic beauty and rhythm of Sōtatsu's work. The earlier work seems to me simply a variation on the theme of "wild geese descending to a sandbar," one of the "eight views of the Xiao and the Xiang" Rivers, a popular subject among the scholarly elite in the Northern Song dynasty.

In Sōtatsu's time, the expression *sembazuru*, "a thousand [origami] cranes," didn't yet exist, nor did *chiyogami*, paper decorated with brightly colored, small woodblock-printed designs to be cut out and arranged. It occurred to me that perhaps the inspiration for the crane scroll painting came rather from Sōtatsu's exposure to ancient Japanese poetry. I turned first to *Japanese and Chinese Poems for Recitation*, a superb Heian anthology compiled by Fujiwara no Kintō that Kōetsu sometimes drew on for the poems he used on Sōtatsu's underpaintings. Sure enough, in Miscellanea, next to "monkeys" I found "cranes." Along with poems by Tang-dynasty poets like Bai Juyi (772–846) and Liu Yuxi (772–842), and Heian poets like Miyako no Yoshika (834–879) and Minamoto no Shitagō (911–983), the section included this well-known poem by Yamabe no

Akahito (fl. 724–736) from the eighth-century *Ten Thousand Leaves* (*Man'yōshū*), written in the tenth month, 724:

> At Waka Bay
> with the rising tide
> the sandbanks vanish
> and cranes fly calling
> toward the reeds on shore

Also listed are poems by two other Immortals of Poetry, Lady Ise (ca. 875–938) and Fujiwara no Kiyotada (d. 938). In his masterful study of the *Man'yōshū*, the poet Saitō Mokichi (1882–1953) describes the poem above as "a first-rate work by Akahito with a clean feeling."[3] The final two lines are outstanding for their clarity of image, he writes, and he also has high praise for their "fluid tone." The third line, "the sandbanks vanish," he frowns on as "slightly explanatory," not fully ancient and at the same time too modern. Despite this caveat, Mokichi chose this *waka* as among the finest in the entire collection of 4,496 poems, and it was undoubtedly a distant source of inspiration for Sōtatsu.

Many other poems in the anthology describe a flock of cranes taking flight as the tide rises or ebbs, including these:

> Toward Sakurada
> cranes fly, calling
> At Ayuchi marsh
> the tide must have gone out
> Cranes fly, calling
> —Takechi no Muraji Kurohito

> Standing at Naniwa marsh
> as the tide goes out
> I cast my gaze about
> and see a flock of cranes
> toward Awaji Island
> —Anonymous

In the evening calm
cranes hunt for feed
When the tide comes in
and waves grow high
they call out for their mates
　—Anonymous

These cranes are surely the same as those that soar and dip with still greater beauty as they head toward the strand in Sōtatsu's long scroll nine hundred years on.

According to Kumakura Isao, president of Shizuoka University of Art and Culture, "After the retired emperor Go-Mizunoo, no emperor would be as devoted to poetry for the next 450 years."[4] *Collection of Retired Emperor Go-Mizunoo* (*Go-Mizunoo-in gyoshū*) includes some two thousand poems by the retired emperor, one of which actually calls out to the cranes in Yamabe no Akahito's poem, asking through a play on words how to restore the way of poetry (*waka*) to its past glory:

I long to ask the cranes
living in Waka Bay
if they know a path
leading to the waves of old

Because of Emperor Saga's (746–842) preference for Chinese poetry, the worlds of the *Kokinshū* and *Shinkokinshū* were tainted by Chinese taste, and the flocks of cranes that once flew *Man'yō* skies were laden with the symbolic meanings they had in the Tang poetry of Bai Juyi and Liu Yuxi, becoming, along with the tortoise, auspicious emblems of longevity or birds who nested in pine trees as companions for exalted persons.[5] Setting aside the Daitokuji triptych *Guanyin, Crane, and Gibbons* by the Chinese painter Muqi (ca. 1210–1269), cranes in the works of Sesshū (1420–1506) and Kanō Sansetsu (1589–1651), as well as those of Ogata Kōrin, Itō Jakuchū (1716–1800), and Suzuki Kiitsu (1796–1858), all have a red crown and do nothing but loiter between trees or at the water's edge.

Here, too, Tawaraya Sōtatsu easily breaks with such makeshift chinoiserie to return to the original scenes of Japanese poetry transmitted long ago by Yamabe no Akahito and the rest. By departing from Chinese symbolism, the great flock of cranes in Sōtatsu's painting wings its way high and low over the rising tide, calling out, with all the more auspiciousness and grace. Mixed with Kōetsu's vibrant calligraphy and exquisite ink shadings, cranes once again appear before me as notes in a musical composition, and bright music resounds.

Is it a piece for strings and traditional Japanese instruments by Takemitsu Tōru that I hear? Something by Debussy or Duparc? No, listening closely I recognize it as the first movement, Allegro, of Mozart's *Concerto for Flute and Harp*, K. 299. The flute expresses the rush of the cranes' wings and their voices calling back and forth, while the low notes of the harp are the sound of the rising tide, filling my ears with distant beauty.

Kōetsu as Understood by a *Japonisant*: The Craze for "Decorativeness" and Its Limitations

To recapitulate, in early Tokugawa Japan, a revival of the flowering of Heian culture was brought about by a pair of brilliant artists who lived in the ancient capital of Kyoto: Hon'ami Kōetsu, who was born into a prestigious family of sword-makers, and the fan-maker Tawaraya Sōtatsu, of ordinary birth. Behind them was the retired emperor Go-Mizunoo, a cultured and broad-minded man who diplomatically dealt with the new government in Edo while continuing to serve as a patron of the arts and an arbiter of taste. Suminokura Soan, son of the wealthy merchant Suminokura Ryōi, also played a role in the movement led by members of the Kyoto bourgeoisie to revive courtly arts and culture.

Kōetsu, Sōtatsu, and Soan did not refer to themselves collectively as "Rimpa" members, nor did their contemporaries. The term came into general use later, with the work of the painter Ogata Kōrin (1658–1716) and his younger brother, ceramicist Ogata Kenzan (1663–1743), sons of the wealthy merchant family that owned the Kyoto textile emporium Kariganeya; "Rimpa" was coined from the second character in Kōrin's name and the character for "school" or "style."

Kōrin was born exactly one hundred years after Kōetsu, and he died in the year that two artistic champions of eighteenth-century Kyoto were born, although they belonged to a slightly lower class of towns-folk: painter Itō Jakuchū (1716–1800) and poet-painter Yosa Buson (1716–1784). Kōrin's dates thus serve as a handy benchmark for the changing times.

Of early modern Japanese painters, the first to become well known abroad, particularly in Europe, were Kōrin and three ukiyo-e artists: Hokusai (1760–1849), Utamaro (d. 1806), and Hiroshige (1797–1858). In the 1850s, not long after Japan was opened to the West, a large number of ukiyo-e prints were dispersed all around Europe, and exported along with them were a fair number of Rimpa-style paintings, small works of fine and applied arts, and albums.

Kōrin was especially popular in France, where the *japonisme* movement began in mid-century and reached its peak at the end of the century. One man, the celebrated art historian Louis Gonse (1846–1921), quite lost his head over Kōrin. An important pioneer of *japonisme*, Gonse published *Japanese Art* (*L'art japonais*), a large, illustrated two-volume introduction to Japanese art in 1883. A lengthy essay of his entitled "Kōrin" appeared in *Artistic Japan* (*Le Japon artistique*, 1888–1891), a trilingual (French-English-German) periodical devoted to international *japonisme* that was published from May 1888 to April 1891. In the essay, Gonse is quite open about his partiality for Kōrin. He begins with an encomium to the artist's name:

> Korin! I love that name. I love the ring and the rhythm of it. The name has a certain undulation, now trailing languidly, now filled with rugged energy—enough by itself to create a certain mental image. Within this true *japonisant*, a devotee of Japanese art in whose soul there has lodged a grain of madness, this name arouses a dizzying sensuality, engendering something like an exceptional trembling that derives from its peculiar, marvelous individuality. . . . The name "Korin" is wonderfully suited to the art its owner represents.[6]

This passage offers ample indication that Gonse was indeed mad for Kōrin—not that he was the only one to fall hard for an admired artist. The novelist Mushanokōji Saneatsu (1885–1976), a key member of the Shirakaba literary coterie in Taishō Japan, idolized Tolstoy and would turn bright red if he so much as spotted on the street the *katakana* used to write the first syllable of the great man's name. A similar phenomenon was at work among Parisian *japonisants* at the end of the nineteenth century. Vincent van Gogh, who frequented the Paris store of Siegfried Bing, a Japanese art dealer and editor in chief of *Artistic Japan*, went into raptures on moving to southern France in 1888 because he felt that the color of the sky, the water patterns in the streams, and even the form of the mountains evoked the Japan of his dreams.

But Gonse was not simply gaga over Kōrin. He wrote, "Kōrin was a painter who pushed the two foundational principles of Japanese aesthetics, synthesis of form and simplification of design, to the furthermost limit." He also placed him correctly in Japanese art history as the successor to "the great seventeenth-century painter" Tawaraya Sōtatsu and the forerunner of Sakai Hōitsu, who was active in Edo in the nineteenth century. Gonse proudly owned several works of art that had been in Kōrin's collection, and he and fellow Parisian *japonisants* of note would get together to show off their prize Kōrin works to one another. He obtained valuable books such as *Kōrin Compendium* (*Kōrin Gafu*, 1802) and *One Hundred Paintings by Kōrin* (*Kōrin hyaku-zu*, 1815). Illustrating his observations with numerous sketches from those books, Gonse writes in the same essay:

> When Kōrin had thoroughly mastered his own technique, he finally made sketches unlike those of anyone else. They are supple, with tenacity and roundness, as well as boldly abbreviated, exhibiting abrupt changes of tone. Within the shadow of a slight awkwardness or seeming carelessness lies the sure touch of a master craftsman.... In their extreme simplicity lies a transfixing charm; a gently permeating, ineffable fragrance; a harmony that clings to one like sensual music.[7]

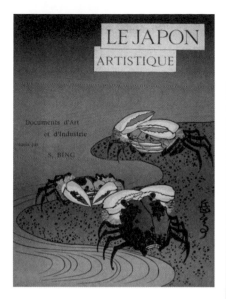

Figure 20. Magazine devoted to *japonisme*. *Le Japon artistique*, vol. 23, cover, and the introduction to an essay on Kōrin.

Gonse is lavish with praise, employing a succession of rhetorical flourishes, as if he cannot find words enough. It is fascinating to know that such keen appreciation of Rimpa art in general and of Kōrin in particular was already widespread in artistic circles of nineteenth-century Europe. This certainly explains the prevalent influence of not only ukiyo-e but also Rimpa-style design and form in Impressionist art of that era and art nouveau at the turn of the century.

One thing bothers me, though, and that is a sense that the *japonisants* were overly focused on the decorative aspect of Rimpa art. In an essay entitled "The Japanese Gift for Decoration" written for the June 1888 issue of *Artistic Japan*, Gonse rapturously declares that "the Japanese are the world's greatest decorators." His appreciation of Kōrin is the natural extension of his belief that "the decorative sense is the essence of Japanese aesthetics." This is a reasonable assessment of the works of the Ogata brothers, Kōrin and Kenzan, and of the Edo Rimpa artists Hōitsu and Suzuki Kiitsu, but what about Kōetsu and Sōtatsu, the seminal geniuses of Tokugawa Rimpa? Of course, they also produced richly decorative art. But the delightful, resounding dynamism of Sōtatsu's *Wind God and Thunder God*; the Mozartesque beauty of *Anthology with Crane Design*, that triple concerto of poetry, calligraphy, and painting; the vast, transcendent tranquility of mist and trees in *Chinese Black Pine and Cypress* (*Maki hinoki-zu byōbu*), rendered simply with ink and silver paint on gold leaf; and the *mono no aware* and *yūgen* (subtle, mysterious beauty) giving life to small ink sketches of dragons, waterfowl, cows, puppies, as well as bracken, edamame, and more—are these not expressions of the great mystery arising from a fundamental interplay between humans and nature, far surpassing mere decorativeness?

Nor can we overlook Kōetsu's hand-modeled black raku ware tea bowls "Amagumo" and "Murakumo," nor his red raku ware tea bowls "Bishamondō" and "Kaga Kōetsu," so heavy and profound, so dark at times, lopsided and rough, yet in their shape and texture and hue brimming with eroticism and infinite complexity, unfathomable joy.

None of the above works were of course yet known in Europe during the age of *japonisme*. Understanding the deepest layers of Japanese aesthetics would have to wait another fifty years, until the second half of the twentieth century. The history of *japonisme* teaches us that in East or West, probing the depths of another culture and discovering the full range of its aesthetics cannot be done without intimate contact and research over an extended period of time.

---

1 AN: Tanabe Katsumi, *Girisha kara Nihon e: Alekusandorosu Daiō to tōzai bunmei no kōryūten zuroku* [From Greece to Japan: Alexander the Great and intersections between Eastern and Western civilization, a pictorial record] (Tokyo National Museum, 2003).

2 AN: Tamamushi Satoko, *Nihon no bijutsu: Rimpa to dezain, sōshoku, kazari* [Japanese art: Rimpa and design, ornamentation, decoration] (Shibundō, 2005).

3 AN: Saitō Mokichi, *Man'yō shūka* [Outstanding poems of the *Man'yōshū*], vol. 1 (Iwanami shoten, 1968), 194.

4 AN: Kumakura Isao, *Go-Mizunoo-in* [Retired Emperor Go-Mizunoo] (Asahi Shimbunsha, 1982), 192.

5 AN: Katagiri Yōichi, *Utamakura uta kotoba jiten* [Dictionary of *utamakura* and poetic diction] (Kadokawa shoten, 1986).

6 Louis Gonse, "Kōrin," *Le Japon artistique* [Artistic Japan], vol. 21, 141. https://hal-bnf.archives-ouvertes.fr/tel-01836592/file/Japonisme%20et%20erudition%20PARTIE%202.pdf. Translated from Haga's translation of the original French.

7 Ibid.

Part

II

4 | ALL ROADS LEAD TO EDO: BASHŌ'S PRAISE OF TOKUGAWA

In the introduction to this book, I quoted a verse by the poet-painter Yosa Buson expressing his weariness with peace. Some ninety years before that, Matsuo Bashō (1644–1694) wrote these haiku:

The Dutch consul too	*kabitan mo*
lies prostrate before him—	*tsukubawasekeri*
springtime of the shogun's reign	*kimi ga haru*
The Dutchmen too	*oranda mo*
have come to see the blossoms—	*hana ni kinikeri*
saddles on horses	*uma ni kuwa*

The first one was written in 1678, when Bashō was thirty-five, and the second was written the year after. Neither of them is particularly famous, nor particularly good. Bashō had become an independent haiku master, but he had not yet established his renowned style. Soon after this, in 1680, he began living a reclusive life in a straw-thatched cottage in Fukagawa, just outside Edo.

From the perspective of comparative literature, these verses are extremely interesting—and not only because Bashō—he of the quintessentially Japanese, austere *wabi-sabi* aesthetic (beauty of transience and imperfection)—chose to write about exotic Westerners, beginning one verse with "*kabitan*," meaning the head of the Dutch trading house in

Nagasaki, and the other with "*oranda*," meaning men of the Netherlands. The verses are interesting because Bashō wrote them in celebration of the Pax Tokugawana.

The particle *mo* (too) is at the end of the first line of each verse and could also be rendered "even": *even* the Dutch consul, *even* the Dutchmen. Paraphrased, the first haiku means something like this: From the Netherlands, a country immeasurably farther away than China or India, way off at the ends of the earth, an envoy called *kabitan* has come to Japan, to Edo, to pay obeisance to the glory of the shogun. How auspicious, the start of this era of peace under the shogun's dominion!

The second one is similar: the cherry blossoms of Edo are now famous throughout Japan and the whole world. Even the Dutch, after traveling to Nagasaki from their land so far away, saddled horses to come here and admire the blossoms in their glory.

Of course, Bashō was perfectly aware that the Dutch mission came to Edo each spring not to view the blossoms but to thank the shogun for granting them permission to do business. The first mission was in 1609, and from 1633 on they were an annual event. By the time Bashō wrote these verses, the visits had been taking place regularly in the second or third month each spring for some twenty years, just as the cherry blossoms were at their peak. The mission was the talk of the town. That's why Bashō wrote poems celebrating the foreigners' having come again to see the Edo blossoms. The use of hyperbole, a deliberate departure from fact, lends interest to the haiku. The verses also express Bashō's "Edoism," pride in his adopted city; now a man in his thirties, he feels himself finally becoming a true Edoite seven years after having left his birthplace in Iga Ueno.

Of particular interest to modern readers is Bashō's image of Japan, albeit exaggerated for poetic effect. However vague in outline the world may be, he puts Japan at its center; the center of Japan is Edo, Japan's new capital at the peak of its heyday; the center of the capital is Edo Castle, with the reigning shogun at its helm. The two verses above can certainly be read that way if taken in a slightly wider context.

In 1666, when Bashō was twenty-three, he wrote a haiku on the crowds of cherry-blossom viewers, referring to the supposed ninety-eight thousand households in Kyoto.

> In Kyoto crowds
> of ninety-nine thousand
> view the blossoms

But after he moved to Edo, his interest and the settings of his haiku turned more and more to the burgeoning capital: the prosperity of merchants' stores shining gold in the moonlight; the liveliness of theaters in Sakai-chō, in stark contrast to the wretchedness of autumn rain. Rather than the Kyoto aesthetic of *miyabi* (elegance), Bashō's taste ran instead toward Edo *zoku* (commonness), and he rejoiced in the capital's flourishing.

> On giant scales
> Kyoto and Edo balance
> in this spring of a thousand years

> Truly the moon
> gilding the prosperous street
> is worth a thousand gold coins

> Rainy day
> The world spends autumn
> in Sakai-chō

> Ten years this autumn
> Now the words mean Edo:
> "my hometown"

> I can see the roof
> of Asakusa Kannon temple
> in clouds of blossoms

> Clouds of blossoms
> Is that the bell in Ueno
> or Asakusa?

In that era, it wasn't strange if even Bashō, later on the poet of *wabi-sabi*, should indulge in such glorification of Edo and praise of its establishment as the capital. Memory of the Osaka winter and summer sieges (1614, 1615), the last challenge to Tokugawa supremacy, was fading, and the Shimabara Rebellion, an uprising in a corner of Kyushu, had been quelled in 1638. Bashō's haiku in praise of the "springtime of the shogun's reign" was written forty years later, in 1678. In all that time, apart from internal squabbles, the archipelago remained quiet, never under attack from within or without. Overseas aggression, foreign incursions and threats, civil war, and religious disputes had ceased, and under the policy of national seclusion (*sakoku*), Japan was set for at least 180 years more of absolute peace.

The first National Isolation Edict was issued in 1633 during the reign of Iemitsu, the third Tokugawa shogun (r. 1623–1651). It laid down regulations governing overseas voyages of Japanese ships and the return of Japanese travelers from abroad. Each new regulation was stiffer than the last, until in 1639, the year after the Shimabara Rebellion and the fall of the rebels' stronghold at Hara Castle, a prohibition against Portuguese ships left Japan almost completely isolated. Japan's "Christian century," which began in 1543 when a Portuguese ship was shipwrecked on the island of Tanegashima, was over. At the same time, Japanese aggression in and invasion of countries in East Asia and Southeast Asia, which had proceeded apace during that century, came to an abrupt end. The various prohibitions also served to isolate Japan from the vigorous expansion of the Western world that had been ongoing ever since the Age of Exploration. This relative isolation protected Japan's still-uncertain cultural and religious homogeneity from the skillful missionary work and strategy for expansion of the Catholic Church, thereby ensuring that the nascent shogun-domainal system could undergo a process of consolidation and strengthening.

In terms of the history of civilization, the period of Japan's seclusion was for other countries in the world, including both Europe and East Asia, a time of historic political, economic, and cultural transformation. From the latter half of the sixteenth century to the early seventeenth century, the Spanish empire rose to hegemony in Western Europe through its monopoly on vast imports of silver from the New World. Iberia took the initiative in the religious movement that arose in opposition to the Protestant Reformation led by Martin Luther and others. One focus of the Counter-Reformation was a fervent mission to spread Christianity not only westward to the Americas but also eastward to Japan in the Far East. Effects of this movement can be seen in the publication of Japanese translations of Jesuit classics such as *The Imitation of Christ* by Thomas à Kempis (*Kontemutsusu munji*, 1610) and *The Sinner's Guide* (*Guía do pecadores*, 1599) by Luis de Granada.

However, just around the time Toyotomi Hideyoshi began restricting the spread of Christianity in Japan and persecuting Christians, the reign of Philip II (1556–1598) saw the powerful Spanish empire's political and economic dominance begin to wane. The fabulous flow of silver from the New World merely brought inflation, and under the reigning conservative regime, new industries aimed at the vast market of the Spanish colonies were unable to prosper.

While the Catholic kingdom in southern Europe stagnated, Protestant countries in the north were developing rapidly. The Netherlands declared independence in 1581 to free itself from decades of Spanish rule and, while continuing to do battle with Spain, swiftly developed into a mercantile nation with a robust shipbuilding and seagoing industry. Elizabeth I (r. 1558–1603) supported the Netherlands behind the scenes. In 1588, the Spanish Armada headed north in a planned invasion of England, only to suffer a huge defeat in the English Channel. This debacle dealt a body blow to the prestige and power of Catholic Spain, leading to its eventual decline.

During this great upheaval, with the rivalry between the Protestant north and the Catholic south heating up in Europe and eventually flipping the status quo, Japan was frequently visited by Spanish ships sailing to or from the Philippines and by Portuguese ships using Macao as a port of call. During Ieyasu's lifetime, a certain amount of trade was allowed although proselytization was forbidden. Then in 1600 the storm-battered Dutch ship *Liefde* anchored off the shore of Kyushu with the

Englishman William Adams aboard, an incident that gave both England and the Netherlands an opening to request trade relations with Japan. The European rivalry between the Catholic south and the Protestant north then played out on a smaller scale in the Japanese archipelago, being resolved in favor of the latter when in 1609 the Netherlands was allowed to build a trading house in Edo, followed by England in 1613. England withdrew a decade later, giving the Dutch East India Company a monopoly on trade with Japan.

Reexamining the contemporary global situation in this light, I am led to conclude that during a time of a great religious and economic upheaval in Europe, the bans on maritime activities and Christianity imposed by the first three Tokugawa shoguns enabled Japan to thread its way through a delicate time when change was on the horizon. In the first half of the seventeenth century, great changes took place in East Asia as well, as repeated civil disturbances caused the Ming dynasty to decline and give way to the Manchu Qing dynasty in 1644. The Tokugawa shogunate limited its relations with the continent to trade in Nagasaki, keeping a safe distance, but sent armed forces led by the Shimazu of Satsuma to the Ryukyu kingdom in an attempt to subjugate that territory. However, Ieyasu acted quickly to improve relations with the Yi dynasty of Korea and sought to repair the severe aftereffects of Hideyoshi's invasions.

Amid unsettled conditions in the East and West during the first half of the seventeenth century, the shogunate's National Isolation Edicts were gradually toughened through repeated trials, evolving into a finished foreign policy that left Japan with only the safest partners in trading and diplomacy. That policy was adopted when three factors achieved a rare state of balance: Japan's fundamental geopolitical situation as an island country in the Far East, political and economic restrictions on European and Asian countries, and the Japanese people's strong desire for peace. It remained in place until that balance was destroyed by the Industrial Revolution in Europe. Japan's self-imposed isolation was a skillful general policy for the promotion of regional security.

This centuries-long policy has long been discussed as if it reflected a lackluster state of lockdown unique to Tokugawa Japan, the dreadful cause of delay and distortion in Japan's modernization. But taking a broader view, Japan's policy of isolation seems little different from similar policies in contemporary China and Korea, and its severity is questionable compared to continuing political, economic, cultural, and communication policies of isolation in the Soviet Union, China, Cuba, Albania, North Korea, and Burma [Myanmar], amidst the far more tightly woven web of international interdependence in the latter half of the twentieth century to the present day. National seclusion, in other words, is a universal phenomenon seen frequently in the course of world history, including our own time. In seventeenth-century Japan, the shogunate took advantage of that historic moment to implement a sensible and bold foreign policy controlling the flow of people and goods, a policy that ushered in and maintained the long Pax Tokugawana and made a cultural ripening possible.

* * *

Now let us return to the haiku of Bashō quoted at the start of this chapter. Written forty years after the establishment of *sakoku* in 1639, they capture the sense of peace, stability, and prosperity that had finally spread in Japan after centuries of strife. Nearly half a century had passed since the Dutch missions to Edo from Hirado and Nagasaki became a fixed annual event in 1633, so regular that they were all but a season-word for spring in haiku circles. In the third month of 1691, Engelbert Kaempfer (1651–1716) accompanied the trading house curator Hendrick van Buijtenhem to Edo for the first time, and they traversed the great Ōdōri Street leading from Shimbashi to Nihombashi. Unlike other towns they had passed through along the way, the townspeople were so used to the Dutch parades and demonstrated such pride as sophisticated urbanites that, Kaempfer wrote, "hardly any people stood in their doorways to watch us go by."[1]

Bashō's haiku, while retaining a sense of exoticism at the arrival of the "red-haired" foreigners, demonstrate that even he had developed a new sense of a centralized order and a hierarchical way of thinking, a growing sense that all roads led to Edo. The years 1678 and 1679, when Bashō composed those haiku, were the final years of the reign of the fourth shogun, Ietsuna; Tsunayoshi was to succeed him in 1680. The consolidation and strengthening of the shogun-domainal system, which had been proceeding smoothly since the reign of the third shogun, Iemitsu, was well advanced. By the start of Tsunayoshi's reign, the abolition or reduction of fiefs and the transfer of daimyo that took place after the battle of Sekigahara were largely complete. The new Edocentric system of government covered the entire nation in a closely woven web, and by the Genroku era (1688–1704), the sense of relief was widespread. Internal peace and freedom from external aggression, the latter thanks to the policy of national seclusion, brought social stability and encouraged domestic industry and trade.

The first century of the Tokugawa shogunate wrought many changes, from the early days when the political system and social atmosphere still bore lingering marks of unrest and violence to the establishment of the Pax Tokugawana at the end of the seventeenth century. Perhaps the best one-chapter summation of those changes is in *Told Round a Brushwood Fire* (*Oritaku shiba no ki*, 1716–1717), the autobiography of the Confucian scholar, historian, and statesman Arai Hakuseki (1657–1725). At the outset, Hakuseki reflects on the life of his father, Arai Masanari (1601–1682).

> Not long after the era of civil wars, when my father was young, men were chivalrous and accustomed to valuing nobility of spirit, and things were considerably different from the way they are now. My father spent years wandering, never staying long in one place.

He describes how Masanari drifted around the country amidst vestiges of the earlier war-ravaged era and finally entered the service of the Tsuchiya family in the 20,000-*koku* domain of Kururi in Kazusa province. Drawing on his father's recollections, Hakuseki recounts various heroic deeds befitting a warrior of old. His father had a fierce mien and was prudent, upright, and strict, clinging to the old ways. In old age, however, "during quiet times he would clean his place, hang old pictures on the wall, and arrange spring or autumn flowers in a vase; then he would sit all day in silent contemplation, or sometimes do some painting." His father's old-fashioned personality and appearance never changed, but when he resigned from service to the Tsuchiya family in 1675 at seventy-five, his surroundings changed, and Masanari incorporated the elegant pastimes of painting and flower arranging into his prudent and honest daily life.

Hakuseki was born in 1657, the year of the Great Meireki Fire in Edo, when Masanari was fifty-seven. He grew up in refined poverty under his father's influence and devoted himself to study, in time becoming a scholar. At the beginning of the eighteenth century, Hakuseki was the top-ranked civil advisor to the sixth shogun, Ienobu, and his Confucian-style government. Hakuseki's autobiography certainly offers a good picture of the transition from the dusty old days to the new era, the "springtime of the shogun's reign" that Bashō praised in verse—a springtime of universal prosperity, peace, and the calm of "Bush clover waves / spilling not a drop / of glistening dew."

> How holy!
> Green leaves young leaves
> in sunlight
>
> Counting them as I pass—
> mansion after mansion
> plums and willows
>
> A village grown old—
> not a house without
> its persimmon tree
>
> Like blossoms
> of the harvest moon—
> a field of cotton

If we could ride in a spaceship equipped with a time machine over late seventeenth-century Japan, the age of shoguns Ietsuna and Tsunayoshi, there under the surprisingly tight rule of the Tokugawa shogunate we might see the society inhabited by Bashō and Arai Hakuseki, the novelist Ihara Saikaku, and the playwright Chikamatsu Monzaemon, the thinker Kaibara Ekiken and the artist Ogata Kōrin, burgeoning steadily beneath us like waves of bush clover. Terms like "tranquility" *(gosei-hitsu)*, "peace in the land" *(tenka taihei)*, and "calm of the four seas" *(shikai nami shizuka)* were used in common parlance in praise of the Pax Tokugawana. The waters surrounding Japan that we would see from our spaceship would not yet be called the East China Sea, the Sea of Japan, or the Pacific Ocean, but they would be laid out with the calm beauty of the traditional "blue sea and waves" design of stylized, overlapping waves that became popular in the Genroku era.

Once a year, around the end of summer, a pair of Dutch sailing ships would come to Nagasaki from the southeast, trailing white wakes in the blue expanse, and return in the early autumn. Thirty Chinese merchant ships would cross the East China Sea to Nagasaki, where they would unload a variety of wares before going home laden with more. Looking closely, we would see lots of small Japanese sailboats, but these would stick close to shore and, after a short run, soon pull into a harbor or slip behind an island before heading for Osaka. On the Pacific side of the islands, very few ships arrived during the Christian era; after that, no ship came from any foreign country.

The seaside scenery that Yosa Buson would later describe in the haiku below was already coming into being.

> The Korean ship
> passes by without a pause
> into the mist
>
> A lightning flash—
> girdled by waves
> the isles of Japan
>
> A lightning flash—
> the isles of Japan,
> boats at anchor

1 AN: Engelbert Kaempfer, *Edo sampu ryokō nikki* [*Geschichte und Beschreibung von Japan* (History and description of Japan), 1777–1779], Saitō Makoto, trans. (Heibonsha, 1977), 173. JWC: Kaempfer's account appeared first in English translation (*The History of Japan*, 1727). The original German was published much later, after his death. There is a new translation by Beatrice Bodart-Bailey in her book *Kaempfer's Japan* (Honolulu: University of Hawaii Press, 1999).

5 | AN ENLIGHTENED PRACTICAL SCIENTIST: KAIBARA EKIKEN, GAZETTEERIST AND NATURALIST

A Visit with Ekiken

If I could go back to the Genroku era, I would love to interview Kaibara Ekiken (1630–1714). There are of course other towering figures of that era; over the last hundred years or so, the names of Matsuo Bashō, Chikamatsu Monzaemon, Ihara Saikaku, Ogata Kōrin, and Arai Hakuseki have increasingly come to represent early modern Japan and Japanese culture around the world. Genroku Japan was truly overflowing with cultural creativity. But those great men in the urban centers of Edo, Osaka, and Kyoto were so engrossed in research, writing, and art, scattering sparks of energy day by day, that I rather doubt they would have had time for an inconsequential visitor from the faraway 2010s. Ekiken, on the other hand, would have at least let this twenty-first-century bumpkin into his drawing room, I am pretty sure.

For one thing, Ekiken lived in Fukuoka, Kyushu, where he served the Fukuoka domain and where the pace of life would have been more leisurely than in the major cities to the north. Also, judging from a portrait of him at sixty-five, he was a calm and generous man with a ready smile. Twenty-seven years older than Arai Hakuseki, Ekiken was, in his encyclopedic knowledge and his lively, lifelong curiosity about all aspects of people and nature, every bit Hakuseki's equal, but he lacked the younger man's severity and aggressiveness and was not a forbidding presence.

Even so, I would assure Ekiken that I was over fifty, or he might refuse to see me after all: in his later years, he believed that people below that age don't amount to much.

> Before fifty, the passions of youth have not yet settled and wisdom has yet to open up. One's knowledge of history being limited, one cannot adapt to changing times. Mistakes in speech are frequent, and actions lead often to regret. The rules and the pleasures of life are still unknown. Anyone who dies before fifty has died too young.   *—Life-Nourishing Principles*

Would this same standard apply to what, from the perspective of Genroku, is our end-times era, with an average life span in the eighties? In any case, as a man over fifty, I must say these words of Ekiken's are music to my ears. Ekiken himself completed his eight-volume *Life-Nourishing Principles* (*Yōjōkun*) in 1713, the year before he died at eighty-three. His words carry the weight of his own experience.

But even if I did go back in time to call at the Kaibara residence in Fukuoka, I might be disappointed to find that Ekiken was gone for the day, or the month, on one of his many field trips. The chances of his being out would be high. Far more so than his contemporary, Bashō, who wrote grandly of those for whom "the journey itself is home, and death comes on the road," Kaibara Ekiken was then perhaps the greatest traveler and the hardiest walker in all Japan.

Chikuzen Gazetteer

In 1648, at eighteen, Ekiken went to Edo with his father, Kaibara Kansai. On returning home the next year, he immediately set off for Nagasaki, accompanying Kuroda Mitsuyuki, the daimyo of the Fukuoka domain. Those trips marked the start of a lifetime of travel. How many trips he must have made overall, and how many thousands of kilometers he must have walked! According to Ekiken's own calculations, counting all the times he participated in daimyo processions and traveled on domain business, he walked to Edo and back twelve times, to Kyoto and back twenty-four times, and to Nagasaki and back five times.[1] In between, with a freedom unimaginable today, he let his legs carry him on lengthy tours of nearby areas. On top of all this, he took many personal trips with his wife, Tōken, and he also set out often on inspection tours of lands owned by the Kuroda family.

Especially from his fifties on, Ekiken produced a succession of travel books and regional geographies, drawing on his experiences and based on his travel diaries and notes. In 1679, at forty-nine, he wrote *Travels in Jōshoku* (*Jōshoku kikō*) and followed it with nearly twenty more books, among them *Record of a Tour of Japan* (*Yamato junranki*) in 1692, written at age sixty-two, and *Record of a Tour of Various Provinces* (*Shoshū junranki*), written in 1713, the year before his death. Ekiken's travel writings bear no resemblance to Bashō's poetic travel diaries of the same era, including *Narrow Road to the Deep North* (*Oku no hosomichi*, final draft completed in 1694, published in 1702) and *Record of Bleached Bones in a Field* (*Nozarashi kikō*, 1684–1685). Writing in a very plain prose style and following his itinerary exactly, Ekiken lists place names and gives the distance between villages, as well as the local scenery, number of households, main sources of income, and the history and condition of local historic sites, interspersed with his personal experiences and impressions. His writings read rather like travel guides. They heralded a new style of objective, observational travel writing in sharp contrast to the tradition of lyrical, subjective travel accounts—a tradition which Bashō knew well—represented by *Tosa Diary* (*Tosa nikki* by Ki no Tsurayuki, ca. 935), *Travel to the Eastern Provinces* (*Tōkan kikō*, anonymous, ca. 1242), and *Diary of the Waning Moon* (*Izayoi nikki* by Abutsu-ni, 1277–1280).

Ekiken's travel writings contain great dollops of human geography and naturalism, and his travels were in a large sense scholarly fieldwork in those areas he visited; however, his greatest achievement was not his travel writings but his regional geography study, the *Chikuzen Gazetteer* (*Chikuzen no kuni zoku fudoki*). The Japanese title indicates that Ekiken saw his work as the Genroku version of ancient *fudoki*, the eighth-century reports on the natural resources, geophysical conditions, and oral traditions of the provinces. With the permission of the newly appointed daimyo, Kuroda Tsunamasa, he began a survey of the Kuroda territories in 1688, at age fifty-eight, and in 1703, at seventy-three, he finally

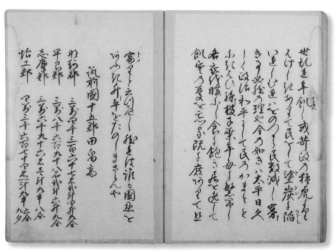

Figure 21. Kaibara Ekiken, *Chikuzen Gazetteer* (*Chikuzen no kuni zoku fudoki*). Fukuoka Prefectural Library.

completed the gazetteer and presented it to Tsunamasa. These thirty volumes are superbly organized, beginning with a general survey of the domain and going on to cover nature and human affairs throughout Fukuoka, Hakata, and all the districts in the Kuroda holdings; it ends with detailed comments on old castles and battlegrounds as well as regional products. In the 1910 edition of Ekiken's complete works, the gazetteer occupies 713 pages. *Chikuzen Gazetteer* is a true lifework.

In the first two volumes, entitled *Synopsis* (*Teiyō*), Ekiken provides the rice output of each district, finely calibrated in *masu*, *gō*, and *shaku*,[2] as well as meticulous records of the number of households, the population, and the number of livestock and boats. His accounts describe the scrupulous administration of domain properties in the Genroku era, although Ekiken's own naturalistic and obsessive focus on gathering data also certainly influenced his detailed descriptions. He set out to gather and record all known facts about the history and status of every village, mountain, temple, and shrine in the domain. The skillfully presented data is infused with details that Ekiken could only have obtained by being physically present in each place. In his sixties, between long trips to Edo and Kyoto, Ekiken was constantly engaged in surveys, accompanied by his nephew and assistant, Kaibara Yoshifuru.

In an introduction that he appended in 1709, Ekiken reflects back on his labors:

> I walked to every village in the Fukuoka domain, climbing high mountains and descending into deep valleys, following steep paths and dangerous ways, getting drenched in rain and soaked with dew, suffering cold winds and hot sun, and making the rounds of more than eight hundred villages. Everywhere I went, I assiduously inquired of the residents concerning all the places around and wrote down all that I saw and heard on paper tucked inside my kimono....I examined many accounts of recent events and inquired of people far and wide concerning them, correcting errors and discrepancies. If anything I had seen or heard seemed unclear, I looked on it with doubt and often went back to resurvey villages and make an exhaustive study of the facts.

This description must be truthful since it matches Ekiken's gazetteer and his activities at that time. This is indeed the approach of an empirical naturalist. Ekiken's work, both qualitatively and quantitatively, is on par with Thomas Jefferson's *Notes on the State of Virginia*, written eighty years later, in 1785.

The Flower of Genroku Practical Learning

In 1709, the same year he wrote the introduction cited above, Ekiken marked his eightieth year by completing another monumental lifework: the sixteen-volume *Japanese Herbal* (*Yamato honzō*) with two supplements and three volumes containing over three hundred specimen drawings. This grand compilation of research is the result of Ekiken's lifetime of travel and fieldwork. These pioneer studies, the first original literature in the field of Japanese *hakubutsugaku* (natural history), demonstrate the cultural strength of Genroku Japan. In his usual style, Ekiken devotes the first two volumes to a synopsis and a discussion of methodology.

The following excerpt is a manifesto of positivism, encapsulating the ideas in the introduction to *Chikuzen Gazetteer*:

Anyone doing a study of this nature must have extensive knowledge, hear and see many things, omit what is doubtful, refer to a variety of sources, and make judgments with care, or accurate results cannot be obtained. One should not blindly trust one's own observations and dismiss the differing views of others. In general, insufficient observation, overconfidence in one's observations, bias in favor of one's own theories, and hasty judgment—these four habits inevitably lead to error.

This sound exposition of the methodology of practical learning has certainly been drawn from Ekiken's long years of research. The researcher must seek broad knowledge and experience, but not blindly trust his own eyes and ears; he needs to be broad-minded enough to listen to others' theories and take them into careful consideration; clinging stubbornly to one's own views and making rash assertions are the root of error: these wise words from the grand old man are equally applicable today, not only in the field of natural history but also in the humanities and social sciences. Young students and newly-minted scholars often clamor the loudest about methodology, but for anyone seriously engaged in creative scholarship, there are vital lessons in these few words, distilled from Ekiken's practical experience.

Ekiken obeys these precepts in his own work, referring to the few Chinese and Japanese books on medicinal plants and agriculture then available, beginning with *Bencao gangmu* (*Compendium of Materia Medica*; Japanese: *Honzō kōmoku*), the seminal Ming-dynasty study compiled by Li Shizhen (1518–1593). Ekiken made full use of the literature, through reference, citations, and frequent criticism. During his Kyoto sojourns he became acquainted with Mukai Genshō (1609–1677) and Inō Jakusui (1655–1715), the top physician and herbalist of the day, respectively, and frequently exchanged views with them. In his notes to *Japanese Herbal*, he comes out with firm praise for their work and acknowledges his intellectual debt to them. Ekiken also cultivated flowers, fruits, and vegetables in his garden and used them in experiments, turning often to acquaintances for information and advice. Here again, as a practical naturalist, he bears a strong resemblance to Thomas Jefferson, designer of the gardens at Monticello. And besides all this, Ekiken drew on the accumulated experience of his dozens of travels around the country over many years.

Japanese Herbal (Yamato honzō)

True to its name, *Japanese Herbal* covers over 1,360 varieties of primarily Japanese plants, animals, and minerals, though not all are necessarily medicinal in nature. For each one, Ekiken gives the name in Japanese and Chinese, including dialectal variations, along with the item's regional origin, form, and efficacy. Generally he follows Li Shizhen's system of classification, adding his own devices and subclassifications. An additional three volumes, as mentioned earlier, contain roughly three hundred drawings. The drawings are fairly unsophisticated and fall far short of the elegant ones in *Sketches of Flowering Plants* (*Kaboku shinsha*) by the eighteenth-century court noble Yorakuin Konoe Iehiro and the woodcut illustrations by Sō Shiseki in Hiraga Gennai's great work *Classification of Various Materials* (*Butsurui hinshitsu*, 1763). Yet they are by no means inferior to the illustrations in *The History of Plants* (*Cruijdeboeck*), the 1554 herbal by Rembert Dodoens (published in Dutch in 1618), which Ekiken may have seen in its Japanese translation, *Kōmō honzō* (*Red-haired Herbal*), and they are far superior to those in Terashima Ryōan's *Illustrated Dictionary of the Three Realms in Japanese and Chinese* (*Wakan sansai zue*, 1712). The explanations range in length from dozens of lines to a single line, but all are written in a clear, expressive style with the needs of people who rely on such books kept foremost in mind. The insights and personality of Ekiken the enlightened thinker are on clear display in this work

Choosing an example is difficult, but here is his entry for the common flowering plant *rengesō*.[3]

> Children in the Kyoto and Kinki areas call this "*rengebana*." In Tsukushi, it is called *pōzō hana*. It blooms in the third month; the color is red and white, the height 3 or 4 *sun* [9–13 centimeters].

Little children gather the flowers and entwine the stems for their play. In hills and grassland, this plant is grown in fields, and the leaves and stems are fed to horses. The young leaves are edible. This plant is listed in *Shokumotsu honzō*[4] and *Kyūkō yafu*,[5] but is not listed in *Honzō*.[6] Some varieties have a white flower that turns red as the day wears on. A lovely flower.

I may have chosen an unusually winsome entry. I am reminded that Ekiken had several grandchildren. This is an example of how studies in natural history can often encourage the development of new styles of prose and painting.

Concerning a bird called *yobukodori* (child-call-bird), Ekiken writes, "One of the three mysterious birds in the *Kokinshū*. Difficult to say what it is based on conjecture." He goes on to cite *Man'yōshū* poems by Kagami no Ōkimi and Sakanoue no Iratsume and refutes popular theories, commenting, "These poems do not indicate that it is a person or monkey or deer. It must be a woods-dwelling bird." Concerning blowfish, which contains lethal toxins, he repeatedly lectures: "Why eat a poisonous fish?" "Anyone careful about their health should not eat it."

In the section on wild boar, he writes:

> People commonly misread 猪 as "wild boar," but this is wrong. 猪 is "pig." To refer to a wild boar, you must write 野猪 as in the title of this entry. In the same way, 鴨 is "duck," not "wild duck." Lard, written 猪油, is from pigs, not wild boar. Sows gestate for four months before giving birth in summer, in the fourth or fifth month. Pigs have litters of eleven or twelve, boars three or four. Eating boar meat stops hemorrhoidal bleeding. It is also an effective cure for skin rash. Roasted, it cures intestinal bleeding. Sow meat is especially tasty after the tenth month. The front legs are delicious. Generally the best way to stew boar or chicken meat is to simmer it a long time the day before with a bit of soy sauce, and the next day to boil it again just before eating. This will tenderize tough meat. Boar meat is not bad for

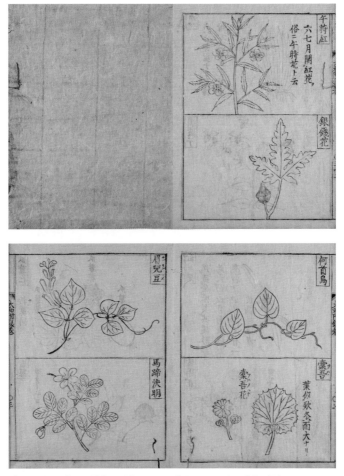

Figure 22. Kaibara Ekiken, *Diagrams of Japanese Medicinal Plants* (*Yamato honzō shohin-zu*). Main Library, Kyoto University.

you. Many people become sick after eating it because it tastes so good that they eat too much.

Japanese people of the time were thoroughly familiar with wild boar, so even though this is a book of natural history, Ekiken does not bother laying out the animal's form, habitat, or other such details, choosing instead to emphasize cooking methods. He himself apparently often ate the meat of the forelegs as treatment for his chronic hemorrhoids. His lively, practical prose is similar to the lucid style of the writer and reformer Fukuzawa Yukichi (1835–1901), and better for people's mental health today than medicinal herbs and wild boar meat are for physical health.

Alongside section headings like "Boiling Water," "Bean-jam Buns," "Salted and Fermented Seafood," and "Boiled Fish Paste," Ekiken includes "*Kappa*" (river imps), "Mermaids," and "Fingernails," and he writes things like this, in the section on leeches: "If a woman's hair is soaked in water for a long time it changes color and turns into small red leeches." Such oddities should be looked on with pleasure as a sign of how enviably rich the world of natural history was in Ekiken's time, when it still mingled with the world of the imagination. If Ekiken could have seen us twenty-first-century humans, he might well have filed us in a subsection of "People" as a strange curiosity.

---

1 AN: Inoue Tadashi, *Kaibara Ekiken*, Jimbutsu sōsho [Library of people] (Yoshikawa kōbunkan, 1989), 106.

2 1 *masu* = 1.8 liter (approximately 0.5 US gallon); 1 *gō* = 1/10 *masu*; 1 *shaku* = 1/100 *masu*.

3 Chinese milk vetch (*Astragalus sinicus*).

4 *Shiwu Bencao* [Edible plant herbal], compiled by Kou Ri in 1620.

5 *Jiuhuang yepu* [Famine relief plant book], edited by Wang Xilou in the Ming dynasty.

6 AN: *Bencao Gangmu* [*Compendium of Materia Medica*; Japanese: *Honzō kōmoku*], compiled by Li Shizhen in the Ming dynasty.

6 | A VISITOR IN THE *SAKOKU* ERA: KAEMPFER AND GENROKU JAPAN

Let us look again at one of the "red-haired" haiku by Matsuo Bashō that I commented on previously:

> The Dutch consul too
> lies prostrate before him—
> springtime of the shogun's reign

In the Japanese original, Bashō uses the word "*tsukubawasekeri*," a causative verb that literally means "is made to prostrate himself." Many readers may assume that Bashō chose this powerful expression as a rhetorical device to exaggerate the shogun's authority. However, it is no mere flourish or figure of speech. In fact, everyone in the Dutch mission was "made to prostrate himself" before the shogun. Bashō, though a mere haiku teacher in Edo, heard about that scene somehow and lost no time incorporating it in a verse. Here we see Bashō's journalistic sense in action.

The journey on horseback from Nagasaki to Edo by the Dutch delegation took an average of thirty days. The head of the Dutch trading company was accompanied by several other Dutchmen including a surgeon, a bookkeeper, and a secretary, as well as the Nagasaki city magistrate, a senior interpreter, a junior interpreter, and several dozen functionaries from the magistrate's office. Along the way, the leader was treated like a daimyo leading a procession to Edo under the *sankin kōtai* (alternate attendance) system and accorded full courtesy. On arriving in the capital, the party entered the Nagasakiya, an inn at Nihombashi

Hongokuchō 3-chōme, next to the bell tower that tolled the hour; they were required to wait there for a week or ten days, confined inside. When the day of their audience finally arrived, at some time after six in the morning they would repair to the castle on horseback or in palanquins. After passing a succession of barriers and made to wait or offer greetings at each stage along the way, they were ushered into a waiting room in the inner citadel of the castle.

For information about what happened during the audience with the shogun, I will cite the description of one who had such an experience in person just thirteen years after Bashō wrote the verse above. (The following is based on translations by Kure Shūzō, Imai Tadashi, and Saitō Makoto.)

> After waiting there for more than an hour while the shogun was settling down in the audience chamber, Settsu-no-kami [Kawaguchi Munetsune, the Nagasaki city magistrate] and two other magistrates came in and led the captain into his presence, leaving us behind. As the captain entered the audience chamber, we heard shouts of "Dutch captain!" This was the signal for him to approach His Majesty and perform his obeisance. The captain then crawled on his hands and knees to a designated spot between the gifts laid out in orderly fashion and the throne, lowered his forehead to the floor, and, still kneeling, did obeisance. Then without uttering a word he crawled backward like a crab. This was all that was involved in the audience we had taken such pains to prepare for.

The consul was thus literally "made to prostrate himself" in the castle. Then, just as they were breathing sighs of relief that the first audience was over, the foreigners were ushered into a different chamber, supposedly having been granted permission to inspect the castle interior but actually becoming objects of curiosity to the shogun, his chamberlains, and ladies-in-waiting from the Ōoku (Great Interior), the women's quarters of the castle.

In a central area with lacquered floorboards and surrounded by several other large rooms, the Dutch crawled in the direction of the shogun, who was seated behind a reed blind, and bowed in the Japanese style. Then the consul expressed his gratitude to the shogun for graciously permitting free trade with Japan, uttering the Japanese words *"Hollanda Capitan oreemoessimas"* (Dutch captain offers thanks). In response, from behind the blind, the shogun began a series of silly questions, conveyed via a steward and an interpreter. "How far is Batavia from Nagasaki?" "Who was mightier, the governor general of Batavia or the prince of Holland?" "What is the latest medicine that prolongs human life?" When the name of a medicine as long and important-sounding as possible was provided, a page or someone behind the blind wrote it down, asking over and over for it to be repeated.

When that exchange ended, the Dutchmen then had to put on a show.

> The shogun ordered us to remove our silk coats and stand up straight so we could be seen. Then we were ordered to walk, stand still, greet one another, dance, leap, act drunk, say a few words of Japanese, read Dutch, draw pictures, sing, put on and take off our coats. We did our best to oblige, and I sang a love song from the German highlands while dancing. In this way we had to perform innumerable monkey tricks for the amusement of the shogun and the rest.

This humiliating monkey show, as the Dutch saw it, continued for two hours. The blinds in the surrounding rooms had gaps that were widened with bits of rounded paper so that those on the other side could get a good look. The bright eyes of the shogun's daughters and women of the court shone through, and the low murmur of their conversation could be heard.

Around three in the afternoon, the consul and the rest of the delegation were allowed to leave the castle, and then they had to go around presenting gifts to senior and junior counselors. Again they were prevailed upon to do a bit of dancing and singing. By the time they finally returned to the Nagasakiya, it was the end of what must have been a very long spring day.

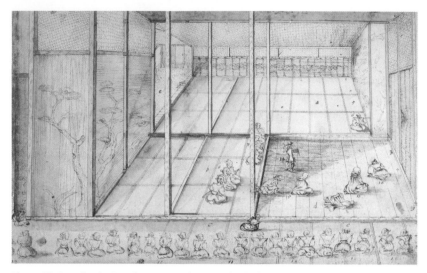

Figure 23. Drawing by Engelbert Kaempfer. "Dancing before Shogun Tsunayoshi." British Museum.

The sole scene of cultural exchange between foreigners and Japanese under the Tokugawa policy of national isolation took place before blinds through which peered numerous pairs of eyes, deep within the inner citadel of Edo Castle in the heart of Edo, the capital of Japan—exactly as described in Bashō's verse on "springtime of the shogun's reign."

This valuable record, which chronicles everything about the Dutch delegation's audience with the fifth shogun, Tsunayoshi (1646–1709), on March 29, 1691, down to the verses of the love song sang before the shogun and his courtiers, was written by the eminent German naturalist Engelbert Kaempfer. He is known as Germany's greatest scientific explorer of the Baroque era. Some have even called him a "fountain of the Baroque." He traversed a world broader and greater in variety than anyone in Genroku Japan could possibly have imagined—certainly not Tsunayoshi or his chamberlain, Makino Bingo no Kami, or Bashō, who would then have been compiling *Monkey's Straw Coat* (*Sarumino*, 1691) by the shore of Lake Biwa, or even the senior interpreter Yokoyama Yozaemon, who accompanied the Dutch delegation from Nagasaki. Kaempfer observed the Japanese way of life and society with eyes trained by his extensive travels and studies, and he wrote down what he saw.

Born in Lemgo, a small town near Hanover in northern Germany, Kaempfer left his birthplace at seventeen to pursue classical and modern studies in schools and universities throughout the Netherlands and northern Germany. Apart from a brief return home for several months in 1680, he continued thereafter to travel widely, even as far as Japan.

In 1683, he left Uppsala University in Sweden to join the Swedish king's trade delegation to the shah of Persia, traveling to Moscow and across the Caspian Sea to Isfahan, the Persian capital. Rather than return to his war-torn homeland, he went on to Bandar Abbas on the gulf of Hormuz to serve as physician with the Dutch East India Company. After a two-year wait, he finally boarded a ship in 1687 and sailed all around India, arriving in Batavia, Java, in October 1689. The following May he sailed from Batavia and stopped briefly in Siam before arriving in Nagasaki on September 24, 1690.

During the twenty-five months of his stay in Japan, Kaempfer went to Edo twice, in 1691 and 1692. He left Japan on October 31, 1692, sailing from Nagasaki via Batavia back to Amsterdam. In mid-October 1693, he set foot on European soil for the first time in ten years. By then he was forty-two. His remaining years until his death at sixty-five in Lemgo were by no means easy, but he completed a doctoral dissertation containing observations about his travels in Persia and Asia that was published in 1712 as *Amoenitatum Exoticarum*. The Japanese translation was called *Kaikoku kikan* (Exotic Spectacles from around the World).

Another Kaempfer manuscript in German that turned up posthumously was purchased by Sir Hans Sloane, an Englishman whose collections were the foundation of the British Museum, and published in English as *History of Japan* in two volumes in 1727. *History of Japan* was quickly translated into Dutch and French, both translations appearing in 1729. It had great impact, both positive and negative, on eighteenth-century Enlightenment thinkers, especially Montesquieu and Voltaire, and even on the *Encyclopédie* of Denis Diderot. The reports of Jesuit missionaries had largely formed the prevailing image of Japan before that, but Kaempfer looked at Japan as a whole, not through the lens of religion or trade, painting a lively picture of an independent, secluded empire with an advanced civilization. His book was truly groundbreaking.

The relativistic values that Kaempfer himself embodied and that Japanese civilization had corroborated later became an important factor in Enlightenment thinkers' skepticism and criticism regarding the invincibility of Christianity and the establishment. For over a century, Kaempfer's book was the best available guidebook on Japan, an essential reference work for the naturalist Carl Peter Thunberg (1743–1822) at Uppsala University and the Japanologist Philipp Franz von Siebold (1796–1866) at the University of Würzburg in Germany. Even Commodore Matthew Perry (1794–1858) pored over it aboard his Black Ship while crossing the Indian Ocean en route to Japan, as he sought ways to negotiate with the Japanese. From the late eighteenth century in Japan as well, scholars of Western learning began to take notice of the book, and in 1801 Shizuki Tadao, a scholar in Nagasaki, translated the chapter on Japan's policy of national isolation. This had considerable influence on the history of ideas in Japan in the years leading to the Meiji era.

Kaempfer remained unknown when he lived in Japan in the heyday of Genroku *sakoku*. The great German scholar and traveler, eager to lessen the intellectual distance between Japan and the West, was dismissed by the Japanese, after being first made to "prostrate himself" before the shogun and perform tricks while curious eyes peered out at him between gaps in blinds. Above I described this as a "scene of cultural exchange between foreigners and Japanese," but in fact the "exchange" was entirely one-sided. Even so, in a complicated and interesting twist, Kaempfer wrote approvingly of Japan's policy of seclusion. Through Kaempfer's great work, Tokugawa Japan's position in the world vis-à-vis other cultures emerges before our eyes in increments, forcing us to reevaluate what we know.

The following lines are the famous opening of Bashō's *Narrow Road to the Deep North*:

> The months and days are travelers of eternity, and the years that come and go are likewise vagabonds. For those who spend their

lives on ships and those who grow old leading horses by the bit, each day is a journey, and the journey itself is home. Many in the past have died on the road.

In this rather solemn mood, Bashō set out on his great journey of seeking, heading for northern Honshu on the twenty-seventh day of the third month of the second year of Genroku, May 1689. At that very time, Kaempfer was aboard a Dutch East Indies ship sailing from Ceylon and Calcutta across the Indian Ocean, bound for Batavia; one year later, he would voyage from Batavia to Japan. By the time Kaempfer arrived in Nagasaki in the eighth month of the third year of Genroku, Bashō's lengthy poetic pilgrimage on the "narrow road" had long since ended. Since the end of 1689 he had been here and there on the southern shore of Lake Biwa and spent three months in his hermitage Genjū-an in Ōtsu before setting out again to explore Awazu, Zeze, and Katada.

I write this out of a rather ironic desire to compare Bashō and Kaempfer, contemporaries and representative travelers of East and West who had nothing whatever to do with one another. Already seven years had passed since Kaempfer left Stockholm, in his own words "*Morbo curiositatis imbutus*" (driven by the sickness of curiosity). Braving daily extremes of hot and cold in fields, mountains, seas, and islands, enduring "the uncertain condition of a traveler," this scholar-explorer journeyed from the Western hemisphere to the Eastern. In comparison, how small in scale appear the travels of our vagabond poet, Bashō! After following the voyages of Kaempfer, one has to squint hard even to make out Bashō's figure.

Bashō, Kaempfer's senior by seven years, set out from Senju at age forty-five, his mood lonely and sentimental: "Thinking of the 3,000 leagues of travel ahead, I felt a knot in my chest. At the crossroads of parting in this dreamlike world, I shed tears of farewell." But no epidemic lay in wait on the road ahead, nor did he face stormy seas or bandits or thieves. The road was well maintained and the going smooth, the hills and fields were pleasant, and post towns offered places to rest at regular intervals along the way. This was the journey of a poet, a journey over roads trodden since ancient times by generations of like-minded travelers, a journey of homage with stops at places made famous by ancient evocative poems. To be sure, sometimes the road was muddy, sometimes there were fleas and lice. But Bashō kept on, finding aesthetic pleasure even in such discomforts, and in the next town he would come upon a welcoming committee of men of culture eagerly awaiting his arrival. This lyrical sightseeing trip through a section of the archipelago, a testament to the serenity of the Pax Tokugawana, ended without incident in only six months.

Narrow Road to the Deep North, the brief record of that trip, is an undisputed classic of world literature, a meditative, poetic travel diary in the vein of earlier classics by Ki no Tsurayuki (ca. 872–945), Saigyō (1118–1190), and Sōgi (1421–1502). Yet set against the enormous two-volume travelogue by Engelbert Kaempfer—cultural explorer, scholar of comparative civilizations, and traveler extraordinaire—*Narrow Road to the Deep North* takes on a different coloration. The two men's approach to travel, and the scale of time and space in their respective works, really brook no comparison. I do not mean to cast aspersions on the master-piece of the "saint of haiku." But from the perspective of comparative cultural history, it is obvious that the hallmark of Bashō's pilgrimage and his written account of it, the fact that he took a meditative, lyrical trip through a remarkably compact, culturally homogeneous space in a small island country self-isolated from the world, sets his writing and his travels quite apart from contemporary Europeans' records of far-flung adventures and observations—adventures motivated by curiosity and observations critiquing their native countries on the basis of what they had seen abroad.

I might be dwelling too much on Bashō. Even if he and Kaempfer had somehow managed to meet, their mentalities were so different that they would have had difficulty understanding one another. But Genroku Japan had no lack of people who, had they chanced to encounter Kaempfer, would have been amazed by his extensive experience and knowledge and full of praise for his ability to synthesize ideas—Japanese people of such towering intellectual stature that Kaempfer would surely have felt a bond with them. In an emerging cultural trend around the turn of the century, such people began to appear in Japan, though in small numbers.

Various names come to mind. Living in Nagasaki, near Kaempfer, was Nishikawa Joken (1648–1724), the finest human geographer and astronomer of his day. He could have used his connections to meet with the man from *Doichiranto* (Deutschland) on one of Kaempfer's botanical excursions outside the city with his young Japanese interpreter. Interviews with the Dutchman could have added greatly to Joken's books *Description of the Japanese Environment* (*Nihon suidokō*) and *A Study of the Chinese Trade, enlarged edition* (*Zōho kai tsūshōkō*). Unfortunately, there is no record that they ever did get together.

Over in Fukuoka on the island of Kyushu, Kaibara Ekiken (1630–1714), pioneer naturalist and the Kuroda domain Confucianist, was also alive and well. If Kaempfer had met him, he might have learned a great deal about the wide-ranging empiricism and ethics of the Japanese people. But during Kaempfer's stay, Ekiken, in his sixties, was hiking around Japan wherever his feet carried him, investigating products, gathering medicinal plant specimens, and writing travel accounts that were as different from Bashō's as night and day. Even if he had been granted special permission to meet Kaempfer, he probably wouldn't have had time.

In Edo, above all there was Arai Hakuseki, a polymath with robust intellectual curiosity about the West who would have been urged by everyone to match wits with Kaempfer. After he became advisor to the sixth shogun, Ienobu, Hakuseki personally interrogated the Italian missionary Giovanni Batista Sidotti (1668–1715). Also, in the course of five years he went to the Nagasakiya inn four times to meet with the Dutch delegation to the shogunate. I like to imagine that if the Kaempfer of Japan (Hakuseki) and the Hakuseki of the West (Kaempfer) had been able to meet at the Nagasakiya inn or somewhere and responded to each other's burning curiosity and doubts, engaging in heated conversation that spilled over to a second day and then a third, they might have become fast friends. Then Hakuseki's three-volume *Tidings of the West* (*Seiyō kibun*, 1715) and five-volume *Observations on Foreign Languages and Customs* (*Sairan igen*, 1725) might have been many times richer, and Kaempfer's two-volume *History of Japan* might have been far more scrupulous and thorough in its coverage of Japanese history, language, and Confucianism.

Daydreaming this way is necessary to understand history. Without daydreaming, or better, without imagination, history doesn't come alive and speak to us. Facts, however, are facts. Hakuseki could never have met with Kaempfer. Kaempfer's first visit to Edo was in 1691, the year when, after having served the Hotta family for ten years, Hakuseki again became a ronin (masterless samurai) at thirty-five. He also separated from his Confucian teacher Kinoshita Jun'an and busied himself with plans to open his own academy in Honjō, an eastern suburb of Edo. Back in the ninth month of 1682, the year he was first engaged by Hotta Masatoshi, he met with a Korean embassy in Edo and composed poetry in classical Chinese, thereby garnering considerable renown in Korea. In the Genroku era, Hakuseki's interest did not yet extend to the West.

Twenty years after Kaempfer's arrival in Japan, Hakuseki did meet with and interrogate a Westerner: the above-mentioned Jesuit missionary, Sidotti. This happened in the winter of 1709, just after Tsunatoyo, the Kōfu daimyo whom Hakuseki had served for many years, succeeded Tsunayoshi to become the sixth shogun, Ienobu. Hakuseki was simultaneously promoted. The interviews took place from the eleventh month on into the twelfth month in the Christian Compound (*Kirishitan yashiki*) in Koishikawa, Edo. Six years later, Hakuseki recorded the contents of the interviews and his impressions in *Tidings of the West*, a masterpiece of documentary literature that he subsequently revised. In the book he sets forth the knowledge of Western geography he gained from Sidotti as well as a criticism of Christianity. Writing in the same style as in his autobiography, a mix of literary Japanese and Chinese, he gives a vivid and thorough account of the scene.

From Sidotti, Hakuseki certainly learned about many important matters concerning world geography and Christian doctrine. Of far greater interest, however, is his reaction to the man himself. Historian Muraoka Tsunetsugu described this historic East-West dialogue as "a negotiation between a statesman who, although a man of Confucian culture, had progressive views rare for his time and a heroic priest from southern Europe who came alone to an island empire in the Far East to propagate his faith at the risk of his life."[1]

One short winter day in 1709, with a world map by cartographer Willem Blaeu between them, the two men faced off. In the next section, I will refer to passages from *Tidings of the West* that describe the razor-sharp exchanges between them and their growing mutual respect and generosity of spirit.

Hakuseki describes Sidotti as a man "far more than six *shaku*[2] in height. An ordinary person wouldn't have come up to his shoulder. His hair was bobbed, the color black, his eyes deep set, his nose prominent." He countered this by describing himself as "a small man five *shaku*[3] tall, every inch bold." A man of exuberant spirit, he was also the preeminent samurai thinker of his day.

---

1 AN: Muraoka Tsunetsugu, *Zoku Nihon shisōshi kenkyū* [Studies in Japanese intellectual history, sequel] (Iwanami shoten, 1939), 72.
2 1.8 meters, or 5' 10".
3 1.5 meters, or 4' 11".

7 | WINTER 1709: EAST-WEST DIALOGUE IN THE CHRISTIAN COMPOUND

Arai Hakuseki's prose style, whether in his autobiography, *Told Round a Brushwood Fire*, or in other works, is concise and supple with a strength and beauty that appeal to the reader's imagination. His account in *Tidings of the West* of his historic interrogation of Father Giovanni Battista Sidotti is a prime example.

On December 22, 1709, day one of the interrogation, as "the sun was tilting to the west" and Hakuseki was about to get up, marking an end to the day's proceedings, "that person" (*kano hito*) uttered these words to the interpreter:

> Since I came here, the year has waned, the weather has grown cold, and soon now it will snow. Even though it is growing cold, here in the Christian Compound you have set guards over me who remain awake all night. I came to this land of my own volition, following the command of the pope, and I am not going anywhere until I achieve the purpose for which I came, so at night please shackle me, put me in prison, and excuse those men from standing guard over me.

The line beginning *Since I came here* has a poetic beauty that puts us immediately in the scene on that cold winter's evening more than three centuries ago. It was just at the winter solstice, when the days are at their shortest. The vast winter sky, darkening with the approach of night, stretches out in the reader's mind.

As I've mentioned, the setting is the Christian Compound north of the castle in Koishikawa, reached by going past Dentsūin temple, turning left just before Myōgadani, and heading down Christian Hill (Kirishitan-zaka) to the bluff on the right. Since the compound was on a small elevation surrounded by trees, it was also known as Christian Hill Compound, and since inside a fenced-off area there was a prison and a guardhouse, it was also called the Christian Prison Compound. Contemporary maps show it was a lonely corner in the northern outskirts of Edo, the sort of place where foxes might well appear.

Hakuseki and Sidotti came face to face in the interrogation room on the north side of the prison, adjacent to the encircling fence. The room faced south and was wide open. Hakuseki sat within on tatami, and Yokota Bitchū-no-kami Yoshimatsu, the magistrate in charge of eradicating Christianity, sat in a row with other magistrates near the veranda. On the wooden veranda to Hakuseki's right sat the chief interpreter Imamura Gen'emon Eisei (1671–1736), who had escorted Sidotti from Nagasaki, and seated respectfully on Hakuseki's left were a pair of interpreter trainees. Sidotti sat outside in a chair in the garden, a meter beyond the veranda, guarded by a police sergeant behind him and two foot soldiers on his right and left, all kneeling on reed mats. (Hakuseki himself scrupulously recorded these details of the seating arrangements.)

On the journey from Nagasaki to Edo, Sidotti had been confined in a palanquin for over a month (from the twenty-fifth day of the ninth month to the first day of the eleventh month), unable to see outside. As a result, he was lame. To sit in the chair he needed the help of the two foot soldiers, one supporting him on either side.

At fifty-two, face to face with a foreigner for the first time in his life, Hakuseki paid careful attention to Sidotti's smallest gestures and facial expressions and even to the sound of his voice. Sidotti had originally shaved the top of his head in a futile attempt to disguise himself as a samurai but had probably not shaved it since his arrival and subsequent arrest on Yakushima, an island off Kyushu, late in the eighth month of the previous year; his black hair had therefore grown out until it appeared "bobbed." He had on a white cotton underrobe and a pongee kimono with a padded brownish garment on top. Over six feet tall, with deep-set eyes and a prominent nose, he appeared haggard as he answered Hakuseki's questions in Italian mixed with halting Japanese as well as Latin and Dutch.

As Hakuseki looked out over the foreigner's head and beyond, the sunset red of the winter sky was gradually fading to dark gray, and the foreigner's figure was becoming a dark silhouette. Sidotti's comment, *Since I came here, the year has waned, the weather has grown cold, and soon now it will snow*, must have impressed Hakuseki deeply. Sidotti addressed the words to the interpreter, who transmitted them to Hakuseki in Japanese. Hakuseki must have gone home that evening and made a note of the remark; his inclusion of it six years later in *Tidings of the West* is telling. The Japanese sentence contains various adverbs (*sude ni*, "now"; *mata*, "too"; *mo hodonaku*, "soon now") that perhaps allowed Hakuseki to empathize all the more. The sentence was surely not embellished or made more dramatic after the fact, as indicated by the words "the year has waned." By the lunar calendar it was still the eleventh month, but for Sidotti it was December 22, the tail end of the year. The Jesuit must have spoken those precise words.

Though *Tidings of the West* is a factual narration, the writing has a peculiar beauty and fascination, due in large part to the quiet sympathy that Hakuseki developed for Sidotti, an understanding tinged with admiration and curiosity about the foreigner, whose sense of mission had driven him to "cross ten thousand leagues of rough seas." Compared to the life and emotion in Hakuseki's blended Japanese-Chinese style of writing, Bashō's *Narrow Road to the Deep North*, though written only a dozen or so years earlier, seems old-fashioned, like the overwrought "elegant prose" of previous generations.

Hakuseki pounced on Sidotti's expression of solicitude for his guards, quoted above, which he felt was hypocritical. After all, Sidotti himself had refused to wear winter clothes, so why all this concern for the guards? Hakuseki hoped to subdue Sidotti's obstinacy with his criticisms and also hoped to show off his own keenness of mind as the shogun's representative. However, leaving that aside, I would like to examine some of the heated exchanges between the two men that followed, with reference to several key passages in *Tidings of the West*.

At the second session, Hakuseki interrogated Sidotti in the Christian Compound for three hours about Blaeu's world map and then toured the prison quarters. He had the magistrates take the day off for the third session while he inquired further about European geography. At the final session, with the magistrates again present, Hakuseki got down to brass tacks, probing Sidotti's basic motivation for sneaking into Japan: Had he come to propagate Christianity? Or was he on a diplomatic mission from Rome? Hakuseki listened to the answers and made his own determination.

Judging from Hakuseki's account, the exchange of questions and answers between the Japanese Confucian statesman and the "heroic" Roman Jesuit was punctuated by laughter and must have been quite a spectacle.

"He had encyclopedic knowledge and a strong memory, and we understood that he was well versed in various academic subjects. In astronomy and geography we were no match for him." This was first and foremost how Sidotti impressed Hakuseki. To show how that strong impression was formed, Hakuseki describes how Sidotti demonstrated his knowledge using Blaeu's map of the world. The incident probably took place during the second interrogation, on the twenty-fifth day of the eleventh month. A large copy of the map, in Dutch, was spread out on the veranda between the two men, and Sidotti used a compass to pinpoint the locations of Rome and Edo, to Hakuseki's great admiration:

> Then they spread out a map of the world printed in the Nether-lands. "Where in Europe is Rome?" I asked, but the foreign lettering was extremely tiny, and the interpreters were unable to find it.
>
> "Do you have a *circinus*?" the foreigner asked.
>
> The interpreters replied in the negative.
>
> "What's that?" I asked.
>
> "In Dutch it is called a *passer*," he said, "in Italian a *compasso*."

"I have one here." I took a compass out of my kimono and gave it to him.

"The joint is loose, and it won't be much use, but it's better than nothing," he said, and when he had found the place he was searching for on the map, he asked for a brush and copied out the letters. Then he took the compass and opened it to the angle he wanted. The map was on the floor, and even though he was seated in a chair in the garden, he reached out and drew something like a spider's web, tracing lines. As he moved the instrument this way and that, counting, it touched a place beyond his reach. "This is it. Take a look." He indicated the compass.

We went over and found the point of the compass marking a spot like the eye of a needle. Next to it, the interpreter said, was the lettering "Rome."

After that I asked where various countries were, beginning with the Netherlands, and using the same technique he was able to locate them all. Then I asked where Japan was on the map, and following the same method, he indicated a place and said, "Here." The lettering said "Edo." It seemed to be a set technique for finding places on a map, but one not at all easy to master.

"Did you study how to do this?" I asked.

"There's nothing to it," he said.

"I'm not good with numbers. I don't think I could do it."

"You don't need to be good with numbers. It's extremely easy to learn."

The incident is mysterious in many ways. Why did Hakuseki happen to have a compass with him that day? It was apparently an imported, Western-style steel compass. Unlike traditional Japanese compasses, those starting to be imported through the Dutch trading company were extremely valuable. And even if place names on the map were in Dutch, surely Sidotti could have easily pointed out the locations of Italy and Rome without going to such extreme lengths—he hadn't been asked the distance, after all. Why make a point of borrowing a compass from

Hakuseki and then, after first protesting that the screw was loose but that it was "better than nothing," put on a grand show of taking measurements? He finished by emphasizing that anyone could learn to do it, even without a facility for mathematics.

Most likely, Sidotti had pored over century-old communications from his Jesuit predecessors before coming to Japan and realized that demonstrations of astronomical and geographical knowledge were an effective means of dealing with the Japanese, especially men of learning. He put on a show for Hakuseki during the interrogation, and the tactic succeeded. Then forty-one, Sidotti had engaged in all sorts of missionary work in the Philippines before arriving in Japan. He must have evolved into quite a showman. I can even imagine that Hakuseki, being favorably disposed toward the foreigner, might have contrived beforehand to stage this little show with him and so brought the compass deliberately to enable him to make such a show and respond to questions in front of the magistrates. The two men, Easterner and Westerner, were in perfect sync.

I wonder if the tiny pinpricks Sidotti made with Hakuseki's compass are still visible on Blaeu's map, which is now housed in the Tokyo National Museum. Someone ought to look into that.

Hakuseki also gave Sidotti credit for being "courteous and circumspect, and careful to show approval even in small things." He includes several interesting examples from the interrogations, painting a vivid picture of the Jesuit's demeanor.

> When [Sidotti] arrived at his chair in the garden, he first folded his hands and bowed. Putting his right thumb to his forehead, he made a sign, then closed his eyes and sat down. Although he remained seated for long periods of time, he was as motionless as a statue. When any of the magistrates or I stood up, he unfailingly rose, bowed, and sat down again. When we returned to our seats, he again rose, bowed, and sat down. Every day he repeated this behavior.
>
> Once, on seeing one of the magistrates sneeze, he addressed an incantation to him and then said to the interpreter, "The

weather is cold. Shouldn't he put on another robe? People where I come from are careful about sneezing, because in the past that form of sickness spread throughout our country."

When the interpreters spoke Latin with an accent, he patiently corrected them, and when they got it right, he heaped praise on them. Hearing me talk, he said, "The interpreters studied Dutch, and old habits die hard. They don't speak Latin as well as you did just now. That must be because you've never studied a European language." He laughed.

Dutch battleships have gunports along the side, in three decks from top to bottom. He wanted to say "each gunport has a cannon sticking out," but he was unable to express himself and was at a loss for words. I held up my left hand sideways and stuck the tips of three fingers on my right hand between the four fingers. "Exactly," he said. Then, turning to the interpreters, he added, "That's very clever." There were other incidents like this.

When I asked, "How far is New Holland [now Australia] from here?" he didn't answer.

I asked again, and he turned to the interpreters and said, "The laws of my religion prohibit killing others above all. How can I possibly enable someone to go to another country?"

I didn't understand his meaning, so I had the interpreter inquire: "What are you saying?"

"It is not appropriate for me to answer questions about other countries in this region," he said. Asked why, he said, "From my observations of this man [Hakuseki], I don't know what he may be doing in this country, but if he were in Europe, he would surely accomplish great things. Australia is not very far from here. If he wanted to invade that land, he could easily do so. My providing detailed information about the route there would be like offering him guidance in taking over another country."

I heard him say this, and so did the magistrates. I laughed. "Even if I did have any intention such as you describe, the laws of our country are strict, and I wouldn't be able to send even one soldier."

In all things, he showed this kind of excess consideration.

I find this to be a splendid evocation of the scene and of the Jesuit's character. Sidotti displays sincere consideration to a degree Hakuseki finds excessive, outspokenly compliments him on his Latin pronunciation and his quickness to intuit the arrangement of gunports on Dutch warships, compliments his ability (*if he were in Europe, he would surely accomplish great things*), and justifies his own refusal to say how far it is to Australia by expressing fear that Hakuseki might invade the country. Sidotti's somewhat reckless determination comes across loud and clear. He may well have sought to butter up the man whom he knew to be the arbiter of his fate. Hakuseki's confidence in recording all this with a casual air and even some relish seems distinctly "un-Japanese."

In any case, the lively exchanges between the two men, via the magistrates and the interpreter corps or at times through their direct participation, reads as vividly as a movie script. It's easy to imagine Sidotti and Hakuseki breaking into laughter more than once as they developed increasing rapport.

Through the four days of interrogation, Hakuseki learned the broad outlines of Western affairs and Christian doctrine, but he did more than expand his knowledge. While developing a high regard for the Jesuit's pluck, humanity, ability, and knowledge, he remained a policy maker of the Tokugawa government and came to this significant conclusion regarding Western civilization:

When [Sidotti] talked about religion, not one word seemed to approach the true way. It was as if wisdom had given way to folly and I were listening to the words of a completely different man. I realized that while the learning of the West may be superior in regard to concrete matters and objects with firm outlines, such learning can only be applied to the so-called physical realm and has nothing to do with the metaphysical.

This view was to influence the attitude of Tokugawa Japanese toward the West in a variety of ways.

Concerning the treatment of Sidotti himself, Hakuseki made full allowance for extenuating circumstances. He advised maximum leniency, writing, "I find it impossible to witness without emotion his firmness of purpose. To follow the laws of our country and put him to death for what is not a crime of his making would stray far from the path of righteous sovereigns of old."[1] The recommendation also implied that he saw Sidotti as not just a missionary but a Roman ambassador.

In the end, of the three possible plans Hakuseki proposed, the middle course was chosen. Sidotti was neither executed nor deported but kept on as a prisoner in the Christian Compound. However, during his imprisonment Sidotti did something to betray Hakuseki's generosity and trust. In the second month of 1714, it was found that he had baptized a husband and wife, Chōsuke and Haru, who were imprisoned in the same compound as the children of Christians and employed as servants. The husband and wife had surrendered to the officer at the compound. All three of them were punished for this breach. Chōsuke died on the seventh day of the tenth month that year, followed soon after by Sidotti on the evening of the twenty-first. Sidotti's remains were buried in the northwest corner of the compound, and a nettle tree planted by his grave was named after him: "Jo'an [Giovanni] Nettle."

Arai Hakuseki began writing *Tidings of the West* in 1715 at the age of fifty-eight, a year after Sidotti's death. The following year, Yoshimune became the eighth shogun, and Hakuseki was relieved of his position in the castle.

---

1 AN: From *Rōmajin shochi kengi* [Proposal concerning possible measures for the Roman], an appendix to *Tidings of the West*.

Part

8 | THE CENTURY OF NATURAL HISTORY: EIGHTEENTH-CENTURY JAPAN AND THE WEST

On the twenty-seventh day of the eighth month, 1714, two months before the heroic Sicilian priest Giovanni Sidotti perished in prison, another great scholar of the Genroku era, the equal of Arai Hakuseki in Edo and Itō Jinsai in Kyoto, died at eighty-four in his Higashihama residence in Kōzu, Fukuoka, on the island of Kyushu, surrounded by his family and disciples. He was the naturalist Kaibara Ekiken (1630–1714), who served the Kuroda family in the Fukuoka domain.

I devoted all of Chapter 5 to Ekiken, and touched on him again in Chapter 6, when after introducing the eventful travels and the travelogue of the German Engelbert Kaempfer I brought up Bashō's poetic travel diary *Narrow Road to the Deep North* for purposes of comparison. Ekiken, a geographer and traveler fourteen years Bashō's senior, tramped the plains and mountains of various provinces at exactly the same time as Bashō's journey north but with even greater vigor, and he wrote a travelogue for the new era in a style utterly different from Bashō's. Confined to the archipelago by the national policy of isolation, Ekiken necessarily did all his journeying within Japan, never setting foot overseas. His attitude toward travel, however, made him a Japanese mini-version of Kaempfer. As I wrote, he was a hardy fellow given to scrupulous scientific observations and record-keeping. Ekiken's wide-ranging, tenacious empiricism definitely made possible the start of Japan's own "century of natural history." Historian Ueno Masuzō put it this way:

The title [of Ekiken's masterwork] *Japanese Herbal* refers to medicinal plants, but as the word '*Japanese*' indicates, the contents are for the most part a superb natural history of Japan. This work bears the distinct hallmarks of natural history, and I regard it as Japan's first step in that field. The one hundred years following the appearance of *Japanese Herbal*...were Japan's era of growth in natural history.[1]

In fact, around the time of Ekiken and *Japanese Herbal*, a succession of fine herbalists and naturalists appeared in Kyoto, Osaka, and Edo, building a broad, robust academic tradition. The research of Kyoto naturalists Inō Jakusui (1655–1715) and Matsuoka Jo'an (1668–1746) relied heavily on books, but in Edo, where Yoshimune, the eighth shogun, promoted new industries, practical research in herbals and regional products (*bussangaku*) was carried out at a quickened pace. Scholars like Noro Genjō (1694–1761), Niwa Shōhaku (1691–1756), Aoki Kon'yō (1698–1769), Uemura Saheiji (1695–1777), and Abe Shōō (d. 1753) pursued practicality and utility to such an extent that they deserve to be called the shogunate's product engineers. Tamura Gen'yū (1718–1780), an authority on ginseng and the famed Hiraga Gennai's teacher, pursued herbal studies under Shōō and the succeeded him as the shogunate physician, also taking charge of ginseng cultivation and production.

Yoshimune's policy of developing new industries, later continued by the chamberlain Tanuma Okitsugu (1719–1788), spurred practical studies of this sort, but that emphasis on practical application resulted in a diminishment of Ekiken's broad-minded approach to natural history— his willingness not just to discourse on things of no immediate practical value, but also to embrace lore and imaginative creations related to flora and fauna. Older works from sixteenth- and seventeenth-century Europe such as Rembert Dodoens' *The History of Plants*, translated into Japanese as *Kōmō honzō* (*Red-haired Herbal*) and Jan Jonston's 1660 work, translated as *Kōmō kinjūgyō kaifu* (*Red-haired Catalog of Animals, Fish, and Shellfish*) were undoubtedly beneficial in broadening people's horizons and allowing a more flexible approach to nature.

The empirical naturalism of Hiraga Gennai (1728–1779), or at least the structure of his Japanese naturalism, stood at the intersection of those two tendencies. Gennai, along with his friend Sugita Gempaku, spoke constantly of "national interest," an idea with great currency at that time. While this concern spurred his studies in regional products and provided the impetus for a more radical approach, it did not apparently confine him to a narrow utilitarianism. At approximately the same time that Gennai was active in Edo, Ono Ranzan (1729–1810), a student of Matsuka Jo'an's, opened and taught in a private academy called Shuhōken on Kawaramachi Street in Kyoto, delivering long lectures that would later be published as *Commentary on Bencao gangmu* (*Honzō kōmoku keimō*, 1803).

What gave eighteenth-century Japan's "century of natural history" in the heyday of the Pax Tokugawana its richness and depth was a crowd of amateur enthusiasts who dabbled freely in the field, influenced and inspired by specialized professional naturalists such as those mentioned above. Many nameless or little-known enthusiasts contributed items to Edo exhibitions of regional products organized by Tamura Gen'yu and Hiraga Gennai or offered assistance when the exhibitions were held elsewhere, as we know from accounts in Gennai's *Classification of Various Materials*.

Also, from the late Genroku era on, horticulture grew in popularity as urban life prospered. People went to great lengths to cultivate azaleas, morning glories, and other plants, and publishers offered a succession of helpful charts and handbooks. The pastime became even more widespread in the first half of the nineteenth century. The streets of Edo were full of greenery, and the back alleys were adorned with potted plants. Some gardeners grew obsessed with making splotched, weeping, or otherwise variegated versions of flowers such as morning glories, azaleas, chrysanthemums, camellias, and sacred lilies, vying to come up with unusual specimens and even to produce beautiful paintings of their creations for woodblock prints. The same thing happened with the breeding of small animals such as goldfish, birds, and mice.

Morning glories—
each flower the color
of a deep pool
——Buson

In a glass bowl
the fish look astonished—
this morning's autumn
——Buson

Cherry blossoms out—
its eyes sewn shut, the bird
sings away
——Issa

Rustling leaves, a summer breeze
blows through a row of
potted plants for sale
——Issa

Hey, look at me!
The sponge gourd grows long
rivaling the cactus
——Issa

Ueno commends the vogue for variegated species: "The rise in interest in unusual plant specimens, during a time of peace, produced actual examples of unusual forms through the widespread collection of variants, an important achievement for herbal studies."[2]

During the "century of natural history," professional and amateur horticulturalists were joined by no less enthusiastic daimyo, shogunal retainers, and other cultured members of the upper class who produced magnificent albums of their own. Among the earliest of these was *Sketches of Flowering Plants* (*Kaboku shinsha*) by Yorakuin Konoe Iehiro (1667–1736), an eminent courtier who would serve as regent, chancellor, and great minister. His Rimpa-style drawings of flowering plants that he collected in his Kyoto residence are finely executed, elegant master-pieces of the genre. But since his sketches belong rather to the realm of fine art, let us instead poke inside collections that are a proper record of research in *hakubutsugaku* (natural history). Such albums are among the most eloquent resources we have to give us a sense today of just how long and strong the Pax Tokugawana was. (Albums of *shunga*, the richly ornate erotic art of the period, are equally valuable, but those fall outside the scope of this discussion.)

Let us turn to three illustrated catalogues of insects and animals edited by the daimyo of the 540,000-*koku* Kumamoto domain, Hosokawa Shigekata (1718–1785): *Illustrated Catalog of Insect Morphology* (*Kon-chū shokazu*), *Sketches of Insects from Life* (*Chūrui ikiutsushi*), and *The Strangeness of Beasts and Shellfish* (*Mōkai kikan*). The first two measure 26.9 × 20 centimeters, the last 33.5 × 29.1 centimeters. All three are in the collection of the Eisei Bunko Museum in Tokyo and are currently on loan to the Kumamoto University Library. Most likely the drawings are the work of a painter in the employ of Shigekata—a great ruler who oversaw the restoration of Kumamoto—or an artistically talented retainer who was commissioned to draw insects and animals that Shigekata himself had collected, nurtured, and observed. The three notebooks are rare documents of enormous value.

Unfortunately, the illustrator of *Insect Morphology* and *Insect Sketches* is unknown. *Beasts and Shellfish* contains pasted-on drawings of animals done at various times and in various places. A drawing of a fish labeled "*kajika*,[3] Katsura River, Shuzenji" gives the date (1784) and the name of the artist: "The sixth month of the fourth year of Temmei, by Shimokawa Sadahira." Another one marked "*kagamidai*,[4] also called *kagami* by locals" records the names of the donor and the artist, as well as the date and place of collection: "Donated by Sata Uto, caught by him in a dragnet on the twenty-second day of the sixth month of the fourth year of Temmei in Namamugi village, Musashi province. Drawn by Mitsui Yasaku." The artists named may simply have been retainers close to Shigekata who happened to like to draw.

In short, Shigekata probably personally oversaw and edited these catalogues. The earliest notations that I am aware of are those for a flying fish in *Beasts and Shellfish*, and this is marked "The ninth day of the eighth month of the seventh year of Hōreki," 1757, and another for a mole, marked the eighth month of the year following. The latest entries are the one for *kajika* and another for white crucian carp, dated the fifth year of Temmei (1785). (A drawing of a whale tooth is dated the sixth year of Kansei, 1794, but that is clearly a later addition.)

In 1757, the year of the earliest entries, thirty-six-year-old Hosokawa Shigekata was busy carrying out the renovation of domain government in Kumamoto (known as the "Hōreki Reform"), ten years after succeeding his brother Munetaka as daimyo. The final entry was made just three months before this intellectually curious daimyo died at sixty-seven. His policy of fostering new industries was reaping results, and he had established a number of fine institutions of learning, including the domain school Jishūkan, the medical school Saishunkan, and the medicinal-herb garden Banjikan. In this way, Shigekata spent half his (long for his time) life involved one way or another in natural history research. He was representative of those eighteenth-century daimyo with a passion for the study of animal and plant life.

Insect Morphology and *Insect Sketches* were apparently created at the same time as *Beasts and Shellfish*. They contain sporadic dated entries, the earliest the seventh month of the eighth year of Hōreki, 1757, and there are also dates from the subsequent Meiwa and An'ei eras (1764–1780). It seems likely that both albums are mainly the work of the same artist. The painting style and the calligraphy in the explanations are virtually identical.

Compared to the drawings of animals and fish in *Beasts and Shellfish*, those of insects are amateurish. However, their focus is not on the number or rarity of the objects of observation, but rather on the metamorphosis in each species from larva to pupa to emergence from the chrysalis and adulthood. The inclusion of the date and sketches of larval food plants as well make these drawings a remarkable source of information. One can only wonder if anyone before Hosokawa Shigekata thought to make such a clear and detailed study of insect metamorphosis and to leave such a meticulous record. I know of no one. The work lacks the rigor of a systematic classification of a natural phenomenon, but even in Europe at that time, taxonomy was in its infancy. Of greater note is the continuous, vigorous exercise of a keen scientific spirit among amateurs and the resultant steady growth in understanding a corner of the natural world.

At one point in *Insect Sketches*, the transformations of a *kuroageha* (spangle, a species of black swallowtail butterfly, *Papilio protenor*) or possibly a *karasuageha* (Chinese peacock, a species of swallowtail butterfly, *Papilio bianor*) are tracked on two pages. First there is a drawing of two tiny larvae barely hatched, still with shells attached: "1. Drawn the eighth day of the seventh month, naked larvae eating kumquat leaves" (Figure 24, right-hand side). This is followed by "2. The thirteenth of the same month, free of the shell, turning green." Two adult green caterpillars are skillfully drawn, their plumpness indicated with the white pigment *gofun* (Figure 24, left-hand side).

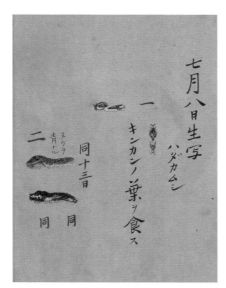 

Figure 24. Hosokawa Shigekata, *Sketches of Insects from Life* (*Chūrui ikiutsushi*), record of the 7th month, days 8 and 13. Eisei Bunko Museum.

Figure 25. Hosokawa Shigekata, *Sketches of Insects from Life* (*Chūrui ikiutsushi*), record of the 7th month, day 20. Eisei Bunko Museum.

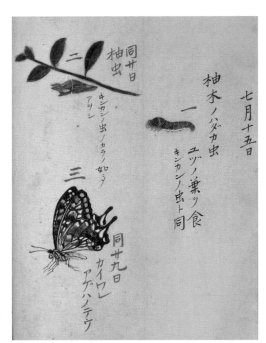

七月十五日

柚木ノハダカ虫

一 ユヅノ葉ヲ食
キシカシノ虫ト同

二 柚虫 同廿日

キシカシ虫ノカラノ
アシ

キシカシ虫ノカラノ如ク

三

同廿九日
カイワレ
アゲハハテフ

Figure 26. Hosokawa Shigekata, *Sketches of Insects from Life* (*Chūrui ikiutsushi*), record of the 7th month, days 15, 20, and 29. Eisei Bunko Museum.

The third section (Figure 25, right-hand side) reads, "The twentieth of the same month, the kumquat larvae turned green and about seven days later looked like this. They are attached this way, hanging from a white thread." The picture shows a chrysalis (bound pupa) dangling from a slender branch by a thread it has spun. Above that is a lateral view of a hatched spangle, drawn no doubt "from life" after carefully counting the veins in the underside of the forewing. The representation is as exact as that in a photograph from a modern guide to butterflies. The same is true of the red spots on the underside of the hindwing. Drawn with what seems to be a specially devised pigment on a rich black with the sheen and depth of velvet, the dark red half-circles are truly beautiful. The white of the forewing, too, has a superb sheen; the tiny scales seem delicate enough to be rubbed off with the touch of a finger.

These drawings and all those in the collection seemed to have been created by an artist who placed each specimen in front of him and, after selecting appropriate pigments, drew while constantly checking the model with his naked eye or a magnifying glass, undoubtedly making new discoveries as he progressed. Each drawing is simple, primitive proof of a rediscovery of nature by Hosokawa Shigekata and his painter. There is also a note attached to the drawing of the spangle: "4. From the insect below [the chrysalis in the third drawing], it took this shape. Unfurled on the seventh day of the eighth month, after seventeen days. Came out back first."

The word "unfurled," *kaiwareru*, is usually used to describe just-sprouted plants, but Shigekata and his partner here apply it to the emergence of a butterfly. Probably the word had never been used in that way before, but it strikes me as beautifully apt. "After seventeen days" refers back to the day the larva became a chrysalis, on the twentieth day of the seventeenth month, seventeen days earlier. One senses how eagerly they awaited the butterfly's emergence. "Came out back first" clearly indicates that they were eyewitnesses to the event.

The observation lasted a full month, from the eighth day of the seventh month to the seventh day of the eighth month. Since other butterflies and moths of different varieties were surely under observation during the same period, the Hosokawa Shigekata Natural History Laboratory must have been a busy place.

Place names besides Edo (indicated by the character for "east," presumably short for "eastern capital") and Kumamoto indicate that the mandatory trips to and from the capital under the *sankin kōtai* system of alternate residence, under which daimyo were required to spend alternate years in Edo, afforded great opportunity for observation and collection. (Other place names include Susaki in Fukagawa, the Kujū mountain range in Hōshū, Yodo in Yamashiro, Fukaya in Bushū, Usui Pass in Jōshū, Mochizuki in Shinshū, and Sasakura in Hishū.) Clearly, the *sankin kōtai* system instituted in 1635 by Iemitsu, the third Tokugawa shogun, not only provided economic and cultural stimulation and facilitated exchange throughout Japan but also had academic uses.

Probably in many cases adult insects were captured and drawn, but as indicated by the entries "Kyoto, sixth month. *Suzume* in piss-pot" and the drawing of a hawkmoth (*suzume ga*) marked "Fukaya, Bushū, the twenty-third day of the fifth month," the pupa was drawn together with its food plants, and then the adult, after emerging, was drawn as well. While traveling, Shigekata and others would gather larvae and pupae along the way, place them in insect cages, and continue to nurture and observe them on the way to Edo or Kumamoto. Sometimes a section of the cage is included in the drawing. The spangle mentioned above was probably not observed in its natural habitat in the garden of the daimyo's Edo residence, but rather fed kumquat leaves in a cage while its transformations were observed and recorded in sequence on the same page.

Other notations concerning the spangle read, "Kumquat *mushi* also turn out this way. This is the same color as yuzu *mushi*," accompanied by a drawing of a blue-green chrysalis suspended from a kumquat branch (Figure 26). This seems to indicate that the protective coloration of the chrysalis changed depending on the condition of the branch. "Yuzu *mushi*" refers to a citrus swallowtail butterfly. Here again there is a beautiful depiction of the larva becoming a chrysalis on the twentieth day of the seventh month and a butterfly unfurling on the twenty-ninth of the same month.

While the "yuzu *mushi*" alone is also called a swallowtail butterfly, other forms, whether butterfly or moth, are identified by the plant the caterpillar feeds on, plus the all-purpose word for insects, "*mushi*": "peach *mushi*," "leaf radish *mushi*," "strawberry *mushi*," and so on. This is undoubtedly a method of classification devised through the experience of breeding insects. At the time, Japanese people made only very broad distinctions such as butterfly, moth, dragonfly, and gold beetle. The author of these notes introduced a new, reasonable (if not systematic) way of looking at insects based on observation of the caterpillars' diet and metamorphosis—a method based on knowledge of *honzōgaku* (botany), traditionally the most advanced area of *hakubutsugaku* (natural history). In other words, we see here something fascinating: botany finding application as a doorway to entomology.

Fifty years before the work of Hosokawa Shigekata, Terashima Ryōan's 1712 *Illustrated Dictionary of the Three Realms in Japanese and Chinese* also contained copious entries on insects in encyclopedic style. Most, however, dealt with insect lore and medicinal uses.

I used to puzzle over notations by Shigekata like "Came out back first," "Cries when touched" (lesser death's head hawkmoth, *Acherontia styx*), and "Lands on the ground" (siren butterfly, *Hestina japonica*) in *Insect Sketches* and *Insect Morphology*. But then, in a graduate seminar on the history of comparative literature and comparative culture that I used to teach at the University of Tokyo, Naitō Takashi presented a paper entitled, "A Consideration of Sketchbooks: Concerning Mid-Edo Illustrated Insect Catalogues." Naitō applied the term "perceptualism" to Shigekata's notations, tying it also to late eighteenth-century natural history writings and drawings. He explained it this way:

> What is being mentioned here are phenomena Shigekata perceived directly through his own senses, primarily the sense of sight. Here the significance of insects is in flux. A discussion of insects is starting to involve only perceptions of insect color, size, cries, and so on—scarcely different from how we discuss them today. Shigekata's simple remarks are the beginning of a gradual detachment of insects from symbolic meaning in folklore (for example, the butterfly as a symbol of death and resurrection) and utility in Chinese medicine.[5]

An illustrated catalog of insects could have been an important symbol of change in modern Japanese intellectual and spiritual history. Satake Yoshiatsu (1748–1785), the lord of the Akita domain with an income of 200,000 *koku*, was a slightly younger contemporary of Shigekata's; he, along with his retainer Odano Naotake, was captivated by Western-style painting under the stimulation and tutelage of Hiraga Gennai and produced, under the name Shozan, a number of fine paintings in the Dutch style, called "Akita *ranga*." He was another daimyo with a bent for natural history. Included in his three *Shozan Sketchbooks* (*Shozan shasei chō*) are *A Summary of Painting Techniques* (*Gahō kōryō*) and other stirring manifestoes of avant-garde painting, as well as sketches of birds, amphibians, insects, and plants in vivid color. However, Naitō's comparative studies show conclusively that of his three hundred-odd sketches of insects, approximately half were copied from Hosokawa Shigekata's *Insect Morphology* and *Insect Sketches*.

As already mentioned, Shigekata nearly always included the date and place of collection and metamorphosis observation as well as the plant food of each insect portrayed in his sketchbooks, but Shozan left out those details and made exact copies of the sketches alone. In some places he did copy Shigekata's notes, which only goes to underscore their connection. Whereas Shigekata sought to gain a fresh understanding of insect life by emphasizing ecology and natural history, Shozan did not hesitate to draw insects into the field of painting, at which he excelled. While copying butterflies, caterpillars, and dragonflies from Shigekata's sketchbooks, he diluted or filtered out the natural history aspect of the drawings and in so doing brought to the fore the fantastic discoveries that result from the close scrutiny of insects. The relationship between Shigekata and Shozan, daimyo respectively of Kumamoto to the far south and Akita to the far north, who would have spent time in the same great hall in Edo Castle midway between, has much to tell us about fascinating aspects of Tokugawa cultural history. A new way of looking at natural history led to important new approaches and visual discoveries in the field of art, the two fields coming together and benefitting from mutual inspiration.

That confluence resulted in the brilliant *Sketches of Flowering Plants* published in the Kyōho era (1716–1736) by Yorakuin Konoe Iehiro, mentioned above; also, later on pictures of flowers and birds by the Chinese painter Shen Nanpin (1682–1760) were imported, and natural history studies became popular, giving rise to the Akita "Dutch paintings" of Satake Shozan and Odano Naotake and the vivid colors of master Kyoto painter Maruyama Ōkyo (1733–1795) in his *Insect Sketchbook* (*Konchū shasei chō*) and *Sketchbook of Flowers, Vegetation, and Animals* (*Kaki sōboku kinjū shasei chō*) as well. Close at Ōkyo's side was *Color Illustrations of Flora and Fauna* (*Dōshoku saie*), a collection of works by Itō Jakuchū (1716–1800), whose deep observations of the varied forms of insects, shellfish, fish, chickens, peonies, and hydrangeas wove a world of magnificent, dreamlike beauty. The lineage of such naturalist paintings includes *Picture Book of Selected Insects* (*Ehon mushi erami*, 1788) by Utamaro, followed in the nineteenth century by Hokusai's *Sketches* (*Manga*) and, in my opinion, reaching its peak with *Sketchbook of Birds, Beasts, Insects, and Fish* (*Reimō chūgyo* [*shasei*] *gasatsu*) and *Album of Insects and Fish* (*Chūgyochō*), late career works of Watanabe Kazan (1793–1841).

While the artworks above reflect the contemporary taste for natural history, it is equally true that natural history studies took on fresh beauty because of their realism. The sketches of small animals in Shigekata's three albums are beautiful precisely because they are so exact. Among the renditions of plant and animal life that cross over most brilliantly into the realm of art are the four *Insect Albums* (*Chūchijō*) of Mashiyama Sessai (1754–1819), daimyo of the Nagashima domain in Ise, which contain drawings of dragonflies and butterflies based on his painstaking observations with a magnifying glass. Equally superb are the studies of shellfish that formed the lifework of Musashi Sekiju (1768–1860), a shogunal retainer in Edo, especially his *Shellfish Catalog* (*Mokuhachi fu*), a masterpiece reminiscent of the pastels of the French symbolist painter Odilon Redon (1840–1916).

Surely the most outstanding examples of such artistic natural history are the thirteen albums of flora and fauna compiled in the 1760s by Matsudaira Yoritaka (1711–1771), the fifth daimyo of the Takamatsu domain in Sanuki province. With titles like *Picture Book of Flowers* (*Shūhō gafu*, Figure 27), *Illustrated Album of Animals* (*Shūkin gachō*, Figure 28), and *Album of Fish* (*Shūrin-zu*, Figure 29), they are damask-bound albums measuring roughly 30 × 45 centimeters and containing brightly colored drawings of over two thousand varieties of flowers, trees, medicinal herbs, vegetables, fish, and birds. After taking infinite pains to make a life-size drawing of a specimen on thin paper, not leaving out one jellyfish tentacle or strand of root hair, Yoritaka would have the drawing cut out and pasted in the album. He compiled this detailed, splendid work, which no one but a daimyo in the Pax Tokugawana could have done, as the de facto director of the Takamatsu Domain Natural History Research Organization.

Here mention must also be made of the one-thousand-plus drawings of Japanese flora chiefly by the Nagasaki painter Kawahara Keiga (1786–ca. 1860) in the von Siebold collection, recently rediscovered in the old Russian capital of St. Petersburg. They, too, are scientifically precise drawings of breathtaking elegance.

Hiraga Gennai, the era's preeminent scholar of regional products and natural history, was kept on as the brains of Matsudaira Yoritaka's research organization even after leaving the domain. Gennai's teacher, the ginseng authority Tamura Gen'yū, was similarly held in high esteem by Hosokawa Shigekata, the lord of Kumamoto frequently mentioned in this chapter, who in 1770 introduced him to another young daimyo with a strong interest in natural history, Shimazu Shigehide (1745–1833), the lord of Satsuma. Since the days of the eighth shogun, Yoshimune, many daimyo had had a deep interest in naturalism, no doubt in large part out of a utilitarian desire to foster the growth of new industries, but over time that often became the mere excuse or stated reason for their passion, as the study of natural history proved engrossing for its own sake. This circumstance endowed Tokugawa natural history, and Tokugawa culture, with resplendent richness.

In and around Edo Castle, daimyo fond of natural history showed each other rare items from their respective domains, traded specimens and information, and proudly showed off their prize albums, freely borrowing and lending in a display of high cultural literacy. Shozan, who had been able to copy drawings of over one hundred species from Shigekata's sketchbooks with much exactitude, must have borrowed the originals for at least six months. Hiraga Gennai wrote in his *Classification of Various Materials* that when his former master Matsudaira Yoritaka showed him an illustrated book containing nearly one thousand varieties of flora on loan from Lord Date of Sendai, he was amazed at how lifelike the drawings were and understood for the first time the true nature of *imake* (*Cynanchum caudatum*), a perennial native to Hokkaido.

These daimyo fond of learning were surrounded by a cluster of scholars and on the outer edges of that circle by countless members of the general public, all devoting huge swaths of time and effort amid the

Figure 27. Matsudaira Yoritaka, *Picture Book of Flowers*,
Corolla No.4 (*Shūhō gafu*), The Kagawa Museum.

Figure 28. Matsudaira Yoritaka, *Illustrated Album of Animals, Water Fowl* (*Shūkin gachō*), The Kagawa Museum.

Figure 29. Matsudaira Yoritaka, *Illustrated Album of Fish*, Vol. 3 (*Shūrin-zu*), The Kagawa Museum.

Pax Tokugawana to everything from the study of butterfly metamorphosis, shell spirals, and regional products to coming up with new and unusual varieties of morning glories, sacred lilies, and goldfish. Mid-eighteenth-century Japan was, to exaggerate a little, in the grip of natural history fever. How this may have been affected by the classification of animals, plants, and minerals undertaken in Europe by their contemporary Carl Linnaeus and his successors is surely a matter of considerable importance. Men like Udagawa Yōan and Itō Keisuke attempted to reconcile the two streams, Japanese and European. Their work may not link easily to the taxonomy of the Meiji era and beyond, but it would be would be the height of modern arrogance, narrowmindedness, and impertinence to deny the fruitful spirit that combined dedication and carefree play—"the élan of play, the spirit of wholehearted abandon"[6]—so abundantly evident in Tokugawa natural history, as well as the freshness of the garden of art and science where those naturalists toiled.

---

1 AN: Ueno Masuzō, *Nihon hakubutsugakushi* [The history of natural history in Japan] (Heibonsha, 1973), 43–44.

2 AN: Ibid., 107–108.

3 Fluvial sculpin (*Cottus pollux*).

4 Mirror dory (*Zenopsis nebulosi*).

5 AN: *Hikaku shisō zasshi* [Magazine of comparative philosophy], vol. 4 (Tōdai hikaku shisō kenkyūkai [Comparative philosophy study group, University of Tokyo], Jan. 1981), 43.

6 AN: Johan Huizinga, *Homo Rūdensu* [*Homo Ludens*], Takahashi Hideo, trans. (Chuo Kōron, 1973), 436.

9 | A LETTER WITH NO ADDRESSEE: SUGITA GEMPAKU, NINE TIMES BLESSED OLD MAN

Portraits are an aid to understanding people. This is true for the portrait of Araki Hakuseki, who proudly described himself as "a small man five feet tall, every inch bold," and for the various photographs of Fukuzawa Yukichi suggesting that the very structure of his brain was handsome. However much I research a person's writings and the achievements and vestiges of his life, without a portrait in hand I always feel that the person never comes quite into focus. And unless I can picture a person's face in all its variety of expressions, writing a vivid history is impossible.

Fortunately, there is a wonderful portrait of physician and scholar Sugita Gempaku (1733–1817). Of all the many portraits painted in early modern Japan, this is one of the finest. I am of course speaking of the famous painting of him by his younger classmate, the Western-style artist Ishikawa Tairō, who took the Western name Tafel Berg, after Capetown's Table Mountain. A high-ranking shogunate retainer and castle guard, Tairō was a man of considerable polish who, hoping to bring a new dimension to traditional painting, associated with *rangaku* (Dutch studies) scholars like Gempaku, Maeno Ryōtaku (1723–1803), and Ryōtaku's disciple Ōtsuki Gentaku (1757–1827). In 1796, together with his younger brother Mōkō, he painted *Flowers in a Vase* (*Heika-zu*), a copy of a 1725 painting ordered from the West by Shogun Yoshimune. Gentaku bestowed high praise on the finished work: "[Viewing it] feels like sitting in a great garden bombarded with sweet-smelling perfume."

Tairō certainly had the proper experience, ability, and technique to

Figure 30. Ishikawa Tairō, *Portrait of Sugita Genpaku*
(*Sugita Genpaku zō*). Waseda University Library.

paint a portrait of the great pioneer of Western learning. The upper left corner of the painting bears an inscription in Gempaku's hand: "New Year's Day, Bunka 9" (1812). The painting is thought to have been completed shortly before that, in anticipation of Gempaku's eightieth year (by the traditional count). The painting overflows with the deep wisdom and quiet passion of the aged scholar who had devoted his life to the study of "true medicine" and the "vast benefit of saving people," as he would write three years later in *Dawn of Western Science in Japan.*

Let us take a closer look at the portrait, which is now in the collection of the Waseda University Library. Measuring 75 × 30 centimeters, it is painted on silk. Gempaku is sitting down, positioned so that his head is in the exact center of the painting. He is wearing a loose-fitting garment of deep blue with a scattered floral design in blue and green. He is shown in two-thirds profile, turned slightly to the right in a posture he must have adopted often in daily life, leaning slightly forward with his left hand resting lightly on his raised left knee. Beside him on his left are a number of Japanese books bound in blue, and in front of him to his right is a beautiful, large Western book with a red spine, which is below a medium-sized Western book lying open to the frontispiece. Behind him on a stand decorated with gold lacquer is a white celadon vase containing one spray each of white camellias and white plum blossoms—auspicious symbols of good fortune and long life. The plum blossom spray is extending upward, nearly parallel with the line of Gempaku's back, scattering its fragrance into the empty space behind him. The color choices and placement of these various props, rendered in deep hues using *Nihonga* pigments, are highly effective. The seated figure, while relaxed and at ease, emanates an aura of alert, focused attention. Is Gempaku following a train of thought, or is he reminiscing about something in the distant past? Is he listening with interest as someone speaks and inwardly preparing a response? Various features combine to suggest the rich inner life of an octogenarian whose mental powers remain as keen as ever: the open Western book, the forward-leaning posture, and above all the expression on his deeply lined face. His eyes are slightly raised and his gaze is far away, his mouth has the ghost of a smile, and the fingers of his right hand curve sensitively, as if stroking the keys of a piano.

The Old Man Nine Times Blessed

A woodblock print of Gempaku's face appeared on the title page of his *Night Talks on Forms and Shadows* (*Keiei yawa*), published in 1810, slightly before the completion of the portrait. There, too, as in the seated portrait, Ishikawa Tairō apparently sought not only to apply Western chiaroscuro but also to demonstrate in the bone structure of the head the anatomical knowledge he had gained from *A New Book of Anatomy* (*Kaitai shinsho*), Gempaku's seminal translation of a Dutch work. The back of Gempaku's head was pointed and his ears were enormous, as he himself acknowledged, purposely including those traits in a cartoonish self-portrait. Tairō keenly observed and recreated not only his subject's lined forehead and cheeks but also the webs of deep wrinkles around his eyes and mouth, the cords in his long neck, and the joints and veins in his curved right hand. As testimony to how true to life this rendition is, we have Gempaku's self-portrait in words from the introduction to *Night Talks on Forms and Shadows*, where he faces his reflection while on call one winter's night:

> In my boredom it occurred to me to pull out the hairs on my chin, and I borrowed a mirror from my wife as she happened by. I took it over by a post, where I hung a lantern, and faced the mirror. A hideous old man was standing there with a face full of wrinkles, eyes rheumy with age, and a scattering of teeth.
>
> "Who might you be?" I inquired.
>
> "I am a shadow, your double," he replied. "You and I are twins, brothers neither older nor younger than one another, one in spirit."
>
> "So that's why you look so much like me," I said in astonishment.

Like the German Romantics E.T.A. Hoffman and Heinrich Heine, Gempaku had an interest in manifestations of a *doppelgänger*. His diary, *Isai's Journal* (*Isai nichiroku*—Isai was a pen name) contains these lines:

"Facing me in a mirror I chanced to pick up was an old man I had never seen before" (1791) and "To my astonishment, facing me in the mirror was a white-headed old man" (1803). *Solitary Talks of an Old Man* (*Yasō dokugo*), published in 1807, also takes the form of a dialogue between his double and himself. These remarks suggest the intense inner life and peculiarly incisive self-awareness of Gempaku the intellectual. In 1809, at seventy-six, he describes himself as having "lived 27,216 days," a description that fits in with a positive attitude of wanting to enjoy each day to the full. In any case, where the old physician disparaged his *face full of wrinkles, eyes rheumy with age, and a scattering of teeth*, his portraitist, Ishikawa Tairō, saw in those signs of old age precious indications of a life well lived for over twenty-seven thousand days and the beauty of a fully mature human being. Something in the eighty-year-old Gempaku inspired that response. The scrupulous rendering of the marks of old age, so different from the broad rendition of the garment folds, give Gempaku's figure its strong presence, conveying the richness of a long life immersed in the joys of the present moment.

Gempaku himself commented on the portrait in a Chinese verse:

> The world of peace continues on and on
> I have maintained the spirit of a beginner
> Once again a new year commences
> Serenely I enter on my eightieth spring
> —Kyūkō Rōjin, New Year's Day, 1812

Add one character to the beautiful word *tenshin*, "spirit of a beginner," and you have Tenshinrō, the name of the private school where Gempaku taught. He used "Tenshin," along with Kyūkō and Isai, as a pen name. The poem reveals the enviable state of mind of a scholar late in life, a state of mind that Gempaku called a "small Shisendō" in admiration of Ishikawa Jōzan (1583–1672), a warrior who renounced military life, built the exquisite Shisendō villa in Kyoto, and dedicated the last third of his life to poetry. This resembles the *Heiterkeit* (spiritual serenity) that Gempaku's contemporary Goethe enjoyed toward the end of his life, far across the seas.

Gempaku signed the poem Kyūkō Rōjin, "Old Man Nine Times Blessed," the name he adopted after he turned seventy. The blessings he claimed were these: living in a time of peace; growing up in the capital; good friends in places high and low; long life; a stipend; not too much poverty; fame; descendants; and health in old age. This expression of contentment by the greatest Japanese intellectual of the late eighteenth and early nineteenth century is fascinating for its expression of an attitude toward life that is individualistic, secular, civil, and has little to do with the strictures of feudal society. Certainly when he sat for the portrait, Gempaku did indeed possess all those blessings.

Memoirs Portraying His Inner Landscape

In 1804, when Gempaku was seventy-one, his only son, Rikkei, turned eighteen and established himself as a Dutch-style eye specialist of such skill that he was able to treat his father's eye disease. Gempaku also had two young daughters of sixteen and fourteen; his elder daughters, Sen and Yaso, were the product of an earlier marriage. Sen and her husband Hakugen, whom Gempaku adopted, had two sons of twelve and four (Kyōkei and Hakugen), and in 1805 a baby girl was born, making the Sugita household even livelier.

That summer, Gempaku was granted an audience with Shogun Ienari, an unheard-of honor. For a domain physician to see a shogun was rare, and for a Western-style physician to do so was unprecedented. Gempaku received a hereditary stipend of 250 *koku* from Lord Sakai, daimyo of the 13,000-*koku* Obama domain in Wakasa, but as his fame increased, he was kept busy running around Edo, seeing patients and dispensing medicine. According to diary entries for the last day of each year, his annual income averaged around 500 *ryō* from the 1790s on. While not wealthy, he thus had a stable income and lived free from want. In 1807, he resigned the official position he had held from age twenty for fifty-five years, and his son-in-law Hakugen succeeded him as head of the family.

A series of deaths of old friends and acquaintances brought home to Gempaku the loneliness of growing old, as the following verses show:

Pummeled by the wind,
left behind, one cries out—
a flock of plovers

Wipe them as I will
my tears only quench the fire
of smoldering embers

Hearing me reminisce
everybody seems to think
it's only idle talk
No one is left who knows
the olden days I describe

Rangaku scholar Maeno Ryōtaku died at eighty in 1803. Katsuragawa Hoshū, Gempaku's friend and collaborator on the translation of *A New Book of Anatomy*, nicknamed Gempaku "Kusaba no kage" (Under the Sod) but died before him in his mid-fifties, in 1809. The following year, Hoshū's younger brother, the *rangaku* scholar and fiction writer Morishima Chūryō, also died. Inamura Sampaku, one of the compilers of the 1796 Dutch-Japanese dictionary *Haruma wage*, died the year after that.

But there was also a stream of good news to cheer Gempaku's heart. Ōtsuki Gentaku's student Yasuoka Genshin turned out to be a brilliant scholar, one whom Gempaku thought so highly of that he married his second daughter, Yaso, to him and adopted him—only to disown him before long due to his dissolute ways. Genshin then faded from the field of Dutch studies, and Gempaku worried about the "lamentable prodigy." However, after the death in 1797 of Udagawa Genzui, the botanist and official physician of the Tsuyama domain and another student of Gempaku's, Genshin succeeded him as head of the family and subsequently reformed, going on to publish a fine book of anatomy in 1805. Through the good offices of Gentaku, he and Gempaku reconciled and were once again like father and son. This was a happy turn of events for Gempaku, who wished fervently for the further development of Dutch studies in Japan. Even happier news came in 1811, as Gempaku's portrait was being painted: the shogunate established the Office for Translation of Barbarian Books (Bansho Wage Goyō Kyoku) in the Temmonkata, a scientific research institution. The first appointees were Baba Sadayoshi from Nagasaki and Ōtsuki Gentaku, Gempaku's prize student and an undisputed pillar of that community of scholars.

The notion that *rangaku* might now become a tool for shoring up the feudal system of Japan, as today's "progressive" students might put it, surely never occurred to Gempaku. He thought quite the opposite: for the first time since the publication of his *A New Book of Anatomy* forty years before, *rangaku* had been officially recognized as a field of study of benefit to the nation, and its position was secure within the government. He was delighted, as he wrote in *Dawn of Western Science in Japan*: "This old man's longstanding wish has been realized," and "seeking somehow to save people, I struggled to establish this difficult field, and finally my labors have been rewarded." That was Gempaku's state of mind around the time his portrait was painted.

I must say that the undiminished radiance of spirit, intelligence, serenity, and vitality so evident in Ishikawa Tairō's portrait of Gempaku find echo in a famous passage from the epilogue to *Dawn of Western Science in Japan*. The content and cadence of that passage make it a fitting accompaniment to the portrait.

> This old man [Gempaku himself] is truly full of joy. I can't help dancing a jig since I know that the establishment of this field will allow many to acquire medical skills that will confer enormous benefit, saving lives for a hundred years, a thousand years, and more to come. Blessed with long life, I have been able to watch with my own eyes as this field has grown from its beginnings until its flourishing state now. My good fortune was possible because of a precious abundance of peace. Despite the many people of goodwill in the world, no one would have had the time for such a vast undertaking if we had tried to build this store of knowledge during the Warring States period.

This passage, and indeed the entire book, is shot through with the deep, powerful spirit of a man looking back at his achievements with exhilaration, bringing his writing alive while never detracting from its logical clarity. Free of the stiff rhetoric of Chinese poetry and prose as well as the wordiness of *kokugaku* (nativist studies) scholars, Gempaku's prose recalls Fukuzawa Yukichi in its natural, modern eloquence. Moreover, it is interspersed with poetic images and touches of color scarcely found in Fukuzawa's writing. Strong attachments to people and sharp observations of them; confidence and pride in his own work, tempered by a keen and humbling awareness of broad historical trends: these form the warp and woof of Gempaku's memoirs.

That is what Gempaku's *Dawn of Western Science in Japan* represents to us. Recently, at a conference on the history of Dutch studies in Japan, Prof. Ogata Tomio[1] and I discussed whether or not that book is indeed a gem of prose. The professor, whom I greatly respect as a translator of old texts into modern Japanese, said no, but I consider Gempaku's prose worth savoring. Though short and overshadowed by Hakuseki's *Told Round a Brushwood Fire* and Yukichi's autobiography (*Fukuō jiden*, 1898–1899), Gempaku's *Dawn of Western Science in Japan*, written midway between them, is in my opinion a masterpiece of modern Japanese autobiographical literature that ranks with the other two and links them together. Moreover, I find that my mental image of the author has at some point blended inextricably with Ishikawa Tairō's portrait of him.

In the painting, the "old man nine times blessed" is leaning forward, looking up in search of bygone times, about to relate his memories of the early days of Dutch studies in Japan.

> Looking back at the beginning, I realize it is going on fifty years since several of my friends and I expressed interest in this undertaking. Never did I suspect things would turn out as they have.

So he begins, ticking off specific memories on the fingers of that right hand. In no time, a stream of recollections turns into a flood. Seen from the halcyon heights of old age, a succession of past incidents reappears before him, all with such clarity that they might have happened yesterday, their significance now more apparent than ever. But returning to those days when he and his comrades devoted themselves with the ardor of youth to the pursuit of new learning, living out fevered dramas of exploration, struggle, and adventure, is of course impossible. That he knows very well—and yet the knowledge causes him great sorrow. An urgent desire to recapture lost time seems to underlie the narrative of *Dawn of Western Science in Japan*, at times rising to the surface and giving the book a literary dimension and depth that set it apart from a simple account of his career or a contemporary history. The same is true of *Isai's Journal*, the diary of his later years. Sugita Gempaku's memoirs depict his inner landscape.

In one 1803 entry, written when he was seventy, Gempaku wrote the following account. He had been heading from his home in Hamachō, Nihombashi, to call on the lord of Obama domain in his residence in Ushigome Yaraichō when, on coming to a certain spot, he suddenly felt the return of his younger self of forty years before.

> Back then I used to come by here often on my way to visit my aged father. I would always judge my progress by the length of the shadow of this tree. When it was high on the wall, my father would be delighted that I had come early, and when it was low he would be cross and want to know why I was late. I quickened or eased my pace depending on the appearance of that tree shadow. I must have been a little over thirty. Young. My father was still in good health for several more years after that. And that was almost forty years ago.
>
> Already the shadow
> has grown so long—
> a winter day

In old age, Gempaku was often surprised when a vision of his past self invaded his reality. With that memory as a springboard, let us travel back into the past that preoccupied Gempaku in old age.

Gempaku reached his early thirties in the first half of the 1760s, more than five years after he left his home in the Obama domain residence in Ushigome Yaraichō and set up a medical practice in Nihombashi. His medical studies still lacked direction, but he studied hard, benefiting from the lively intellectual stimulation. Already he had heard the news that the physician Yamawaki Tōyō (1705–1762) had conducted Japan's first dissection of a human body in Kyoto in 1754, and *On Internal Organs* (*Zōshi*), Tōyō's findings from that dissection, had already been published. The physician Yoshimasu Tōdō (1702–1773) was also well known. Such men rejected the abstract system of Tang-dynasty Chinese medicine that ruled in Japan and instead promoted the rising School of Ancient Medicine (*koihō*), which called for first-hand experimentation on treatment and pathology. Tōyō's experiments and ideas cast doubt even on pre-Tang medical texts and held that true treatment was possible through a correct understanding of the body's internal structure. This had a powerful impact on the young Gempaku. Through a chance reading of Ogyū Sorai's *Secrets of Military Tactics* (*Kenroku gesho*), he discovered an illuminating connection between Tōyō's thoughts about anatomy and treatment and the relationship between military theory and tactics.

With so many giants in the field of internal medicine appearing in western Japan, Gempaku wrote in *Night Talks on Forms and Shadows*: "I didn't want to get ahead by following others' lead, and since I had the good fortune to be the son of a surgeon, I made up my mind to establish myself in that field." That was Gempaku's reaction to the changes then sweeping through the field of medicine. In 1758 he published two books, *A Handbook of Surgery* (*Yoka taisei*) and *An Introduction to Syphilis* (*Kōsō sōron*), containing excerpts from various Chinese books on surgery that were the fruit of his studies at this time. The inclusion of Chinese medicine points to a youthful skepticism that went so far as to challenge the Sugita family tradition of Western-style or "red-haired" medicine.

Friendship with Hiraga Gennai

Gempaku's lifelong friendship with Hiraga Gennai (1728–1779) also began during his early thirties. The two men probably came to know each other through Nakagawa Jun'an (1739–1786), Gempaku's friend and colleague from the Obama domain, who studied *honzōgaku* with Gennai under Tamura Gen'yū (1718–1780). In 1762, when Gennai held an "Eastern

Capital Pharmaceutical Convention" to display products from around the country, Gempaku and Jun'an helped out by contributing rare items from their collections. The previous year, when they called on the Dutch embassy at the Nagasakiya inn in Edo, Gempaku watched the prodigy impress the Dutchmen with his knowledge of *slangensteen*—"snake stone." In *Dawn of Western Science in Japan*, Gempaku fondly wrote, "A specialist in herbal studies, [Gennai] was quick to grasp theory and had outstanding ability; he was just the man for the times."

At that time, Tanuma Okitsugu, a new government minister, had just come on the scene and was beginning to display his talents. While carrying out various plans for the centralization of economic power, he also sought to improve the state of the country through the promotion of industry. While signs of social unrest were steadily increasing, including the Post Horse Rebellion of 1764 (a village uprising of unprecedented scale that Gempaku, in his 1787 *Essays in Hindsight* [*Nochimigusa*], described as an "unrestrained rampage") and the Meiwa Incident[2] three years later, in the big cities the freshness of cultural liberalism was in the air. The figure of Hiraga Gennai striding in the vanguard of that movement, sowing fresh ideas wherever he went, must have left Gempaku, five years his junior, goggle-eyed. Gennai was probably the first person with whom Gempaku discussed Dutch studies. They met often to trade news, talk over their latest plans and ambitions, and wax indignant over the state of society. Sparks from the fire in Gennai must have set young Gempaku, "filled with youthful ardor" as he was, aflame as well. The following passage from *Dawn of Western Science in Japan* beautifully and nostalgically captures the nature of the exchanges between the two scholars in those early days.

> Whenever I got together with Hiraga Gennai, we would talk over what we had recently seen and heard. Western science was full of such astonishing things; if Japanese translations of the Dutch texts were made available right away, so much could be gained; it was such a shame that no one had yet expressed the intention to do so; wasn't there some way to open the door?

Nothing to be done here in Edo. If only we could get an interpreter in Nagasaki to read and explain a text! If even one book could be made available, it would be of enormous value to the country. Each time we met, we would lament our inability to do any of this. All we could do was complain in vain about the situation.

Even though he does not use direct quotations, Gempaku skillfully conveys the pair's impassioned manner of talking and their frustration over their inability to realize their high hopes. As he wrote these words late in life, Gempaku must have had vivid recollections of his friend's expressive face and the life in his voice, which was said to be beautiful. Gennai eventually suffered a succession of failures and in 1779 died a miserable death in prison. Filled with "fury and despair" at his friend's sad fate, Gempaku used his own funds to erect a monument to him bearing this epitaph: "An extraordinary man who loved the extraordinary and did extraordinary things. Why did you die an extraordinary death?" Gempaku identified intensely with the feelings of Gennai the pioneer—the man who called himself "the greatest trickster of all time"— and fully understood the significance of his life and accomplishments. As he approached seventy, Gempaku wrote that poignant memories of days when he, Gennai, and others used to get together to sing, dance, drink sake, and trade insults would return all of a sudden.

Although Gennai and Gempaku together sang the praises of Western science and shared the dream of one day translating Dutch books into Japanese, their paths diverged. Gennai undertook mining surveys around the country, visited Nagasaki again courtesy of Tanuma Okitsugu, and developed various products, "throwing himself into" practical activities in the national interest. Gempaku, at the invitation of another physician, Maeno Ryōtaku, visited a Nagasaki interpreter, Nishi Zenzaburō (ca. 1717–1768), only to be advised that the Dutch language was impossibly difficult and they should forget about trying to learn it. Nevertheless, despite this and other setbacks, he and Maeno persisted in the task of acquiring Western medical knowledge directly through the Dutch language and finally achieved their goal.

In the spring of 1771, Gempaku obtained through his colleague Nakagawa Jun'an a copy of his very first Dutch book: *Anatomical Tables* (*Ontleedkundige Tafelen*, 1734); this was a translation of the German *Anatomische Tabellen* (1722), an illustrated encyclopedia of human anatomy. Delighted with his new possession, Gempaku spoke these heartfelt words, "Perhaps now the time has come when this field of learning will be available to us!" Soon after, an invitation came for him to observe the dissection of a human body the following day at the execution ground in Senjū Kotsugahara. He invited Jun'an and Ryōtaku to join him, and when they gathered early on the morning of the fourth day of the third month, Gempaku saw with surprise that Ryōtaku was clutching a copy of the same Dutch book. Amazed and impressed by all they had seen and convinced of the accuracy of the illustrations in *Ontleedkundige Tafelen*, the shaken three resolved on the way home to translate the book, a decision that led to years of miserable toil and quiet joy. All of this is well known from Gempaku's extremely moving and beautiful account in *Dawn of Western Science in Japan*.

Afraid that health problems would prevent him from living long enough to see the project to completion, Gempaku spurred his colleagues on, and he devoted himself fully to the work of translation under Ryōtaku's leadership. This, too, is well known.

"In advancing any new theory," Gempaku wrote decades later, "fear of criticism from posterity is a useless frame of mind that will keep you from accomplishing anything." That famous line from *Dawn of Western Science in Japan*, so expressive of the adventurous spirit of someone spearheading change in an era of cultural innovation, matches Gennai's thinking to a degree I find astonishing. For Gennai, the self-proclaimed "great trickster," took this as his motto: "Thinking keeps you from doing anything. We just jumped in and bungled our way through."

Where *Dawn of Western Science in Japan* is the retrospective chronicle of a great scholar looking back more than forty years from the lofty heights of a nine-times-blessed old age, *Questions and Answers on Dutch Medicine* (*Oranda iji mondō*, 1795) is a vivid and dramatic account written in the thick of the early struggle to establish *rangaku*. It consists of a set of four letters exchanged between Gempaku and Tatebe Seian, the physician who served Lord Tamura of the Ichinoseki domain in the northern province of Mutsu. In late 1772 or early 1773, as *A New Book of Anatomy* was nearing completion, Gempaku received a long letter with no addressee. It was dated the eighteenth day of the intercalary sixth month, 1770, a full two and a half years earlier; someone named Tatebe Seian had entrusted it to a student of his traveling from Ichinoseki to Edo. Gempaku opened the letter with skepticism and read it with astonishment.

The writer castigated so-called Dutch-style medical knowledge being passed on in medical families everywhere, declaring it juvenile and bogus, nothing more than old knowledge from the Sino-Japanese medical tradition (*kampō*) mixed with a smattering of Dutch hearsay. Just as Buddhist sutras had once been translated in China, wasn't there some knowledgeable person now in Japan who could translate Dutch medical books and transmit proper Dutch techniques of surgery, gynecology, and pediatrics? The writer had long lamented his inadequate knowledge of Western medicine but had never seen a Dutch medical book, nor was he capable of reading one. And yet to abandon Western medicine and rely solely on Chinese medicine was unthinkable. "Edo is a big place, and there must be someone who has already established this field or translated a Dutch medical book. . . . Such a great undertaking will not be realized unless some bold person in the capital rises up and speaks out." If there was such a book, he would like to see it as soon as possible, but he was getting on and Edo was far away, so he had written this letter as a last testament and sent it from deep in the hinterland to an unknown person in the capital.

By coincidence, the contents of the letter perfectly mirrored the genesis of the translation project and the translators' intentions in carrying it out. In an age when means of communication were not yet fully developed, there were surely many dramas, and yet what could be more dramatic than for Seian's letter, the equivalent of a stick of wood thrown into the ocean, to have drifted into Gempaku's hands? Just as Hiraga Gennai was connecting with samurai painters in Akita,[3] Gempaku would, through this letter, establish a lifelong connection with the Ichinoseki domain in a corner of the Tōhoku region in northern Honshu, demonstrating the breadth and depth of the ongoing cultural shift taking over the nation.

Determined to be a Pioneer

In the first month of 1773, Gempaku, much excited, sat down to write a reply: "Dear Tatebe Seian-sensei, I have read about your concerns regarding practitioners of Dutch medicine with great interest. You and I are far apart and have never met, but your understanding of our work strikes me as a once in a thousand years coincidence." After carefully responding to Seian's various questions regarding Dutch medicine, he wrote that he and his colleagues had been so impressed by the accuracy of a book on human anatomy that they had begun to translate it, and a first draft of the five volumes of *A New Book on Anatomy* was now completed. He included a flyer entitled "Anatomical Diagrams" (*Kaitai yakuzu*) that had just been published at the beginning of the year.

Three months later, a second letter arrived from Seian. This was not just a message about medicine, but a human document bursting with powerful emotion:

> I don't know about other schools of medicine, but for your work on Dutch medicine, I believe that the greatest hero of all time is not King Wen[4] but you. That is the opinion of this old and foolish man. When I saw the "Anatomical Diagrams" you so kindly sent, I couldn't help shouting out in a frenzy of excitement. My mouth hung open, my tongue cleaved to the roof of my mouth, and my old eyes opened wide in astonishment as I wept for joy.

When *A New Book of Anatomy* was finished, he went on to say, untold millions would reap infinite benefit, not only in Japan but in all the countries of Asia where *kambun* was the common medical technique. Gempaku was not just the founder of a school of surgery but a bodhisattva of great compassion. He had heard that Gempaku was forty, still in the springtime of life; he, an old man of sixty-one, wished him and his entire young and promising team all success in their further endeavors.

Nothing could have meant more to Gempaku and his colleagues than these lines of sincere encouragement. The joy of encountering a true kindred spirit was thrilling to Gempaku. In the tenth month of that year, he wrote Seian again to explain further about Dutch medicine and ended with these words:

> Thank you very much for pointing out that lately the new medical practices (*koihō*) have come under heavy criticism and urging me to be on guard against similar ignorant reaction to *A New Book of Anatomy*. Certainly many are waiting with swords held high. But one cannot function as a spearhead unless one is prepared to take a beating. If our spear should reach even one person, I will be satisfied.... As long as the theory we put forward is sound and fully substantiated, then the errors of the past thousand years will, I believe, be corrected in time.

His resolve is truly praiseworthy. *A New Book of Anatomy* was published in the eighth month of the following year, 1774. Undoubtedly a copy was sent to Seian, but although he and Gempaku both expressed a desire to meet in their letters, they never did get together in person. But as Seian indicated he would do in his first letter of the previous year, in 1778 he sent his favorite student, then twenty-one, and his youngest son, then fifteen, to study with Gempaku. These two were of course Ōtsuki Gentaku—Gempaku and Ryōtaku's most eminent successor—and Hakugen, who was to marry Gempaku's daughter and become his adopted son, eventually succeeding him as head of the family. One can only marvel at this and at the mystery of human connections in general.

The portrait of the serene old man rich in blessings told of eighty years filled with many such dramas. Gempaku, too, was an extraordinary man, no less so than his friend Hiraga Gennai, for whom he wrote that epitaph. It took one extraordinary man to recognize another. I am unable to touch on all of Gempaku's writings here, but three works in particular—*Essays in Hindsight*, a record of his observations of society in the Meiwa and Temmei eras (1764–1788); *Solitary Talks of an Old Man*, written in 1807 when he was seventy-four; and his diary which covers the subsequent twenty-plus years—show that behind his seemingly quiet and studious life, he harbored a burning passion and a complex psychology that fostered both deep thought and depression. With his gaze keenly fixed on the fluctuations in contemporary society, he often sensed impending doom. In this way, Sugita Gempaku was a modern intellectual.

> The cries of insects
> from the depths of the grass—
> How long the evening is!

The cry of insects that Gempaku heard on an interminable autumn evening in his later years, long after the deaths of Gennai, Jun'an, Ryōtaku, Shūho, and Seian, was, I now think, the deep inner voice that so absorbs the attention of the aged scholar in the portrait.

---

1 Ogata Tomio (1910–1989) was the great-grandson of Ogata Kōan (1810–1853), a physician and *rangaku* scholar noted for establishing an academy (Tekijuku) that later developed into Osaka University.
2 Yamagata Daini (1725–1767), author of an essay criticizing the shogunate for usurping the emperor's power, was arrested and executed with another man for plotting rebellion, an effort by the government to suppress the growing *sonnō* ("Revere the Emperor") movement.
3 Gennai was invited to the Akita domain as a consultant on the management of copper mines. A *ranga* (Dutch painting) artist as well as a physician and scholar, he mentored the domain lord and his retainer in techniques of Western painting, giving rise to the Akita *ranga* school.
4 King Wen (1112–1050 BCE), founder of the Zhou dynasty, was known as the "greatest of all kings."

10 | READING SUGITA GEMPAKU'S MEMOIR: DAWN OF WESTERN SCIENCE IN JAPAN

I used to recommend particular books to college freshmen as an introduction to learning or as an introduction to the life of a scholar. Students around the age of twenty invariably want to read Max Weber or Karl Marx (or more recently, Michel Foucault or Jacques Derrida), and when they have finished, they imagine that they now understand society and the life of the mind. That is an empty delusion. Reading crude translations of dry-as-dust treatises on sociological methodology or philosophy only dulls the brain and the senses. Instead, I urge all students, whatever their major, to read books by the finest thinkers of early modern Japan: books that fascinate, books to savor, books that capture the essence of a way of thinking in idiosyncratic and beautiful Japanese. Specifically, I recommend four books that are firsthand accounts of the intellectual adventures of men who were pioneers in their disciplines: *Master Sorai's Responsals* (*Sorai sensei tōmonsho*, ca. 1717) by Ogyū Sorai;[1] *First Steps into the Mountains* (*Uiyamabumi*, 1798) by Motoori Norinaga;[2] *Dawn of Western Science in Japan* (*Rangaku kotohajime*, 1815) by Sugita Gempaku;[3] and *An Encouragement of Learning* (*Gakumon no susume*, 1872–1876) by Fukuzawa Yukichi.[4]

A cocky student might initially look down on all these books as too easy. However, every one of them is a classic that, on careful reading, offers a gentle challenge to the brain, the heart, and the senses.

The works by Sorai and Norinaga should by rights be discussed in this book, but as my emphasis here is not on Confucianism or nativist

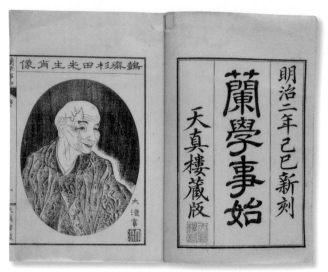

Figure 31. Sugita Genpaku, *Rangaku Kotohajime* (*Dawn of Western Science in Japan*). Tamagawa University Museum of Education.

studies but on Western learning, I will focus on Gempaku's book, examining select passages in their literary and historical contexts. Let's begin with a description of one of Gempaku's visits to the Nagasakiya inn, where Dutch traders in Edo stayed on their annual tribute mission to the shogun. This visit is estimated (by Ogata Tomio) to have taken place in 1769.

> From then on I visited [the interpreter] in his quarters every day. One day I observed the Dutch physician [George Rudolf] Bauer, whom I mentioned earlier, treat a medical student named Kawahara Gempaku for a boil on his tongue and also perform a bloodletting operation. It was quite an involved procedure. The physician calculated ahead of time how far the blood would jet out and placed a vessel to catch it. The jet of blood landed exactly in the vessel. This was the first bloodletting in Edo.

Assuming this happened in 1769, Sugita Gempaku was thirty-six. For the first time in his life, this established "Dutch-style" surgeon came into direct contact with the medical practices of a Westerner. His astonishment and admiration are clear. Gempaku had by then been frequenting the Nagasakiya for some three years, but he was all the more persistent in his visits that year because he had heard that the senior Dutch interpreter, Yoshio Kōzaemon (1724–1800), was an able surgeon, and he hoped to study under him.

Bloodletting, also known as phlebotomy or venesection, entailed the insertion of a needle into a vein to release "bad blood." Europeans continued to trust the effectiveness of that treatment until the mid-nineteenth century and were quick to employ it on the slightest pretext. Most likely, Kawahara agreed to be used for a demonstration of the bloodletting technique in return for having the boil on his tongue treated. Under everyone's watchful, curious eyes, blood spurted out and landed perfectly in a metal or ceramic bowl placed a meter or two away. The experiment must have made a profound impression on Gempaku, since he remembered the details forty-five years later.

A jumble of factors were operating on Gempaku that day: his growing premonition and expectation that Western medicine was entirely different from—far more deeply thought out and precise than—the Dutch-style treatments, such as applying plasters to cuts, that he had learned from his physician father; the persuasive power of a live demonstration of advanced techniques being held right before his eyes; his secret desire to be persuaded; a faint willingness to accommodate the moment. Mixed with these was a professionalism seemingly impressed less by the bloodletting itself than by its flawless execution, the accuracy with which the spurting blood hit the mark. And there was the vivid thrill that the sight of spurting blood never fails to arouse. Gempaku's brief description of the event, written years later, well conveys this welter of impressions and also attests to his mounting inclination to enter directly into the world of Dutch medicine.

The text continues as follows:

> This old man was, at the time, young and energetic. During the Dutchmen's stay I constantly visited [the Nagasakiya], and one day Kōzaemon showed me an unusual book that he said was

Heister's *Chirurgie*,[5] which he had first brought over the year before. I begged him to let me have it, and he offered to swap it for twenty barrels of Sakai sake.

Although I couldn't read a single letter when I opened the book, I could see that the illustrations were markedly different from those in Japanese or Chinese books; just seeing their exquisite precision made me feel I was being enlightened So, I borrowed the book for a time as I wanted to at least copy the pictures, and by working day and night I managed to finish the task while Kōzaemon was in Edo. Sometimes I would work through the night and hear the cock crow at dawn.

This passage, too, has an unforgettable charm, perhaps because of the opening words: "This old man was, at the time, young and energetic." At eighty-two, Gempaku is looking back with nostalgia on the single-minded dedication of his younger self.

The book that Yoshio Kōzaemon showed him, considerably inflating its price, was the famous introduction to surgery by Lorenz Heister. Edo scholars often were shown or managed to obtain new "red-haired" books through Nagasaki interpreters. Every year, Hiraga Gennai and others contrived to raise the money to purchase costly Western books in the same way.

Although Gempaku was as yet unable to read any of the text of the thick book, just looking at the many copperplate prints made him feel he "was being enlightened"—a particularly apt expression. As his scholarly uncertainty of many years dissipated like mist, he must have felt a pleasurable sensation, as if now at last he could see plainly. The drawings were indeed "markedly different from those in Japanese or Chinese books"; using perspective and shadows, they showed the various body parts and their workings with a precision and definition that must have seemed unquestionably real. As Gempaku studied them, he must have felt his image of his own internal anatomy undergoing expansion and revision.

Although this is an unintended consequence, the passage above accurately shows the crucial importance of visual features in intercultural communication. Gennai, Gempaku, and the other early seekers of Dutch learning were initially fascinated above all by the illustrations in Dutch books. Before they could understand the Dutch language, those pioneers experienced a literal "enlightenment"—the light of truth banishing the dark of ignorance—through their senses. Gempaku, caught up in that intensely exhilarating sensation, spent many a spring night eagerly copying illustrations during the remainder of Kōzaemon's short stay. "Sometimes I would work through the night and hear the cock crow at dawn": the words convey the image of a scholar surrounded by darkness, copying away by lantern light, his mind alive with a thousand new possibilities.

Psychologically "Somehow" Turning to the West

Gempaku's contact with Heister's book took him unawares a step closer to the world of *A New Book of Anatomy*. One of the great achievements of *Dawn of Western Science in Japan*, at least in Part I, is its skillful evocation of numerous small incidents showing the gradual change in the mood of the times and the activities of others that led Gempaku, a scholar in his thirties, first to the Dutch, then to Dutch books, and finally to the field of *rangaku* without conscious planning or intention on his part.

From the late 1760s, Edo scholars moved with increasing intensity toward *rangaku* and *A New Book of Anatomy*; Gempaku, still without any conscious effort, was motivated only by vague presentiments and curiosity to make his way in that direction. Writing in old age, he perfectly captures this rather mysterious, fortuitous coming together of the age and the individual through the repeated use of the adverb "somehow" (*nantonaku*). That word is, I believe, a key to deciphering Part I of *Dawn of Western Science in Japan*. Several examples follow (emphases added). The reader is encouraged to open a copy of the book and ponder along with me.

> From around then, items from the Netherlands were *somehow* regarded as curious, and all sorts of instruments imported from

there were popular; people known to love novelty would collect and cherish them, whether their collection was large or small.

This passage comes just after a description of how three years earlier, in 1766, Maeno Ryōtaku suddenly invited Gempaku to join him in calling on the senior interpreter Nishi Zenzaburō at the Nagasakiya. They requested instruction in the Dutch language, only to quickly abandon the idea when told their efforts would be useless. As soon as he heard what an arduous chore learning Dutch would be, Gempaku, impatient by nature, "lost all desire to study" the language; yet he reports that around that same time, the atmosphere in society was "somehow" changing. Society was in motion, passing him by.

"Especially when the late daimyo of the Sagara domain [Tanuma Okitsugu] was in power, society was at a peak of extravagance and magnificence," Gempaku explains. And so, people scrambled to acquire equipment like the *weelglas* (weather glass), *thermometer*, *donderglas* (thunder glass), *vochtmeter* (moisture meter), *donkerkamer* (camera obscura), *tooverlantaren* (fairy lantern), *zonglas* (sun glass), and *roeper* (megaphone), fussing over them as well as over clocks, telescopes, glasswork, and other "red-haired" rarities and curios. It is interesting to note that many of those objects had counterparts in Monticello, the far-off Virginia home of Thomas Jefferson, in inventions suggestive of a "quirky ingenuity," in the words of historian Kenneth Clark.[6] Moreover, one begins to see how the spirit of the age could have inspired the polymath Hiraga Gennai to become the hero of the Tanuma era (1767–1786)—when Tanuma Okitsugu as senior counselor encouraged Western learning— and invent an *erekiteru* (static electricity generator).

"People's hearts were supremely moved by curiosities and awed by the subtlety of the natural laws": Gempaku's words well express the spirit of the age (the working of the collective consciousness). By the 1760s and 1770s, the policy of national seclusion had continued for nearly one hundred fifty years, and Japanese people had finally begun to tire of the endless repetitiveness of their island country's daily life. That was why their curiosity was so piqued by foreign inventions and why they thrilled at the exoticism of even the smallest encounter with Dutch oddities. Undiminished by the long period of isolation, Japanese curiosity perked up as if on cue. Gempaku describes it as a natural awakening, like that of hibernating insects at winter's end.

And as a result, "a great number of people came *naturally* together in the Dutch quarters during the annual tribute mission in the spring." According to Gempaku, this new attitude had "somehow" developed and inspired more annual visits to the Nagasakiya by physicians like himself and product developers like Gennai. Here "naturally" is a variation on "somehow," another key to Gempaku's sense of history. He himself was among the "great number of people" who gathered at the Nagasakiya, where the bloodletting experiment had so impressed him that he borrowed the Heister book from Yoshio Kōzaemon and night after night copied its illustrations until dawn.

More than eighty years had passed since Bashō's haiku:

> The Dutch consul too
> lies prostrate before him—
> springtime of the shogun's reign

In the interval, Edoites' attitude toward the Dutch had undergone a sea change.

I cannot comment on each passage in detail, so from here on I will simply list the various passages that showcase Gempaku's "somehow" view of history. Directly after the passage cited above, Gempaku goes on to point out that *rangaku* enjoyed a bit of a groundswell in popularity after Maeno Ryōtaku struck up a friendship with Yoshio Kōzaemon and went to study in Nagasaki in 1770.

> As it gradually became known that the Dutch were skilled not only in medicine but in all manner of arts, people's interest *somehow* turned that way.

Curiosity about and a taste for "red-haired" novelties and curios gradually led intellectuals to become more focused in their studies of Dutch science and technology and of Western civilization in general.

As a result, more and more people joined the annual "conversations with the Dutch" (*Oranda taiwa*) at the Nagasakiya inn in Edo. Restrictions on entry were gradually eased and became freer "naturally." Hiraga Gennai took a leading role, solving a puzzle ring in one go and showing the foreigners a *slangensteen* (snake stone).

> Despite this trend, there wasn't anyone who knew a lot about the West. However, *somehow* the tendency to avoid things Western disappeared. Possession of Dutch books was no longer strictly regulated, and occasionally people could be seen carrying them about.

As scholars continued to seek out, with some hesitation, Dutch books and the like, objections died away. It was as if before anyone knew it, winter had turned to spring. The change didn't come about by decree but through a general thawing that happened "somehow." Amid this gradual transformation, Gempaku felt as if Dutch books came to him, rather than the other way around. In the spring of 1771, Nakagawa Jun'an, who was also from the Obama domain, brought back from the Nagasakiya two books on anatomy translated into Dutch, *Ontleedkundige Tafelen* and Caspar Bartholin's *Anatomia*. He showed them to Gempaku and invited him to purchase them. Even then, Gempaku did not leap at the chance. But eventually he came round:

> I could not of course read a word of the text, but the depiction of the viscera, joints, and so on was superb, unlike anything I had ever seen or heard before. I learned that the drawings were based on actual dissections, and I knew *somehow* that I had to have them. As my family practiced Dutch-style medicine, I wanted at least to have them on my bookshelf.

The continued repetition of "somehow" tells us that Gempaku used the word in a special sense. While essentially an extremely vague word, "somehow" in Gempaku's usage is an intentional expression of what was inherently vague and uncertain, and so the wording is exact.

To sum up, Gempaku is writing as an old man in his early eighties, reminiscing about events some forty years before when he was groping toward the seminal translation of *A New Book of Anatomy* and the establishment of Dutch studies in general. He remembers a general shift in atmosphere and attitude that he was not necessarily aware of at the time. This shift took place amid the languid "*sakoku* peace" of the mid-Tokugawa period, unmarked by any prominent, milestone event. That, however, only makes the shift all the more obvious and spontaneous. The word "somehow" beautifully captures the changing tone of the times, a change visible only from the perspective of distant recollection, and conjures up the figure of the memoirist, writing of a time when, with no idea where the changes were heading, he merely responded in a passive manner to the arrival of this new culture. Even as this impending change began to have an immediate impact on Gempaku's surroundings and *rangaku* became more attractive, he tells us that when presented with the chance to obtain a copy of *Ontleedkundige Tafelen*, he merely thought "somehow" that he had to have it. He had no inkling that his encounter with this book of anatomy would change the trajectory of his life and that of Japanese scholarship.

If a single brush stroke can bring a painting to life, then in *Dawn of Western Science in Japan*, the word "somehow" corresponds to just such a stroke. This casual word vividly conveys the subtle interaction between the age and the individual, and brings into relief the figure of a man groping his way forward through the half-light of history. The passage describing Gempaku's climactic experience on the third day of the third month, 1771, the night before the autopsy of a female criminal executed by beheading, has all the greater immediacy precisely because it comes after the frequent repetition of "somehow." He thought the temper of the times had "somehow" changed, that he was "somehow" attracted to Dutch books, and then he discovered that these things were after all no mere random hodgepodge of "somehows." Sugita Gempaku saw that the times and the force of history had progressed steadily toward a certain node, a connecting point, in an ever richer context. Recalling as if it were yesterday the deep emotion with which, after a long time of groping in the dark, he saw a ray of light, the old man wrote these words:

And so, having by some miracle obtained the Dutch book of anatomy, I wanted before anything else to compare its illustrations with the real thing. That path of learning was about to open. I must say, my obtaining the book that spring was truly strange and wonderful. I remember that it was the third day of the third month [1771].

In a narrative voice very close to ordinary idiomatic speech, Gempaku captures his extraordinary emotions: deep emotion that all the "somehows" until then had been the work of an invisible hand guiding him to the fullness of knowing "That path of learning was about to open"; joy at being freed from the indefiniteness of "somehow"; disbelief; bewilderment. Shortly after this, when he was invited to the human dissection, Gempaku repeats and underscores his excitement. "I was overjoyed at the timing of this exceptional good fortune and ready to fly off [to Kotsugahara] on the spot."

Gempaku's memoir, though only a slender paperback booklet, leaves a deep, indelible impression on readers, and not only because the events it describes are in themselves so moving. Rather, I believe that because the style of writing is so natural, neither polished nor precious, it brings to life the speech of the aged scholar, a man who "thought deeply and felt deeply," by conveying something close to his actual voice. This style gives the work an inner dimension, making it much more than a simple factual documentary or a tale of heroic exploits. The use of the idiomatic "somehow" and "I must say . . . [it] was truly strange and wonderful" (*fushigi tomo myō tomo iwanka*) are typical of the colloquial style of the whole, which is written freely without any of the stiffness or posing of the classical *kambun* style. This is what imbues the old scholar's memoir "in search of lost time" with a uniquely poetic freshness and truth.

The uncertainty of the adverb "somehow" is, moreover, an expression of humility. By using it, Gempaku acknowledges that he is a small being at the mercy of history's machinations. Founders of academic disciplines are generally more inclined to use words boasting of their foresight. The word "somehow" rather conveys the dignity of someone capable of admitting his own smallness. Above all, it is indicative of the keen, mature sense of history of a thinker who, even as he was being driven by the times, evolved into a driver of the times. No less vividly than the passage expressing his youthful amazement at the sure hand of the Dutch physician demonstrating bloodletting or the celebrated passage describing his excited conversation with Maeno Ryōtaku and Nakagawa Jun'an on the way back from the dissection at Kotsugahara, the single word "somehow" conveys the profound impression of a man who lived history.

In this chapter, I have delved into Sugita Gempaku's *Dawn of Western Science in Japan*, which historians turn to only as a historical source and scholars of literature take up rarely if at all. I, however, have examined it from the perspective of the history of comparative culture, and by now the reader will understand why I recommend this work so strongly to young university students.

---

1 Samuel Hideo Yamashita, *Master Sorai's Responsals: An Annotated Translation of Sorai Sensei's Tomonsho*, Center for Southeast Asian Studies Kyoto University (Honolulu: University of Hawaii Press, 1994).
2 Sey Nishimura, "First Steps into the Mountains: Motoori Norinaga's *Uiyama-bumi*," *Monumenta Nipponica*, vol. 42, no. 4 (1987), 449-493.
3 Sugita Gempaku, *Dawn of Western Science in Japan: Rangaku Kotohajime*, Ryōzō Matsumoto and Tomio Ogata, trans. (Hokuseido Press, 1969).
4 Fukuzawa Yukichi, *An Encouragement of Learning*, David A. Dilworth, trans. (New York: Columbia University Press, 2012).
5 Lorenz Heister, *Heelkundige Onderwijzingen* [Surgical teachings], a Dutch surgical textbook published in 1741.
6 Kenneth Clark, *Civilisation* (New York: Harper & Row, 1969), 264.

11 | PICTURES OF PEACE

Tawaraya Sōtatsu's Early Spring and Early Fall:
Puppy and *Edamame*

A chubby puppy as cute as a stuffed animal, its adorableness emphasized by the rounded, shortened portrayal of the four paws, as if it were wearing socks: of all the pictures of puppies Tawaraya Sōtatsu (ca. 1570–1640) painted, *Puppy* (*Koinu-zu*) is the most appealing.

A stuffed animal would be so lightweight that you could pick it up by the toes, but Sōtatsu's creature looks as if it would be fairly hefty if you did manage to pick up the protesting pup. Along with the feel of thin fur and warm skin at the throat, belly, and tail, the painting conveys a live animal's solidity and combative nature. *Tarashikomi*, seen in overlapping splotches of darker and lighter ink, and *horinuri* (painting-by-carving), seen in the white outlines of the ear, the front right shoulder, and the rump, are two techniques that Sōtatsu tried around the same time in a pair of hanging scrolls entitled *Oxen* (*Ushi-zu*), but here he used them more effectively and with a lighter touch. These techniques are particularly striking in rendering the sheen of the puppy's skin in the early spring sun and the vital strength inside the plump body.

The black puppy has paused in its progress and lowered its head—a head that seems disproportionately large, like that of human babies. What is the dog doing? It is sniffing the scent of spring, newly emerged from the soil. Sōtatsu, who along with Hon'ami Kōetsu (1558–1637) led the

Figure 32. Tawaraya Sōtatsu, *Puppy* (*Koinu-zu*).
Private collection.

classical revival and *yamato-e* revival in Kyoto in the Kan'ei era (1624–1644), has divined the nature of a puppy and infused this soft, gentle ink painting with a distinctively Japanese delight in early spring.

We know that this is not just spring but early spring because under the figure of the puppy, which is slightly above center on the scroll, are the silhouettes of six or seven spring grasses, none of which is even included in the traditional "seven herbs of spring." Three or four slender stalks of bracken, what looks like a thistle or dandelion, and a couple of Chinese milk vetches rise from the light black soil as if doing a little dance. Who but Sōtatsu, in Kyoto in that era, could have come up with the combination of a black puppy and these tender young herbs and wildflowers? The rustic flavor, mixed with a refined humor, cannot be found in classical paintings from China and Korea nor in puppy paintings by Yosa Buson and Itō Jakuchū.

Sōtatsu may have been the first painter in Japanese art history to include bracken in one of his works. Perhaps the celebrated poem in praise of spring by Prince Shiki (d. 716) in Japan's first poetry collection, the *Man'yōshū*, dimly echoed in his mind:

> Above the cataract
> running over the rocks
> bracken shoots
> have come out—spring
> is here, at long last!

The body and the actions of Sōtatsu's puppy express the joy of early spring in Japan. Some critics have claimed that this scroll painting illustrates the Zen koan "Jōshū's dog,"[1] but such an interpretation seems stiff and pedantic.

Sōtatsu was an extremely versatile painter. His *Bugaku Dance* (*Bugaku-zu byōbu*) in the Daigoji temple in Kyoto shows nine dancers on a rhythmic background of gold leaf, with a pine tree in the upper left corner and drums and a pavilion in the lower right. Stillness and motion are spaced out in an unobtrusively geometric arrangement of amazing precision. Had Henri Matisse, the painter of *La Danse* (1910), seen this painting, he would have been full of praise.

The collaborative works *Calligraphy of Poems from the "Kokinshū"* (*Kokinshū wakakan*) and *Calligraphy of Poems from the "Shinkokinshū" on Colored Paper* (*Shinkokinshū shikishichō*), featuring calligraphy by Kōetsu and underpaintings by Sōtatsu, are trios of poetry, calligraphy, and painting so breathtakingly beautiful that one wonders if there is anything more exquisite. On his gold-leaf screen painting *Wind God*

Figure 33. Tawaraya Sōtatsu, *Edamame* (*Edamame-zu*). Private collection.

and Thunder God, meanwhile, the two gods dance with energy enough to make heaven roll with thunder and the earth move, and their expressions are so humorous, that even now, four hundred years after they were painted, they radiate liberation and cheer. One look at them and the painter of *Guernica*, Pablo Picasso, might well have felt daunted and laid down his brush for a while.

Between these powerful masterworks in color, Sōtatsu also painted an array of large and small masterpieces in monochrome ink, including *Dragons and Clouds* (*Unryū-zu*), *Water Fowl in the Lotus Pond* (*Renchi suikin-zu*), the aforementioned *Puppy* and *Oxen*, as well as *Shennong* (*Shinnō-zu*) and *Peonies* (*Botan-zu*): the power of his imagination truly knew no bounds. Some ten years ago, when I first saw an exhibition at Tokyo National Museum entitled *Treasures by Rinpa Masters: Inheritance and Innovation*, the scroll painting *Edamame* (*Edamame-zu*) filled me with surprise and admiration. In contrast with his delightful portrayal of early spring bracken at the feet of a roly-poly black puppy, in *Edamame* Sōtatsu works with only a couple of soybean plants, one spindly with leaves and branches spread to the right and left, the other off in the lower left-hand corner, showing only beans and leaves. That's all.

Has any other painter in the world created a rich tableau out of one and one-third edamame plants growing in a field? This scroll painting has a sublimely bracing air. Only about thirty oval leaves are rendered in varying shades of ink, using *tarashikomi*. The clusters of plump, ripening beans hang darkly and slightly heavily next to the stem. The dark shadows of the beans and the graceful, translucent leaves suggest that a bright moon is shining tranquil beams over the field. In this elegant painting, Sōtatsu, the painter of *Wind God and Thunder God*, captured the *mono no aware* of early autumn in Japan.

According to the exhibition catalogue, the former owner, artist Yasuda Yukihiko, loved this painting and would hang it in his *tokonoma* alcove on a night of moon-viewing. He wrote on its box "Moon-viewing Beans." One can only applaud such excellent taste. These two stalks of edamame perfectly convey the beauty and calm of moonlight.

Kusumi Morikage's *Enjoying the Evening Cool under an Evening Glory Trellis*

Sometimes I jokingly say that immigration inspection sites in Japan's airports should hang a large reproduction of Kusumi Morikage's (1620–1690) screen painting *Enjoying the Evening Cool under an Evening Glory Trellis* (*Yūgaodana nōryō-zu*) on the wall. Anybody who views this work with admiration or relief should be allowed in the country, visa or no visa, no questions asked. With a piercing beauty, Morikage's painting expresses the sensitive emotions deep within the hearts of the

Figure 34. Kusumi Morikage, *Enjoying the Evening Cool under an Evening Glory Trellis* (*Yūgaodana nōryō-zu*). Tokyo National Museum.

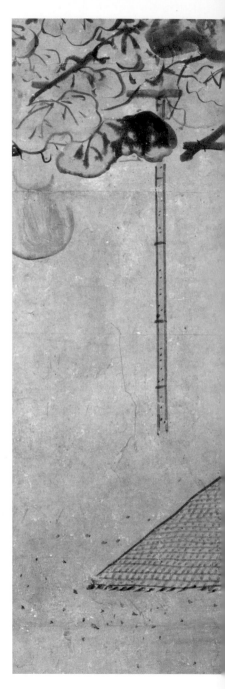

Figure 35. Kusumi Morikage, *Enjoying
the Evening Cool under an Evening Glory
Trellis* (*Yūgaodana nōryō-zu*), detail.
Tokyo National Museum.

Japanese people, so anyone who empathizes with the scene should be regarded as Japanese.

Few if any other paintings express so well the sense of quiet, cool refreshment and relaxation that Japanese people love, as well as the desire for a frugal yet happy life—a life happy *because of* its very frugality. Such a desire was embraced generally in Japan until not so long ago.

Nowadays the title of the painting is often shortened to *Enjoying the Evening Cool*, omitting mention of the evening glory. This is apparently because while "enjoying the evening cool" is associated with summer-time, the trellis is decked not with flowers but with round fruit, and on the upper left of the painting is a pale full moon, associated with autumn. The seasonal references do not match.

But the farming family that seems emblematic of "honest poverty" is under a trellis decorated not with the modest and beautiful white flower made famous in the "Yūgao" chapter of *The Tale of Genji* but with its fruit, a kind of gourd. Amid the lush growth of palm-shaped leaves, rendered lightly in shades of black and gray, six or seven round gourds already hang from the trellis, which is supported by several slender bamboo poles. The season is definitely late summer or early autumn. Soon the inner flesh of the gourd will be cut into strips and hung to dry for use in cooking, and the outer shell will be dried and used as a container for charcoal and the like. The trellis and vine extend over the straw-thatched roof of the small house, though only the wickerwork door and a small window are visible. The space below the trellis, seemingly larger than the house's interior, makes a pleasantly breezy place to relax.

Spread out on the ground under the trellis by a scattering of small stones is a large straw mat, the size of two or three tatami mats. A family of three is relaxing there, sitting or lying down, cooling off after the labors of a hot day. Perhaps they have had a quick bath and a simple supper. The father, nearly middle-aged, is reclining in the center of the mat, wearing an indigo-dyed under-kimono that is so thin and gauzy his loincloth shows through. His legs are stretched out comfortably behind his wife. His eyes are pensively downcast, and the long fingers of one hand prop up his chin. The young mother was perhaps last to use the bathwater; her still-wet long black hair is cascading down her naked back, and just below the pit of her arm is the suggestion of a round breast. She is wearing only a *koshimaki*, a wraparound underskirt. Her face is winsome, with slits for eyes gazing into the distance and a small red mouth.

These people seem too refined to be an ordinary farming family. Even the child, a little boy of five or six sitting behind his father with one shoulder bare, isn't seeking attention. Perhaps for some reason they had to give up their samurai status and are living secretly in this house. Or perhaps they reflect the state of mind and high aims of the painter himself: once the top disciple of Kanō Tan'yū (1602–1674), the first official painter of the shogunate, Kusumi Morikage was forced by the misconduct of his daughter and son to leave Edo and wander around Kanazawa in Kaga province.

Rice cultivation has always been very important in Japan, the "Land of Abundant Rice," and artists have depicted scenes of labor in farming villages throughout Heian and Kamakura times (794–1333). Such scenes appeared in *yamato-e* paintings as settings of pilgrimages in illustrated biographies of eminent monks like Hōnen (1133–1212) and Ippen (1239–1289); illustrated legends of shrines and temples; and depictions of activities associated with the months of the year (*tsukinami-e*) or the seasons (*shiki-e*). In the Muromachi period (1336–1573), *kōshoku-zu* (paintings of cultivation and sericulture) and *shiki kōshoku-zu* (paintings of cultivation and sericulture in the four seasons) were introduced from Song-dynasty China, both titles and actual works showing farmers at work. Paintings on such themes entered the mainstream in Tokugawa Japan, as rice cultivation was the principal industry.

Such agricultural works were produced by many artists and schools of painting, from forerunners of the Kanō school to Tan'yū and his pupils, as well as the Unkoku school, founded by Unkoku Tōgan (1547–1618); Iwasa Matabei (1578–1650); Hanabusa Itchō (1652–1724); and the late eighteenth-century Maruyama-Shijō school. Kusumi Morikage, one of the most important painters of the pivotal Genroku era, left a particularly large number of fine screen paintings of rice cultivation in the four seasons. The popularity of such paintings was concurrent with the vogue for paintings of cities. Both types of painting convey the diligence of Japanese people in the Pax Tokugawana and the joy of labor; they also functioned as *kankai-zu* (pictures of advice and admonishment), showing the hardships of labor to members of the warrior class, who had little knowledge of the daily lives of the populace.

The theme of farming life was not taken up in ukiyo-e but rather in the works of Asai Chū (1856–1907), through the influence of Antonio Fontanesi (1818–1882), an Italian who painted in the style of the French Barbizon school and who taught in Japan's government-sponsored Technical Fine Arts School. Working in the style of Barbizon painters Jean-Francois Millet (1814–1875) and Theodore Rousseau (1812–1867), Chū painted watercolors and oil paintings of farmers, farmhouses, and farm villages. In the Taishō era, this line of art represented a kind of physiocracy, a belief that the country's economy should be based on agriculture. It continued thereafter in the pastoral paeans of painters like Ogawa Usen (1868–1938) of Lake Ushiku; Shimizu Toshi (1887–1945), who studied in the United States and Europe; Sakai Sanryō (1897–1969) of Aizu; Noguchi Kenzō (1901–1944) of Ōmi; and Fukuda Toyoshirō (1904–1970) of Akita. This in a nutshell is my view of the development of the genre through the ages in Japan.

Enjoying the Evening Cool, while clearly deriving from the above tradition, is in a category all its own. Plenty of other paintings of farming life, in both Japan and China, contain scenes of fishing, circling the house singing to scare off birds (*torioi*), and the like, as well as scenes of people relaxing at a riverside or at home. Such scenes soften and lend interest to the paintings. Morikage's masterpiece, however, doesn't paint an exact picture of farming life, nor does it offer "advice and admonishment." Rather, this contemplative work is filled with deep empathy.

The painting is generally considered to allude to a poem by the samurai poet Kinoshita Chōshōshi (1569–1649), who had connections to the powerful Toyotomi clan:

> Under the eaves
> where evening glories bloom

they enjoy the evening cool
he in an under-kimono
she in an under-skirt

The setting in the painting may be similar, but the level of refinement is vastly different. The poem, as well as a number of other paintings that also allude to it, simply takes pleasure in the notion of a couple lounging in dishabille. Morikage's painting is a far more genuine tribute to country life. I would say that he shows us a family enjoying the repose and deep peace of the Pax Tokugawana. Few if any other paintings convey so directly the repose and happiness afforded by a life of modest means.

What makes that repose all the more palpable is the white light of the large full moon of early autumn in the upper left corner. The bottom half of the moon is hidden by evening mist, the remains of the steamy heat of the day. Soon the mist will dissipate and the cool of twilight will prevail. I am reminded of the pleasurable sensation of evening cool on my skin long ago as I sat with my parents and younger sisters. I remember, too, the occasional sharp discomfort from a stone underneath the matting and the dampness of the ground.

Kusumi Morikage's masterful ode to the simple life reminds us in the twenty-first century of this example of basic Tokugawa wisdom: "Appreciate having enough; be satisfied with your circumstances." (My only quibble with this painting is the lack of smoke from a mosquito coil.)

The East-West Peregrinations of a Rhinoceros

Let's get in a spaceship equipped with a time machine and be off.

Our destination is the Malabar Coast of India at the start of the sixteenth century. In May 1498, with a commission from King Manuel I of Portugal, Vasco da Gama discovered the sea route to India. A dozen years later, in 1510, Afonso de Albuquerque (1453–1515), the governor of Portuguese India, launched a fierce assault on the island of Goa, slaughtering the Muslim residents and making Goa the headquarters of Portuguese supremacy in the Indian Ocean.

Self-interest soon prompted neighboring Hindu and Muslim states to seek amicable relations with Portugal. In a gesture of goodwill, Sultan Muzafar II of Cambay (modern Gujarat, in western India) presented King Manuel I with a rhinoceros, through Albuquerque. The strange beast resembling an armored car was transported via the just-opened sea route, going around the Cape of Good Hope and Cape Verde and landing in Lisbon on May 20, 1515, after a voyage of somewhere between six and ten months.

The rhino created a sensation in Lisbon—no doubt even more so than the arrival of the first pandas did in Tokyo in 1972. Ganda (Sanskrit for "rhinoceros"), the first rhino ever to set foot on European soil, was taken as a living symbol of the victory of Portugal and Christendom over the Muslim world. Ever since the days of Pliny the Elder (23–79 CE) in ancient Rome, it had been said that if a rhinoceros and an elephant fought, the rhino would win by ripping open the elephant's belly with its horn. To test this theory, an experiment was conducted in a Lisbon arena, and Ganda won by default when the elephant bolted. Following this victory, Manuel I decided to present the animal to Pope Leo X in Rome. Unfortunately, the ship sank in a storm off the Genoa coast and Ganda, along with the entire crew, drowned.

This might seem to be the end of the story, but it is only the beginning. Around the time Ganda set sail for Rome, a printer in Lisbon wrote to a colleague in Nuremberg, informing him about the enormously popular beast. He enclosed a sketch by an unknown local artist. His friend in Nuremberg happened to show the letter and sketch to none other than the great painter Albrecht Dürer (1471–1528), who was the friend's adopted son.

Dürer lived and breathed art. Struck by the sketch of this enormous, exotic animal, he promptly set about copying it, and he included the explanation for good measure. Within the year he printed a woodcut of his sketch—the familiar picture we so often encounter in albums today, including the words "1515 Rhinoceros," his monogram, and the explanation.

The original sketch by the unknown Lisbon artist is now lost, so it is impossible to know how closely Dürer adhered to or departed from it.

Most likely, he was unable to escape his preconceptions and wonderment at the idea of the monstrous animal from India. The head and throat have overlapping folds similar to gills. Each section of the metallic-looking hide, so closely resembling the armor of the knight in Dürer's 1513 painting *Knight, Death, and the Devil*, serves to emphasize the awesomeness of the beast. What appears to be a second, dorsal horn, scarcely noticeable in the sketch, is larger and more prominent in the woodcut—a strong indication that Dürer, having never seen the real thing, was drawing from his imagination.

In any case, although Ganda traveled all the way from Cambay, India only to perish off the Genoa coast, he enjoyed a long afterlife in Dürer's print. For the next nearly three hundred years, he continued to live in the pages of European books of natural history before journeying back across the Indian Ocean to pop up in late eighteenth-century Japan.

An enlarged print of Dürer's rhinoceros was reproduced in *History of Animals* (*Historiae animalium*, ca. 1558) by the Swiss naturalist Conrad Gessner (1516–1565), greatly enhancing the image's credibility and increasing its renown. Probably Gessner inspired the French surgeon Ambroise Paré (1510–1590) to publish another print in his *Unicorn's Speech* (*Discours de la licorne*, 1580) with the caption "a rhinoceros, its body sheathed in armor." The second horn was even larger than before, and Ganda was transformed into a savage beast built like a tank with a machine gun attached. There was undoubtedly a chain of other images in between, but eventually in 1653 Joannes Jonston (1603–1675) produced a full-page copperplate print in his monumental *Natural History* (*Historia Naturalis*).

Ganda arrived in Japan in 1663, three years after the publication of a Dutch translation of Jonston's work. The book was presented to the shogunate during the reign of Ietsuna, the fourth shogun, by the Dutch consul Hendrik Indjic. For half a century it lay unopened in the Edo Castle library, until the 1716 appearance of the eighth shogun, Yoshimune, a ruler of enterprising spirit with plans to promote Japanese industry. Thanks to him, the book played a central role in inspiring Japan's "century of natural history," along with Dodoens' 1554 work *The History of Plants*.

Figure 36. Sō Shiseki's drawing of a lion in *Thicket of Ancient and Modern Pictures* (*Kokon gasō*). Waseda University Library.

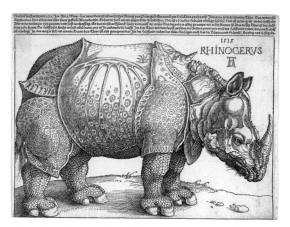

Figure 37. Albrecht Dürer, *Rhinoceros*. National Gallery of Victoria, Melbourne.

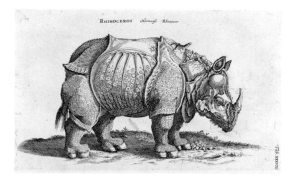

Figure 38. Joannes Jonston, rhinoceros in *Historia Naturalis*. Tenri Central Library, Nara.

Figure 39. Tani Bunchō, *Rhinoceros* (*Sai-zu*). Private collection.

The herbalists Noro Genjō (1693–1701) and Aoki Kon'yō (1695–1769) both purchased the book. In 1768, Hiraga Gennai "sold his furnishings and bedding"[2] to buy a copy. Gennai looked at the illustrations and merely dreamed of his own future book of Japanese natural history, but his friend Sō Shiseki (1715–1786), a painter of the Nanpin school, quickly made thirteen woodcuts of a lion, donkey, sheep, camel, and other animals, which he included in his album *Thicket of Ancient and Modern Pictures* (*Kokon gasō*, 1770)—unfortunately, he mistakenly gave the lion the bushy tail of a fox. Jonston's lion proved especially popular. Odano Naotake (1750–1780) and Shiba Kōkan (1747–1818) both based their renditions on the Jonston image. (Jonston himself had based his image on a lion in the Rubens painting *Daniel in the Lion's Den*, ca. 1615.)

As a result, Japanese people saw the figure of a Western lion, not the Chinese *shishi*, for the first time. And through a reproduction of the Dürer rhinoceros, they encountered the overall image of a rhinoceros, rather than merely the horn, which was used at the time as protection from floods and as a detoxicant.

The first painting of the rhinoceros in color on silk was a 1790 work (40 × 64 centimeters) by the literati painter Tani Bunchō (1763–1840). Where Bunchō may have encountered Jonston's rhinoceros is unknown. By then Gennai had already died in prison; perhaps his precious copy of Dodoens' book—inscribed in red, "the first copy in Japan"—passed into the hands of someone who showed it to Bunchō. Or, because he succeeded his father as a retainer of the Tayasu family, one of the branch families of the Tokugawa, and as such enjoyed the protection of the powerful senior counselor Matsudaira Sadanobu, perhaps Bunchō was able to view the book in Edo Castle. In any case, he painstakingly reproduced Jonston's illustration—that is, Dürer's rhinoceros—in detail with a brush, capturing everything from the hideous wrinkles on its face to the scales on its limbs, the roundness of its torso, and even the hairs sticking out of its ears.

Taking a closer look, the folds of flesh on the face and neck do look like wrinkles, as if Ganda were wrapped in a *furoshiki* cloth wrapper. A rhinoceros is a perissodactyl (odd-toed ungulate), but this one has retrogressed to the order of artiodactyl (even-toed ungulate). Appropriately enough, Ganda looks as if he is wearing Tokugawa footwear: *koma-geta*, low wooden clogs with white thongs. The second horn protruding from his back has grown still bigger and thicker. This painting on silk clearly demonstrates the distortions that accompany cultural transfer, as easily observable traits become exaggerated in proportion to the distance they have traveled from the original.

The most hilarious example of this phenomenon is the scaly spots on the rhino's legs and torso. The spots are actually from a skin infection the animal suffered during its confinement in close quarters on the long voyage from India. Dürer picked up on the pustules from the nameless Portuguese painter, and every natural history book from then on included them as an innate rhinoceros characteristic. Such books were eventually transported back across the sea to the Far East, so that the spots appear even in Bunchō's painting.

Nietzsche, taking his cue from a line in an English translation of a Buddhist hymn, wrote in his aphoristic book *Daybreak* (*Morgenröte*, 1881), "Thus I wander, lonely as the rhinoceros." (*So wandle ich einsam wie das Rhinoceros.*) Certainly Ganda wandered far and wide. Skin infection and all, he migrated from East to West and back again, across three long centuries of history.

Rousseau's and Hiraga Gennai's Ginseng

Appended to one French edition of *Reveries of a Solitary Walker* (*Les Rêveries du promeneur solitaire*, 1782) by Jean-Jacques Rousseau is a recollection of Rousseau by Bernardin de Saint-Pierre (1737–1814). It is apparently an excerpt from Bernardin's book on Rousseau's life and works.[3] Several years ago, I read that excerpt and was brought up short.

A disciple of Rousseau, Bernardin de Saint-Pierre was also the author of a book that many have heard of but nowadays few have read: *Paul and Virginia* (*Paul et Virginie*, 1787), a sweetly sentimental novel set on the French island of Mauritius in the Indian Ocean. Along with his major work, *Studies of Nature* (*Études de la nature*, 1784), it appealed to contemporary Europeans' taste for natural history and exoticism, as well as their sentimental streak, and catapulted him to fame. Bernardin himself lived on Mauritius for two and a half years (1768–1780) and based the book on his experiences there. The island took on sudden importance at the time due to conflict with Britain over colonization. One year before Bernardin was sent there as a senior engineer, control over the island had just been transferred from the French East India Company to the French state. When Bernardin finally returned to Paris in 1771, he was unknown and penniless. A friend introduced him to Rousseau in June of the following year.

Bernardin and his friend went to visit Rousseau in his modest fifth-floor apartment on Rue Plastrière in Paris. The room held a variety of potted plants and plant specimens, and a birdcage suspended from the ceiling contained a siskin. A few days later, Rousseau paid a return call at Bernardin's house. Bernardin showed him flora he had brought back from the island and shared some samples with him. As he walked Rousseau home, they passed through the Tuileries Garden and smelled, out of nowhere, the aroma of coffee. Rousseau confessed that he had a weakness for two luxuries: ice cream and coffee. The next day, Bernardin sent him a bag of coffee beans he had brought back from the island of Bourbon (present-day Réunion), near Mauritius. The gift was marked "a sample of seeds of foreign flora."

At first, Rousseau sent a polite note of thanks. The next day, however, he wrote in a markedly different vein: "If I accept such a gift from you, someone whom I have only just met, we can no longer continue an ordinary association. Either you take back the coffee or we never meet again." Rousseau's peevishness was on full display. This unexpected foofaraw was resolved and the friendship restored when Bernardin accepted two gifts in exchange: a book on fish and "*une racine de ginseng*" (ginseng root).

When I read about the ginseng, it struck me that Rousseau and two Japanese herbalists who were his contemporaries, Hiraga Gennai and his teacher Tamura Gen'yū, were truly birds of a feather. In that century of natural history, they were on opposite sides of the globe and had no way of knowing that they were slightly yet definitely connected through their interest in ginseng. I was surprised and delighted to discover this.

Hiraga Gennai devoted enormous effort to domestic production of high-quality medicinal ginseng, with considerable success. When he was in his twenties, Tamura Gen'yū acquired ginseng seeds at the behest of Shogun Yoshimune and attempted to grow them in Kanda, Honjō, and Nikkō. He also wrote several books on ginseng, including a 1747 study of the plant's pharmacological properties. An expert on ginseng and a keen student of regional products (*bussangaku*), Tamura became head of an official institute for ginseng production under the direct control of the shogunate. Gennai faithfully carried on his mentor's work, seeking ways to domesticate production in order to make ginseng widely and cheaply available without relying solely on Korean imports. His 1763 work *Classification of Various Materials* contained an appendix explaining the cultivation of ginseng, complete with illustrations.

So the development of ginseng research in Japan is well documented, but where did Rousseau's ginseng root come from? Possibly some ginseng imported to China or Japan from Joseon-dynasty Korea made its way to Europe from Nagasaki in a Dutch ship or from Canton in an English ship. The *Encyclopédie* of Diderot and d'Alembert contains a detailed four-page article on ginseng by the Jesuit priest Louis Chevalier de Jaucourt (1704–1779), according to which ginseng was first introduced to Europe in 1610 when a Dutch East India Company ship brought some back from Japan. Ginseng was also included among items presented later to Louis XIV by a Siamese envoy and so became known in France as well. In his article, Jaucourt estimates that products imported on Dutch ships accounted for the bulk of European consumption in the latter half of the eighteenth century.

However, the ginseng Rousseau had on hand could well have been Canadian in origin. As Jaucourt mentions, in 1712 the Jesuit missionary Joseph-Francois Lafitau (1681–1746), who worked with the Iroquois, discovered ginseng in a forest in Canada, which was then a French territory. Lafitau was a scholar made famous by his ethnographic studies of the Iroquois. He searched for ginseng in Canada after he learned about its shape and curative properties in a report by Jaucourt on missionary work in China. His eventual discovery of the costly medicinal herb touched off a Canadian "ginseng boom." Ginseng from all over was collected in Quebec and as early as the 1720s and 1730s was being exported by the French East India Company, mainly to Canton. Jaucourt's article indicates that by 1757, the amount of Canadian ginseng exported in this way was around 2 tons.

The French Academy recognized the word "ginseng" in 1762. At the end of the Seven Years' War the following year, France ceded Canada to Britain by the Treaty of Paris, but it is safe to assume that Canadian ginseng continued to enter Europe. In my opinion, that explains the ginseng root that Rousseau sent his new friend in return for the gift of coffee beans from the French-owned island of Bourbon. If so, the mysterious connection between Rousseau and contemporary Japanese herbalists could deepen even more.

Beginning in 1747, Chinese merchants had taken advantage of the scarcity and high cost of ginseng in Japan to export Canadian ginseng to Nagasaki, calling it "Cantonese ginseng." As the product became widely available, a debate similar to one that Jaucourt touched on in his *Encyclopédie* article arose in Japan as well: was Canadian-Cantonese ginseng as effective as the Korean product? Naysayers won the day. The import and use of Cantonese ginseng was banned in 1763. The work of Tamura Gen'yū and Hiraga Gennai in domesticating production also may have influenced this decision.

As Cantonese ginseng became better known, it was ultimately judged equal in quality to ginseng from Korea, and in 1788 the ban was lifted. In any case, I find it fascinating that Rousseau and Gennai, on opposite sides of the globe, had an unknown connection through their involvement in the international economic and cultural affairs associated with the medicinal herb ginseng. As is well known, Rousseau, a devoted botanist, was a fervent admirer of the naturalist Carl Linnaeus (1707–1778); when Linnaeus' pupil Carl Thunberg went from the Swedish Uppsala University to Japan in 1775, he taught then state-of-the-art Western natural history to two of Gennai's friends in Edo, Nakagawa Jun'an and Katsuragawa Hoshū.

Pursuing contemporaneous ties such as these between eighteenth-century Japan and the West lends freshness and intimacy to the faces of those involved. This is one of the great merits of what I call "comparative cultural history."

Hiraga Gennai's *Portrait of a Western Woman* and the Woman's Younger Sisters

Among the brilliant men of Meiji was the literary scholar Fujioka Sakutarō (1870–1910). An associate professor of literature at Tokyo Imperial University, Fujioka wrote several novel surveys of Japanese literature that are still read today, including *A Comprehensive History of Japanese Literature: The Heian Period* (*Kokubungaku zenshi Heianchōhen*), and *Literary History of the Kamakura and Muromachi Periods* (*Kamakura Muromachi jidai bungakushi*). Another colorful masterwork is his 1903 *History of Early Modern Painting* (*Kinsei kaigashi zen*).[4]

Fujioka's history of painting begins with a chapter on "The Kanō School at Its Zenith" (*Kanō zensei*) and proceeds on to "Sideways and Downward" (*Ōryū kakō*) and "Innovation of Old Style" (*Kyūfū kakushin*), touching on the Rimpa school, Hanabusa Itchō (1652–1724), ukiyo-e, Ike no Taiga (1723–1776), Yosa Buson, and the recently popular Soga Shōhaku (1730–1781) and Itō Jakuchū (1716–1800). In the next chapter, "Competing Schools" (*Shoha kakuchiku*), he writes in considerable detail about Hokusai (1760–1849) and his school, Shiba Kōkan (1747–1818), and others, prefaced by a short but astute criticism of Hiraga Gennai's *Portrait of a Western Woman* (*Seiyō fujin-zu*). This is probably the first mention of Gennai by any Japanese art historian. He begins by mentioning that he "once saw an old painting" in the possession of Shikata Seishichi of Osaka and proceeds to describe it:

> It was an oil painting on canvas of a Western woman. Although probably done in imitation of Western paintings, Japanese techniques were employed, and Gennai, the artist, was not skillful. The simple, rough execution and the woman's intrepid expression seemed a reflection of the character of Gennai himself.[5]

This succinct, crisp assessment perfectly sums up the painting. Even

Figure 40. Hiraga Gennai, *Portrait of a Western Woman* (*Seiyō fujin-zu*). Kobe City Museum / DNPartcom.

Figure 41. Gaseo, *Portraits of a Western Man and Woman* (*Bijo to ōgon-zu*). Kobe City Museum.

Figure 42. Emily Eastman,
Young Girl with Stylish Coiffure.
Peter Tillou Collection.

today, nothing more need be said. In the tenth month of 1770, Tanuma Okitsugu granted Gennai permission and a small stipend to travel to Nagasaki for a second time to study Dutch translation. Gennai remained in Nagasaki approximately two years, until the autumn of 1772. At the home of a Dutch interpreter there, he was given a broken *erekiteru* (static electricity generator). As Fujioka surmised, it's likely that on being shown a portrait of a Western woman, he hastily boned up on the fundamentals of oil painting and copied the work. "Simple" and "rough" indeed— the collar and frill of the woman's dress are paper-thin, and the red beads of her necklace, too, are vague. Only the head is rather magnificent. The hair piled up rococo-style has great luster, as if he mixed lacquer into the black oil paint. Here and there he scraped the hair with a knife to make it shine, and the blue beads in the hairband sparkle too. Above all, the intensity of the gaze from the wide-open eyes, tinged red in the inner corners and with a few lashes drawn in at the outer corners; the long curve of the thick eyebrows, extending down to the dignified line of the nose; the firmly shut red mouth—all of these do indeed express an intrepid spirit.

Fukuzawa Yukichi, Fujioka's younger colleague in Western studies, also liked to speak of an "intrepid spirit." Having found the two characters used to write "Gennai" in the signature, Fujioka is convinced that the powerful depiction of that spirit in the painting "is indicative of the character of Gennai himself." This positive appraisal comes from a historian who describes the freedoms of the Meiji era.

A Nagasaki painting of a Western woman depicts the identical hairstyle, features, and dress, although below her neck frill she wears a cross, and her head is turned in the opposite direction. To the left is a grinning, shrewd-looking man with a large purse in his hand; despite this considerable difference, the painting is estimated to date from about the same time as Gennai's or a little later. It is signed "Gaseo" in Roman letters, which Koga Jūjirō suggests in *A Complete History of Nagasaki Paintings* (*Nagasaki kaiga zenshi*, 1944) could be read as the Japanese name "Gashō"; however, no artist of that name is known in late eighteenth-century Nagasaki. Still, the painting is evidence that Gennai and "Gashō" used the same Dutch painting as a model.

About thirty years ago, in an album of American folk art, I found the image of a woman who could be the little sister or cousin of the "intrepid" woman in Gennai's painting. This 1820s watercolor by Emily Eastman is entitled *Young Girl with Stylish Coiffure* (35.5 × 23.5 centimeters). The subject's hairstyle, curls, ribbons, dress, frill, and above all her lively and attractive features suggesting an intrepid spirit are exactly like Gennai's painting. The Eastman watercolor was created some fifty years after Gennai's oil painting, in Loudon, New Hampshire, and is now part of the collection of Mr. and Mrs. Peter Tillou.

I believe that the women of Gennai, "Gashō," and Eastman share a common mother, or rather a grandmother or possibly an aunt; perhaps this common ancestor was among the ladies in rococo portraits of aristocratic women in eighteenth-century France or Britain, the center of such portraiture. Recast in a framed miniature or a mezzotint woodcut, one made its way across the Atlantic Ocean to the American East Coast, while the other went across the Indian Ocean to Nagasaki. Each ended up on the rim of another world. I have long searched in the art museums of the United States and France for an image of that grandmother or aunt, but I have not yet found one.

The Edo "Farting Man" and a Comparative Theory of Farting, Centered on Hiraga Gennai

When I was a boy, New Year's at my grandparents' house always meant playing *iroha-garuta*, a matching game with cards. Someone would read out the first half of a proverb, and players would compete to grab the card with the second half. I used to get absorbed in the game, along with a crowd of cousins. One proverb that I never missed was "Squeezing the buttocks after farting" (*he o hitte shiri subomeru*). As soon as my grandmother called out in a ringing voice, "*He o...*" the card was mine.

As a child, I didn't yet realize the meaning of the saying, but I was intrigued by the appearance of the word "fart" (*he*) in the game, and I liked the accompanying picture. I'm sure the pictures were much the same in other versions of the game: a grown man on his stomach, the hem of his kimono hauled up to expose his raised rear end, letting loose a fart through his loincloth. To my child's eye, the picture was at once repulsive and funny. My grandmother was an avid reader of Hani Motoko's magazine *Women's Friend* (*Fujin no tomo*) and a member of a "friends' association."[6] That set of cards could have been published by such a respectable association, but even so, a card with a proverb beginning with the sound "*he*," could only have only one off-color ending. This is an admirable aspect of the Japanese *karuta* tradition, educating children in non-Puritan aspects of life.

Little boys normally go through a stage of inordinate interest in farting and other bodily functions. Director Ozu Yasujirō's wonderful film *Good Morning* (*Ohayō*, 1959) highlights that boyish propensity with skill and great humor. Two young brothers and their classmates who live nearby, convinced that eating pumice stone makes one fart more, engage in a farting contest. They push one other's foreheads to produce the desired effect, and each time, like clockwork, the reward is a gentle "pfff." The losers are those who can't make the sound. One boy eats too much pumice and gets an upset stomach. The film shows the

Figure 43. Illustration from Hiraga Gennai, *On Farting* (*Heppiriron*). Waseda University Library.

charming earnestness and playfulness, innocence and ridiculousness, of the world of little boys of long ago. Added to this is the drollery of an elderly man who farts a greeting each morning, making this great film an essential contribution to the cultural history of flatulence in Japan.

A pair of eighteenth-century literary works features an illustration that could be the prototype of the farting man in the card game of my childhood and takes as its subject a man who could be the prototype of the boys in Ozu's *Good Morning*. I am speaking of *On Farting* (*Heppiriron*), which Hiraga Gennai wrote in the seventh month of 1774 at forty-six, and its follow-up, *On Farting, Part II* (*Heppiriron kōhen*), which he wrote three years later.

When did farting first appear as the subject of a work of Japanese literature? I haven't yet made a thorough study of the matter, and an academic field called "the literary history of farting in Japan" seems nonexistent. Nakamura Yukihiko, editor of Gennai's collected works,[7] notes that a book with the beautiful title *Collection of Fragrant Echoes* (*Kunkyōshū*) was published in 1757, in Osaka, not far from where Gennai lived. Apparently Gennai had access to the book and helped himself to several of its expressions. However, due to the breezy charm of Gennai's style as he discusses flatulence and the quirky, delightful way in which he develops his "hot air" arguments, it is safe to say that his work is the premier example of the genre in Japanese medieval and early modern literature. The proverb "Neither lighting incense nor farting" (*jinkō mo takazu he mo hirazu*) describes someone mediocre and uninteresting, worthy of neither praise nor blame—a description entirely at odds with Gennai's life and work. Precisely because he was a man of such strong personality and humor, he was able to write these remarkable works.

On Farting was included in Part I of the collection *Six Pieces by Fūrai Sanjin* (*Fūrai rokubushū*), published in 1780, along with a full-page woodcut illustration. "Among the countless attractions of long-prosperous Edo," it begins, "there was once, in the vicinity of Ryōgoku Bridge, a flatulist whose feats provoked widespread discussion and rumors." The illustration shows the entrance to a freak show featuring a performance with the billing, "The Man who Parts Mist, Making Blossoms Bloom."[8] The identity of the artist is unknown, but the scene is depicted with considerable artistry, in the ukiyo-e style of Hishikawa Moronobu (1618–1694).

In front of the hut hung with reed screens is a large banner, with the performer's name partly legible. The signboard on the roof is decorated with the farting man's image; he is shown lying with his bottom raised, in the posture of the man on the old *iroha-garuta* card of my youth. Over his exposed behind is something like a modern-day cartoon "speech balloon" containing images that represent four different types of farts—drawn in gray shading—that he can produce on demand. This is indeed the prototype of the picture of my childhood. Gennai, who was knowledgeable about painting, wrote that "because the depiction is in gray shading, in the manner of the illustration of dreams, an unsuspecting bumpkin happening by might conclude in amazement that the man dreamed with his behind."

Gathered around the benches outside the hut is a lively crowd of people expressing various reactions: men who apparently just saw the show and are offering embellished critiques; a man wearing a headband, calling to potential customers; and a cluster of assorted onlookers, gazing up at the sign. This typical scene in the amusement district of Ryōgoku Hirokōji is the very center of what Gennai calls "Edo prosperity" in an age of widespread peace.

The much acclaimed show put on by this professional fart artist, also known as Blowhard Fancyfart (Kyokube Fukubei) actually began its run in Ryōgoku Hirokōji in the fourth month of 1774. Four years later, it was shown in Osaka as well. Gennai went to see the show and promptly set down his observations and interpretations. The essay shows Gennai's journalistic skills, seen also in his debut *gesaku* (playful vernacular) novel *Rootless Weeds* (*Nenashigusa*); in the summer of 1763, the *onnagata* (kabuki actor specializing in female roles) Ogino Yaegiri drowned in the Sumida River, and *Rootless Weeds*, offering a satiric take on the incident, was published five months later. Like *On Farting*, it is a true tour de force.

Let's join Gennai in taking a peek inside the freak show:

> I entered by the wicker gate, and there was the flatulist, seated under a red-and-white curtain on a slightly raised platform, flanked by his accompanists, flutists, and drummers. He was of medium build and fair-skinned, with a shaven head and crescent-shaped sideburns. He wore a light blue unlined kimono over a red crepe undergarment. After introducing himself in a smooth and amiable way, he began with the curtain-raiser drum pattern, *toppa-hyoro-hyoro-hih-hih-hih.* After that he imitated a rooster that crowed at length, *boo-boo-booh-boo*, and after that a waterwheel—all this while farting continuously, *booh*, and turning cartwheels, creating the effect of water pushing down on one side and turning him around and around.

How delightfully cheerful and carefree! The account is surprisingly inoffensive; some readers may be let down because it doesn't make more of a stink. This sort of amusement perhaps flourishes in a time of peace. As Gennai writes, all sorts of performing arts began to flourish at this time: everything from kabuki, sumo, and *gidayū-bushi*, the music of the bunraku puppet theater, to *karakuri* mechanized dolls, children's kyōgen farces, imitations of actors' gestures and voices, and comic sermons. In the Tanuma era, when Senior Counselor Tanuma Okitsugu was in power, everyone in Edo, including samurai, monks, merchants, and migrant workers, would watch, listen to, and mimic these performances. Perhaps the ultimate performer, however, was Farting Man, who could fart out a dog barking, the boom of Ryōgoku fireworks in summer, popular songs, and even, on request, the revenge play *Chūshingura* or the ballad composed by Hiraga Gennai himself, "Miracle at the Yaguchi Ferry" (*Shinrei yaguchi no watashi*).

On the way home after the performance, the narrator—Gennai—debates with his friends whether the man used a drug to cause flatulence, or whether it was some sort of trick. He offers this extravagant praise:

> We had got wind of this flatulist before, but now we have seen him with our own eyes. In all the 2,436 years of our nation's proud history, from the beginning of Emperor Jimmu's reign to this third year of An'ei, there are no records or legends about anyone like him. His accomplishments are unique, not only in Japan but also in China, Korea, India, the Netherlands, and many other countries. Ah, what art! What farts!

Dragging Emperor Jimmu and even the Netherlands into this discussion of a lowly topic like farting and marveling that the performer shows an originality unprecedented in world history of course marks this writing as *gibun*, "playful literature." But another character in Gennai's tale, the priggish country samurai Ishibe Kinkichirō (his name means something like "Goody-goody Stonehead"), turns pale at this encomium, declaring that even in this appallingly money-grubbing modern society, it is outrageous and shocking beyond belief that anyone would make a public show of farting, an act so shameful that any samurai would perform seppuku and any woman would take her own life if they ever "let loose" in front of others. This display of indignation propels the narrator's praise of farting to new heights of erudite eloquence. The exchanges between the two men; the ever-increasing pace of the writing as they slip into higher and higher gears of chopped logic (*herikutsu*, "fart logic"); and, alternating with the voice of Blowhard Fancyfart, the voice and face of Gennai himself emerging with the greatest clarity since his *Life of Dashing Shidōken* (*Fūryū Shidōken den*, 1763)—these are certainly the outstanding features of this short eighteenth-century work.

Gennai has unending admiration for the performer's spirit of daring and originality in elevating the fart, that which "comes from the void and disappears into the void, without serving a mite of purpose," into a previously unexplored form of art. Herein lies the difference between *On Farting* and the absurdity of the merely noxious literature of flatulence written in all other times and places.

> This flatulist created his art through his own ingenuity, without benefit of tutelage or tradition to guide him. He taught his inarticulate rear end, his uncomprehending rear end, the rhythm of breathing, that is, opening and closing, then supplied it with the pentatonic scale and the twelve-pitch scale and enabled it to combine them all with skill. Compared to a third-rate chanter of ballads, he is far and away more talented. Strange and wonderful indeed! He is truly the founder of the Way of the Fart.

After provoking laughter with this high praise, the text shifts into the venomous, satirical tone for which Gennai is well known, in a tirade against scholars, men of culture, doctors, and masters of the performing arts:

> But these days, not only musicians are incompetent hacks. Scholars are buried in wastepaper, the cast-off leavings of continental Chinese learning. Those fond of Chinese poetry and writing gather up wood shavings of Han Yu, Liu Zongyuan, and those in the earlier golden age of Tang, and try to make a pillar. Our native poets go nowhere in search of inspiration, preferring to sit back and collect sticky rice on the soles of their feet. Physi-

cians swear either by the new style of medicine or the old, and loudly debate the merits of each, but they are powerless to cure disease, and so influenza wipes out the population. Self-styled haiku masters only lick the spittle of Bashō and Kikaku,[9] and tea masters affecting an elegant style only nibble the turds of Rikyū and Sotan.[10] The other arts are all deteriorating as well. People who practice them lack talent and ingenuity, and their efforts to imitate the ancients fall painfully short because they do not apply their minds. The flatulist, however, by working his ass off like no one before him, has pulled off feats of farting unknown to the ancients and thereby achieved fame throughout the land.

This is a self-serving line of argument. Three years later, in the sequel to this work, Gennai boasted,

> Seeking to fashion things that most people knew nothing of, I gave up my property and abandoned my stipend, used all my ingenuity and went through all my money, and succeeded in making the *erekiteru* as well as in discovering quite a few products that had never been produced domestically before.

He continues in a self-mocking tone: "Having used up my money on useless inventions, I am penniless." In this later essay, he assumes the name Penniless Poorman (Hinka Zeninai), and we can see that identity already cropping up in *On Farting*: Gennai finally climbs down from his soapbox, and slowly his arguments for an "encouragement of talent and ingenuity" or "encouragement of learning" return to the essay's original humorous vein.

> In this way, by applying one's mind and being disciplined, one can achieve greatness even by farting. Ah, if only those seeking to reform our world or engage in the arts would apply themselves with such single-mindedness, their fame would resound even more than farts! I have merely appropriated the sound of flatulence in order to awaken from their torpor those who are

in despair or immature or lacking in industry; but perhaps my argument smells suspicious. Tell me my ideas aren't worth a fart if you like; I don't give a shit.

Gennai doubtless dashed this piece off in one sitting, as he often did. It is bursting with energy and quite well done. In its quick changes of pace, jesting, irony, hyperbole, and successive fabrications, as well as the confidence and intense focus it shows, the style resembles that of Fukuzawa Yukichi's *An Encouragement of Learning* (*Gakumon no susume*, 1872– 1876) and Natsume Sōseki's *I Am a Cat* (*Wagahai wa neko de aru*, 1905– 1906): this is my long-standing opinion. In *On Farting, Part II*, written in a tone that Gennai's disciple Hezutsu Tōsaku (1726–1789) called "a mix of indignation and despair," Gennai's tone of mingled self-confidence and self-deprecation comes through even more clearly. Apart from the introduction, the content changes into a *gesaku*-style autobiography of Fūrai Sanjin (Gennai's pen-name) with no connection to flatulence.

Gennai's essays perhaps only use the flatulist as a prop to discourse on the invention of various arts and disciplines, and lack the "aroma" befitting the literature of flatulence. To be sure, such aroma is not entirely lacking. The epilogue to *On Farting* states, "The sound comes in three varieties. Those that sound like *bu* are refined and round in shape, while those that last a little longer are less refined and irregular in shape; silent farts are vulgar, and their shape is long and a bit flat." The author uses the basic classification system that every Japanese schoolboy knows, and he even defines the shape of each type. The introduction to Part II is full of wordplay and puns, and even contains a parody of a famous poem from the *Kokinshū*:

> The spring hill-farts
> where mists arise
> are far away
> yet the spring wind blows
> bringing the blossoms' scent

This is, however, hardly enough to rival the stench in "The Miller's

Tale" or "The Summoner's Tale" in Chaucer's *Canterbury Tales*, or the roar of breaking wind in Francois Rabelais' *Gargantua and Pantagruel*. The treatises of this eighteenth-century Japanese herbalist are simply too theoretical, too lacking in earthy physicality. *Ainu Folk Tales* (*Ainu mindanshū*) contains many stories involving flatulence, beginning with "The Story of Panampe's Farts." Like so many folktales from Japan, Korea, and China, they are generous and silly, droll and warm-hearted, and provoke genuine laughter. Needless to say, they are utterly unlike Gennai's discussion of the showman Blowhard Fancyfart. Flatulence apparently differs by country, people, culture, and the times; I am increasingly drawn to the idea of a comparative study of flatulence, but first let's consider a writer extremely close to Gennai.

The poet and playwright Ōta Nampo (1749–1823) was a precocious writer who studied under Gennai from age eighteen, beginning in 1767. His *One Hundred Poems on Farting* (*Hōhi hyaku shuka*) may have the same topic as his mentor's comic essay, but Ōta's work is far earthier and, shall we say, more pungent.

> Seven farts eight farts
> I fart away and yet
> as for kerria roses of Ide[11]
> not one has appeared—
> I'm clean as a whistle!

> This morning I saw
> that sometime in the night
> I cut a fart
> How sleepy/smelly is
> the blossom in my summer bed!

> In my poor abode
> I light a smoky fire to smudge
> mosquitoes away
> and keep the smell of farts[12]
> from coming near[13]

The tendency of writers of comic or "wild" verse (*kyōka*) to put themselves in a bad light and indulge in self-pity are on full display here. Also, the verses underscore the difference between the ronin scholar Gennai, lively and strong-willed even when discoursing on flatulence, and his quick-witted student. Contrast their works with the following haiku by Kobayashi Issa (1763–1828):

> The farting contest
> begins again—
> winter confinement

Issa's approach to farts evokes the simple rural world of Japanese folktales and the sketch *Fart Wars* (*Onara gassen shitae*, 1921) by Ogawa Usen (1886–1938). Having studied the portrayal of farting in literature into modern times, I find increasing depth and humanity, as in the play *The Screens* (*Les Paravents*, 1961) by Jean Genet, which captures the pathos of soldiers farting on a dead lieutenant, and in *Notes on Farting* (*Hōhishō*, 1979) by Yasuoka Shōtarō (1920–2013), which is filled with poignant memories of breaking wind. Perhaps the closest in spirit to Gennai's work is the strange and pedantic *Manual of the Crafty Artillerists* (*Manuel de l'artilleur sournois*) by Comte de La Trompette, in Salvador Dalí's *Diary of a Genius* (*Journal d'un génie*, 1964). I will have to put off the pleasure of comparing that to Gennai's work till some other time. I used to own a copy of the work by Dalí's Comte de La Trompette. I searched for it in my library, intending to further develop the comparative study of breaking wind, but unfortunately could not find it. I will simply add here that the French word "*trompette*" (trumpet) is itself suggestive of farting, *pet* being the noun form and *péter* the verb for the act.

Yosa Buson: *Mt. Fuji Seen beyond Pine Trees*

The painting shows a forest of pines, each tree leaning slightly to the left, with trunks and needles as strong and hard as those of a sago palm or a cactus. The line of trees rises and dips as in a dance, and just where it dips the lowest is the distant, majestic shape of Mt. Fuji, pure white with snow, solid, mighty, and reaching to the heavens. The sky is rendered with a light layer of the white pigment *gofun*, made from pulverized clam-shell, covered by a thin wash of India ink against which Fuji's size and whiteness stand out with all the more clarity. Is the sky the deep, clear blue of late fall and early winter, I wonder, or the moist, bright blue of early spring? I can't tell, but in the upper right portion of the sky a bit of white underneath shows through like a trailing cloud, and on the left, a quarter-section of the pines on this approximately 1.4-meter long scroll painting is pale, dissolving into a sudden misty rain or autumn shower sweeping in. So this must be late autumn or, judging also from the depth of the snow cover, early winter, displaying the grandeur of Mt. Fuji "sitting alone, a sublime peak."[14]

In the early eighteenth century, haiku poet Uejima Onitsura wrote an interesting haiku using the slang word *nyoppori*—"jutting high":

> Jutting high
> dominating the autumn sky
> Mt. Fuji

Buson's painting brings Onitsura's haiku to mind, and yet Buson's Fuji is far more elegant. The haiku also makes the mountain's silhouette stand out too distinctly against the autumn sky. In Buson's painting, along the outlines of the mountain's slopes, descending right and left from the peak, the white pigment of the mountain blends into the ink wash of the sky, subtly suggesting the softness of the snow and the gentleness of the majestic mountain. Fuji is a sacred mountain and the painting beautifully expresses the deep love and reverence Japanese people have felt for it from ancient times, a feeling rather like that inspired by a Madonna, a stunningly beautiful woman.

The construction of the painting—pines in the foreground, Fuji in the background, and nothing between—recalls this masterful summer haiku by Buson:

> Only Mt. Fuji
> is not engulfed
> by young leaves

Figure 44. Yosa Buson, *Mt. Fuji Seen beyond Pine Trees* (*Fugaku resshō-zu*).
Kimura Teizō Collection, Aichi Prefectural Museum of Art.

He emphasizes the mountain's uniqueness by writing its name with non-traditional characters that mean "matchless," followed by *hitotsu*— "one" or "only." The haiku captures the energy of the young, fresh green leaves that surround the great mountain and emphasize its towering majesty. The same sort of image is at work in this painting of Buson's later years. The immovable snow-covered mountain is exalted by the forcefulness of the pines, which are seemingly engaged in a line dance with arms spread wide, and this, mixed with the changing weather in the sky from the left, gives this long horizontal painting a surprising dynamism.

In autumn 2013, the Shizuoka Prefectural Museum of Art held a special exhibition of paintings of Mt. Fuji to commemorate the mountain's listing as a UNESCO World Heritage Site. The exhibition was brilliantly organized by Fukushi Yūya, a very young curator. Among eighty masterpieces, great works, rarities, and curiosities by painters ranging from Kanō Tan'yū (1602–1674) to Yokoyama Taikan (1868–1958), *Fuji Seen Beyond Pine Trees*, bearing only the simple inscription "Buson," stood out with utter radiance, delighting viewers' eyes even now.

Tiny Birds that Flew Over from the Netherlands

Odano Naotake's *Shinobazu Pond* (*Shinobazu no ike-zu*) is a good painting with a quietude that never fails to draw me in. Naotake was a samurai of Kakunodate in the Akita domain. In late 1773, when he was twenty-three, he went to Edo for the first time, following Hiraga Gennai, whom he had met through his work inspecting domain mines. By the following summer, at the request of Gennai's friend Sugita Gempaku, he had completed a volume of precise drawings to accompany the publication of *A New Book of Anatomy*. Over the next five years, Naotake lived in Edo surrounded by people knowledgeable in Dutch studies, and he quickly learned to paint in the Western style. His masterpiece *Shinobazu Pond* was completed during that time.

Drawn large in the foreground, using a traditional style that featured flowers and birds, along with Western-style shadowing, are a potted peony and a standing tree. In the background is Benten Island amid the smooth waters of the pond, and spreading over all is a spacious sky of pale blue.

The painting conveys the young Naotake's keen sensitivity to Western things, his ability to learn new techniques, and his conscientiousness.

Close examination shows that on the left, flying above the Hongō plateau, there are three birds that seem to be crows or kites, depicted as simple V-shapes. They definitely animate the quiet sky. It occurs to me, however, that I can't recall a single earlier painting in China or Japan that shows the tiny outline of birds in flight in this way. Certainly cranes, herons, sparrows, crows, swallows, wild geese, Mandarin ducks, and so on have frequently been made the subject of ink paintings and partition paintings (*shōhekiga*), but none of them were shown flying high in the sky. Without exception they were portrayed perched on a tree branch or amusing themselves at the water's edge.

With this in mind, I examined other paintings by Naotake and discovered that in each one, birds are flying in the sky. The same is true for paintings by Naotake's patron, Satake Shozan, the lord of Akita domain. Then what about Shiba Kōkan, whom Naotake instructed in Western painting? Sure enough, in all his engravings and oil paintings, V-shape birds are flying. This technique must have been picked up by studying Dutch engravings. Those birds first flew from Western skies into Eastern ones in Akita *ranga.*

I then quickly looked at works by seventeenth-century Dutch landscape painters Rembrandt, Ruysdael, and Hobbema. And there they were! Birds exactly like those in Nobutake's paintings, flying together in the sky. Come to think of it, Flemish skies painted in the sixteenth century by Pieter Bruegel the Elder (ca. 1525–1569) have them too. His famous painting *Magpie on the Gallows* (1568) shows numerous tiny birds dotting the sky above the trees.

In this way, a line can be traced directly from Flemish landscapes of the sixteenth and seventeenth centuries across time and space to the Akita *ranga* of eighteenth-century Japan. Just to be sure, I opened the voluminous *Dawn of Western Painting in Japan* (*Nihon yōga shokō*, 1930) by *Nihonga* painter Hirafuku Hyakusui (1877–1933) of Kakunodate. The frontispiece was a Dutch copperplate print of a harbor scene that had belonged to Naotake, and in the sky was the tiny figure of a bird in flight.

Figure 45. Odano Naotake, *Shinobazu Pond* (*Shinobazu no ike-zu*).
Akita Museum of Modern Art.

Figure 46. Pieter Bruegel the Elder, *The Magpie on the Gallows*.
Hessisches Landesmuseum, Darmstadt.

Watanabe Kazan's Later Work: *Book of Birds, Insects, and Fish*

Watanabe Kazan (1793–1841) added sketches of insects and fish to his sketches of birds and also added drawings of vegetables and fruits that were delivered to him, ending up with two albums not always neatly sorted by category. The first page depicts a moth and a locust, dated the seventh day of the fourth month, 1838. The following year, imprisoned in the government crackdown on scholars of Western studies, he made no sketches. He resumed sketching in the first month of 1840, after being spared the death penalty and sentenced to house arrest in his home domain of Tahara, on Atsumi Peninsula. The final entry is dated the twenty-second day of the eighth month, 1841.

In the late 1830s, Kazan, who was passionate about coastal defense policy, formed and headed a group dedicated to Western learning called

Figure 47. Watanabe Kazan, *Album of Birds, Beasts, Insects, and Fish*. Soun Museum of Art.

Shōshikai (Old Men's Society), in association with Takano Chōei (1804–1850), Koseki San'ei (1787–1839), and other leading *rangaku* scholars who had studied with Philipp Franz von Siebold, as well as shogunate retainers Egawa Tarōzaemon (1801–1855) and Kawaji Toshiakira (1801–1868), who supported enlightened learning. The period when Kazan was most active in that group corresponds to the time when he began the sketches for *Book of Birds, Beasts, Insects, and Fish* (*Reimōchūgyo-satsu*). In 1838–1839, he wrote a series of essays that were virulently critical of the shogunate, including "Answers Concerning Western Affairs" (*Seiyō jijō okotaegaki*) and "A Cautious Argument" (*Shinkiron*), writings that presaged the end of the Pax Tokugawana. Because of these writings, those opposed to Western studies got up false charges against him, and he was imprisoned for a time in the detention center in Edo's Temma-chō. Finally, after nearly two years of house arrest in Tahara, he took his own life on the night of the eleventh day of the tenth month, 1841. The final entry in *Book of Birds, Beasts, Insects, and Fish* is dated two months before his suicide. The sketches in the book, made during a period of extreme mental anguish in Kazan's final year, are his most beautiful works of art.

In 1979, when the Tochigi Prefectural Museum of Fine Arts in Utsunomiya held an exhibition of works by Tani Bunchō, I contributed an article to the catalogue and paid a visit to the museum. That is when I first held Kazan's *Book of Birds, Beasts, Insects, and Fish* in my hand. The book was on display as an example of the work of Bunchō's students, since Kazan studied with Bunchō in his late teens. Wearing a pair of white gloves loaned to me by Ueno Kenji, the museum curator, I opened the book and marveled at what I saw. The sketches had such beauty and power that I remember thinking, "If I have these, what need do I have of Cezanne's watercolors or pieces by Klee?"

Like many Japanese youngsters, I was crazy about insects as a boy, and Kazan's superb drawings of dragonflies and grasshoppers captivated me. Kazan's dragonflies, *koshiaki tombo* and *shiokara tombo*, were drawn with their four translucent wings stretched taut, showing a touch of color at the base of the wings and black spots at the tips, just as in real life. With their elegant bellies wrapped in bands of light blue and yellow, they looked as if at any moment they might push off with their six legs and fly away. I could well imagine the delight of catching such rare specimens; the flutter of their wings in the net seemed to register in my own fingertips. A stunning sketch of a *kuruma batta* grasshopper poised to jump also caught my eye, especially the length, girth, and strength of the bent rear legs. In the autumn section, a katydid missing several legs looked pitiful, and a mantis with body raised and wings outspread looked fierce. There were also sketches of fish that someone must have sent while Kazan was under house arrest—mackerel and whiting, the deep blue and light pink of the skin fresh and beautiful.

From the Genroku era on, countless albums containing color sketches of Japanese flora and fauna enriched Tokugawa civilization. Clearly Kazan was conscious of that line of natural history studies, as his notes scattered throughout the albums demonstrate, but I would say that his *Book of Birds, Insects, and Fish* is the most valuable and exquisite of them all.

The French poet Paul Claudel (1868–1955), who served as ambassador to Japan in the 1920s, wrote a comparative study of Japanese and European culture; he was full of praise for the "grace of soul" with which Japanese poets and painters "endeavor to portray the life force with even greater glory in creatures small and weak." (*The Black Bird in the Rising Sun* [*L'oiseau noir dans le soleil levant*], 1927). Watanabe Kazan's *Book of Birds, Insects, and Fish* very poignantly conveys the *mono no aware* of the lives of such tiny creatures, even more so than his *Album of Insects and Fish* (*Chūgyochō*), which appeared the same year with the sketches transformed into paintings.

The samurai painter Kazan knew perhaps better than anyone else the peril facing the peaceful isles of Japan, and he had foreknowledge of his own demise as well. Such knowledge surely sharpened and strengthened his art at the end of his life.

---

1 A starter koan of the Rinzai sect of Zen. When asked, "Does a dog have Buddha-nature?" the Chinese Zen master Jōshū answered only, "*Mu*," meaning "No" or "Nothing." This would appear to contradict the central Buddhist tenet that all

living things have buddha-nature. The student must meditate on the seeming contradiction as a means of gaining enlightenment.

2 AN: Fujioka Sakutarō, *Kinsei kaigashi zen* [History of early modern painting] (Kinkōdō shoseki, 1903), 316.

3 AN: The excerpt is included in *Kodoku na samposha no musō* [*Les Rêveries du promeneur solitaire*], Imano Kazuo, trans. (Iwanami shoten, 1960).

4 AN: See note 2.

5 AN: Fujioka, op. cit., 316.

6 Hani Motoko (1873–1957), considered Japan's first female journalist, was also a co-publisher of the women's monthly magazine *Fujin no tomo* [*Women's friend*]. "Friends' associations" (*tomo no kai*) were formed by readers of the magazine. Hani's work emphasized Christian ideals and promoted women's independence, self-esteem, and personal freedom.

7 AN: Nakamura Yukihiko, ed., *Fūrai Sanjin shū* [Collected works of Fūrai Sanjin], *Nihon koten bungaku taikei* [Compendium of Japanese classical literature], vol. 55 (Iwanami shoten, 1961). JWC: Fūrai Sanjin was Gennai's pen name.

8 The reference is to "Hanasaka jiisan" [The old man who made blossoms bloom], a folktale about a man with the magical power to make cherry trees burst into blossom.

9 Takarai Kikaku (1661–1707), Bashō's disciple.

10 Sen no Rikyū (1522–1591) and his grandson, Sen no Sōtan (1578–1658).

11 Yellow stains (of excrement). Bright yellow kerria roses are especially associated with the Ide Tamagawa, a river near Kyoto.

12 "*Ka*" means both "mosquito" and "smell"; "the smell of farts" can also be rendered "whining mosquitoes."

13 AN: Ōta Nampo et al., *Kyōka manzaishū, saizōshū sen* [Best selected wild poems of ten thousand generations] (Fuzambō, 1904).

14 When the Zen master Ekai Zenji (720–814) was asked, "What above all else should we be thankful for? What is the greatest happiness?" he replied, "Sitting alone, a sublime peak." Existence itself is the greatest mystery, the greatest happiness.

Part

IV

12 | POET OF THE PAX TOKUGAWANA: YOSA BUSON

I was in my mid-thirties when I first examined the haiku and letters of Yosa Buson.

From fall 1965 to fall 1967, I was a visiting scholar in the East Asia Studies program at Princeton University. Before I left, the violent protests against the United States–Japan Security Treaty that had broken out at the start of the decade[1] were still rippling through Japanese society, and so when I mentioned in the faculty lounge of the University of Tokyo at Komaba that I would be going to the United States, an assistant professor of German who was older than me immediately said, "You're going to prostitute yourself to the American empire?" Looking back now, I can only be grateful to the College of General Education (now College of Arts and Sciences) for sending a young French instructor off to the United States for two years to do research on the culture of Meiji and Tokugawa Japan.

My invitation to study at Princeton came from Marius Jansen (1922–2000), a central figure in the groundbreaking studies of Japan's modernization then being pursued by American scholars. Jansen had written two acclaimed works, *The Japanese and Sun Yat Sen* (1954) and *Sakamoto Ryōma and the Meiji Restoration* (1961). He had gone to Princeton intending to write a thesis on the question of time in medieval European theology, but during World War II he studied Japanese as an army officer and afterward went to Harvard University to study medieval and modern Japanese history under the direction of Edwin O. Reischauer.

Before long, Jansen was the leader of his field. Born in the Netherlands, he could read the complete works of the historian Johan Huizinga in the original. When he invited me and my family over for dinner, he would always play Mozart and Chopin on the piano in a corner of the dining room after the meal. He was, in short, a brilliant man of high culture.

Far from prostituting myself to the American empire, I got to know the members of Jansen's graduate seminar in Japanese history, occasionally gave talks in Japanese or English at other Ivy League schools, and was otherwise free to pursue my own research. In addition to the main library, there was an East Asian library known as the Gest Library, open until midnight every night. During my undergraduate years in Japan, I had taken no courses in Japanese literature or history, so the Gest Library was a trove of unknown treasures.

I came across a thick clothbound book called *The Complete Works of Buson, Revised and Enlarged* (*Kaiteizōho Buson zenshū*, 1925), edited by Ebara Taizō. Surprised at the size of the book, I borrowed it and took home. I had long admired Buson's works as quoted by writers such as novelist Satō Haruo (1892–1964), poet Hagiwara Sakutarō (1886–1942), and poet Tachihara Michizō (1914–1939), so I was more than happy to come across a fine edition of his complete works.

I took the book back to where I lived on the edge of campus and began to read it, pausing now and then to look up at the late autumn sky from my room. The days that followed were a sheer delight, mingled with nostalgia. I loved Buson's haiku, but I was also struck by his letters, which were new to me. In the spring of 1777 (twenty-third day of the second month), when he was sixty-one, Buson wrote a letter to his student in Fushimi, Kyoto. This letter was sent along with several copies of the collection *Midnight Melodies* (*Yahanraku*), which contained the long poems "Spring Breeze on the Kema Embankment" (*Shumpū batei kyoku*) and "Yodo River Songs" (*Dengaka*); their publication in a New Year's album named *Shunkyō* had been delayed due to Buson's illness. Here are the opening lines of the letter:

> The spring is a cold spring. How are you getting on? I am sure

you are managing with your usual charm. In any case, *Shunkyō* has finally been published, and I couldn't wait to show it to you.

A while after returning to Japan from Princeton, in the first essay I ever wrote on Buson,[2] I quoted those lines and added this comment:

> These few lines may read like a standard greeting of the season, but in fact they glow like silk with deep, tender sympathy. I would even say this courtoisie conveys a bit of graceful coquetry. This is the epistolary style of a Japanese haiku poet, very different from that of a Nerval or Rilke.

My opinion is unchanged. However, later on I noticed that in the Iwanami Bunko edition of Buson's letters, annotated by Ōtani Tokuzō and Fujita Shin'ichi, the opening line has been changed to "This is certainly a cold spring." I checked a reproduction of the original, and it appears that the later version is correct. Ebara, the editor of the version I read, must have misread Buson's cursive handwriting as *haru mo* (spring) instead of *sate mo* (indeed, certainly). But I like the repetition of "spring," which lends a certain softness to the expression, and I still recite the line by heart that way.

The same collection of letters contains several that Buson wrote to his beloved disciple Teramura Hyakuchi (1749–1835), the son of a textile dealer, who was thirty-three years younger than him. Buson was living at the time in Kyoto's Bukkōji temple at Karasuma Nishi-iru, not far from the textile store at Teramachi Shijō-agaru. One undated letter made me smile and feel even greater affection for Buson, a fondness mixed with envy. It goes like this:

> I borrowed this lantern from you intending to return it immediately, but yesterday I took the family out on an excursion and came back at night. Excuse the delay. Today is another impossibly fine day, and staying home doing nothing is a sin. If you agree, you must come with me this evening to see the cherry blossoms on Mt. Kachō. Send a line with your thoughts. That's all! Yahan.

As usual, Buson had the maid take this letter from his house to the Sakaiya on Teramachi. The previous day, the maid had accompanied Buson and his family on an all-day excursion to view cherry blossoms on the city outskirts, bringing along picnic lunches, and since they returned late, he was only now sending her to return the lantern he had previously borrowed. Buson writes apologetically, but then his tone turns playful.

Who wouldn't love to receive a charming invitation like this from "Yahan" (short for his pen name, Yahantei)? Hyakuchi may have groaned, "Not again!" but even so, surely he sat right down and wrote, "I will gladly accompany you."

An image comes to mind of two men in silhouette, one old and one young, jesting and improvising verses as they stroll in Higashiyama of a spring evening, the warm air fragrant with blossoms. If the letter beginning, "The spring is a cold spring" conveys the fine sensibility nurtured by a mature civilization, this invitation to view cherry blossoms in the evening gives a palpable sense of the deep peace that had settled over the nation, especially over the ancient capital of Kyoto, in late eighteenth-century Tokugawa Japan.

Buson's mention of his family's outing makes me wonder if they perhaps went to the Ninnaji temple (also called Omuro), in the northern part of the city. Buson wrote a pair of haiku about that temple:

> I saw Matahei![3]
> The blossoms at Omuro
> now at their peak

> Drowsy spring
> starts with the blossoms
> at Omuro

Or perhaps they wandered farther afield, spending the whole day visiting Sagano and Arashiyama.

> A day in Saga—
> the cherry blossoms
> of the house of Kan'in[4]

The fragrance of blossoms
at Saga, after the lamps
go out

While there, perhaps this happened:

Exhausted
he goes home to sleep—
the lord of blossoms

And then the next morning, perhaps the poet and his wife and daughter ended up like this:

Straw sandals
that trampled blossoms—
sleeping late

Going from Buson's letters to his haiku, from his haiku to his paintings and back again, we can spend many hours reconstructing the beauty and richness of Buson's world. With all our senses, we discover the entirety of the peace of Tokugawa Japan, a peace then identified with the phrases "tranquility" and "calm of the four seas."

While absorbed in reading Buson's complete works at Princeton, I also admired works by Buson's friend Ueda Akinari, including the ghost stories *Tales of Moonlight and Rain* (*Ugetsu monogatari*, 1776), *Tales of Spring Rain* (*Harusame monogatari*, pub. 1907), and essays, and enjoyed gazing at the art of his painter friends Maruyama Ōkyo, Ike no Taiga, and Itō Jakuchū. I delighted in the extraordinary talent of the Edo ronin Hiraga Gennai in everything from natural history to *gesaku* fiction. I reread *Dawn of Western Science in Japan* by Gennai's friend, Sugita Gempaku, and was highly drawn to the rococo *mono no aware* of the full-color woodblock prints made by Gennai's neighbor, Suzuki Harunobu (ca. 1725–1770).

At first I believed that these new movements in literature, art, and thought in the latter half of the eighteenth century showed the exercise of the modern mind in Japan, and I gave talks on that topic in Marius

Jansen's seminar at Princeton and John Hall's seminar at Yale. But eventually, after returning to Japan, I read more deeply in the works of Buson and found a more fruitful and interesting approach that in no way reduced the significance of the Japanese population moving together toward a more modern way of thinking: I saw these changes as signs of the maturation of Japanese civilization during the Pax Tokugawana.

"Pax Tokugawana" is the term I coined in reference to the total peace that Japan built, maintained, and enjoyed both at home and vis-à-vis other countries under the Tokugawa shogunate. The term is modeled after the Pax Romana of ancient Rome—two hundred years of peace and stability that lasted for five generations, beginning with the reign of Augustus (63 BCE–14 CE), the first emperor after Caesar—and the Pax Britannica of nineteenth-century Britain. The Pax Tokugawana began in 1603, when Tokugawa Ieyasu established the shogunate in Edo, and it lasted for the extraordinarily long period of two hundred fifty years, until the arrival of Commodore Matthew Perry and his Black Ships in 1853, which led to the opening of the country. The shogun-domainal system provided political stability through an adept balance between centralized and decentralized power, and the wise policy of national seclusion preserved peace with East Asian and Western nations. This basic system allowed industry and the economy to develop steadily, enriching life in cities and villages. In the absence of religious unrest, learning, literary arts, drama, the fine arts, and even horticulture developed in rich and varied ways throughout the land. The long stability and productivity of the Pax Tokugawana, which compares favorably to the Pax Romana and Pax Britannica, were praised by foreign observers such as the German explorer Engelbert Kaempfer and the British diplomat Sir John Rutherford Alcock (1809–1897).

Haiku, born during this halcyon time, was a truly democratic genre "for the people and by the people," from its origins with Matsuo Bashō in the Genroku era to Yosa Buson a hundred years later and Kobayashi Issa (1763–1828) in the early nineteenth century. Domestic peace was at its peak during Buson's lifetime in particular, and his works express that peace with supreme clarity and depth.

Buson's most famous haiku, universally known in Japan, expresses the essence of peace:

Spring sea—
all day long the waves
gently rise and fall

But it's probably not enough to read this as a paean to the beautiful, restful sweep of the sea on a seemingly endless spring day, with waves rhythmically breaking and ebbing, over and over again—a scene with all the lyricism of "Spring Sea," Miyagi Michio's 1929 composition for koto and flute. The sea in this haiku was the same yesterday and the day before, and all of today. It will be the same tomorrow and the day after, and no doubt next year and the year after too. The boredom of such tranquility and calm lurks below the surface of the poem.

Sighs arise from the deepening discontent and disappointment at being left behind on islands where nothing will ever change:

A Korean ship,
not stopping, passes on
into the mist

Mustard flowers—
not even a whale comes by
as the sea darkens

Buson imagined a spectacular aerial view from high above the earth reflecting his forlorn awareness that on all sides, the archipelago was fenced in only by foaming waves, an awareness heightened at dusk by a bolt of lightning in the early autumn sky.

Lightning—
girdled by waves
the isles of Japan

Other haiku contain the discovery of particular losses, emphasized by the passage of spring:

Washing my feet
in a leaky tub, the water
running out like fading spring

Fading spring—
glasses that don't suit my eyes
have disappeared

As he further internalizes negative sensations of loss, weariness, abandonment, stalemate, and the like, the "cloistered poet," as I call him, slides into a deeply isolated "small world" resembling the *fin de siècle* ennui of poetry and one-act pantomimes in nineteenth-century Europe.

Fading spring—
the lute in my arms
feels heavy

Spring evening—
as the incense burns down,
I add more

After a nap
awakening to find
the spring sun has set

Slow spring days
piling up, so far away
the past

Path ending
the fragrance grows closer—
wild roses

A fallen peony—
petal on petal
in twos and threes

Buried embers—
my hermitage too
buried in snow

Under a low roof
the pleasure of hiding at home
wintering

Cocooned in a protracted peace, the precocious Tokugawa poet knows the weariness of coping with his solitary self—a full century before his counterparts in Europe.

In an essay, Marius Jansen pointed out that the era of Buson, Jakuchū, Gennai, and Harunobu was 170 years after the battle of Sekigahara and nearly 140 years after the Shimabara Rebellion—a time when living memory of the turbulence of war had vanished in Japan. Tales of war were set deep in the past, the stuff of legend. Whichever way one turned, daily life offered only scenes of languorous peace. Furthermore, after the 1770s, peace would continue to hang over Japan, close to the ground and heavy, for another eighty years. Buson stayed cloistered in Kyoto, capturing the texture of that peace in hundreds of marvelous haiku and new-style poems (*shintaishi*). The Edo inventor, Hiraga Gennai, tried in "frustration and despair" to do whatever he could to break out of that feeling of entrapment.

Buson, moreover, did something neither his predecessor, Bashō, nor his successor, Issa, ever did. In the following celebrated poem, which we have already quoted several times, he skillfully captured the essence of Tokugawa peace:

Buried embers—
finally simmering
the stew in the pot

Like buried embers, Japanese society before the Industrial Revolution definitely had low productivity and low growth; its fires burned low. At the same time, there was low consumption amid a culture of appreciating what was merely sufficient, being satisfied with one's circumstances.

The poem describes gathering leftovers, tossing them in a clay pot, setting the pot over a low fire and then forgetting about it until a delicious aroma reveals a well-simmered stew. "This is the rich flavor of civilization, so unlike the barbarism of barbecuing," I imagine Buson murmuring.

In the autumn of 1804, on hearing that a Russian fleet was approaching far-off Nagasaki, Issa, the proletarian Edo poet, composed the following haiku:

> Be more like
> the land of spring breezes,
> Russian ships

Only about twenty years after the death of Buson, the poet of peace in Japan's ancient capital, Issa wrote this prescient poem foreseeing the beginning of the end of the Pax Tokugawana. I see in this poem a sentiment similar to that found in the songs in praise of peace sung at 2015 protests against the security bill that expanded the role of Japan's armed forces abroad; this was seventy years after the end of the Pacific War.

---

1 In May and June 1960, the government of Prime Minister Kishi Nobusuke passed legislation ratifying the revised security treaty with the United States, causing massive protests that led to the cancellation of a state visit by President Dwight Eisenhower.

2 AN: Haga Tōru, "Yosa Buson no chiisana sekai" [The small world of Yosa Buson], *Kōza hikaku bungaku* [Lectures on comparative literature], vol. 3 (University of Tokyo Press, 1973), 212.

3 The painter Matahei, a character in a popular puppet play by Chikamatsu Monzaemon (1653–1725), is known for a scene where he dances for joy.

4 A princely house established in 1710.

13 | BUSON'S YOUTHFUL ELEGY: "MOURNING THE OLD SAGE HOKUJU"

No matter how many times I reread Yosa Buson's new-style poem "Mourning the Old Sage Hokuju" (*Hokuju Rosen o itamu*), I am always moved by the honesty of its poetic sensibility and the freshness of its expression of grief. And afterward, I am inevitably left feeling that the celebrated Meiji-era new-style poems of Kitamura Tōkoku (1868–1894) and Shimazaki Tōson (1872–1943) are old-fashioned and coarse by comparison.

"The old sage Hokuju" refers to Hayami Shinga (1671–1745), a sake brewer and haiku poet who lived in the Yūki district, Shimōsa province. He was apparently a poet of considerable renown in local haiku circles. In 1742, while Buson was still a young man, his Edo teacher Yahantei Hayano Soa passed away, and Buson spent nearly ten years wandering through northern Kanto, with the help of haiku associates in Yūki and Utsunomiya. During that time, the elderly Shinga took an interest in the young poet and treated him with kindness and generosity.

Three years after they met, on the twenty-eighth day of the first month of 1745, Shinga died at seventy-four. Buson, then just shy of thirty, had demonstrated talent in both poetry and painting, but his prospects were far from clear; he was a young man with an uncertain future. Yet the elegy begins, "You left in the morning," using a familiar form of address. Buson also writes, "I had a friend. He lived on the other side of the stream," calling Shinga his "friend" and treating him as an equal. These choices seem odd, based on the relationship between the two men. In mid-Tokugawa society, using a familiar form of address to one's elder and mentor would definitely have been considered inappropriate.

The surprisingly complex structure of the poem and the sophistication of its vocabulary also make it hard to believe that this eighteen-line elegy could be the work of a thirty-year-old beginner.

The poem was first made public in 1793, when it was included in *Flowers on the Shore* (*Iso no hana*), a memorial collection edited by Shinga's son Momohiko for the forty-ninth anniversary of his father's passing. However, it seems likely that Buson composed the poem well before that, for the thirty-second death anniversary. Publication was delayed for some reason until ten years after Buson's death.

The literary scholar Ogata Tsutomu (1920–2009) first theorized that Buson had composed the poem late in life.[1] Most likely Ogata was so struck by the brilliance of the poem that he found its appearance and origin hard to explain and, after a great deal of wavering, he concluded that it was composed for the thirty-second death anniversary, in 1777. Buson was by then an old man in his early sixties and had already published two masterful linked poems (*haitaishi*) in a New Year's album: "Spring Breeze on the Kema Embankment" and "Yodo River Songs."

These are the opening lines of "Mourning the Old Sage Hokuju":

> You left in the morning. In the evening my heart is in a thousand pieces—
> why so far away?

According to Ogata's theory, those youthful lines of such poignancy and grace were written in the same period, with the same voice, as these opening verses of "Spring Breeze on the Kema Embankment":

> Servants' holiday—
> leaving Osaka, I reach
> the Nagara River

> Spring breeze—
> the riverbank is so long
> and home so far

In the above work, the aged poet and the young woman, whom he finds "very attractive" and who seems equally drawn to him, have an exchange that is portrayed with mature skill. Ogata believes that the same poet, just past the age of sixty, also wrote those other lines, lines filled with such piercing anguish that they suggest the heartbreak of first love.

The theory certainly provides a reasonable explanation for how Buson came to write "Mourning the Old Sage Hokuju," and I feel that Ogata's argument has some merit. And yet, every time I reread the poem, I find myself doubting Ogata's theory. There is no questioning the richness, depth, and breadth of Buson's creations in poetry and painting from around the time of "Spring Breeze on the Kema Embankment" and "Yodo River Songs" to the end of his life. And yet, "Mourning the Old Sage Hokuju" seems to me altogether too youthful and fresh, too intense and wholehearted to be lumped together with the mature works of Buson's later years.

The poet's grief, moreover, is described with extraordinary skill, the words seamlessly connected, the imagistic progression—flowers–bird–hills–stream–hut—swift and smooth. This poetic artistry is surely not attainable only in the full maturity of later life; more likely it grew out of the boldness and discoveries of a young poet groping his way forward.

Let us examine the poem in some detail, at least the opening lines, and savor the wonders of this youthful elegy, a work rare in the history of Japanese poetry of the eighteenth century and indeed in the history of world poetry.

> *kimi ashita ni sarinu yūbe no kokoro chiji ni*
> *nanzo haruka naru*

A literal rendering:

> You left in the morning. Evening heart-mind a thousand pieces why so far?

A paraphrase:

> You died this morning, and ever since my heart that was alive because of you has been shattered into a thousand pieces; now

I can only wander in search of you, beyond the evening sky.

How suddenly the poem begins! The suddenness is extremely effective, underscoring the importance of the one addressed as *kimi* ("you," familiar), and the enormous place that *kimi* holds in the poet's heart. Apart from his name, "the old sage Hokuju," the one being mourned has no attributes. Knowing only that he is a friend who used to live "on the other side of the stream," someone with whom the poet presumably often went walking in the surrounding hills, we are all the more persuaded of the great admiration and love, and the deep grief filling the poet's heart and being.

The opening two lines clearly form one stanza (although there is no space between these and the next two lines), and the enjambment is extraordinarily effective. The enjambment makes it unclear what is far away. Is it you who left in the morning, or is it my own heart, broken in a thousand pieces and searching for you, or perhaps both? The ambiguity makes the poet's vast sadness all the wider and deeper.

In tracing the meaning of a poem's chain of images and words this way, the poem's translations into other languages often provide more useful suggestions than commentary in Japanese. Translations into European languages are particularly revealing because of the need to be clear about the grammatical subject and the distinction between singular and plural.

I happen to have two English translations of Buson's elegy on hand. Following the fine translations of Buson's haiku into English by Basil Hall Chamberlain (1850–1935) at the end of the nineteenth century and into French by Paul-Louis Couchoud (1879–1959) in the early twentieth century, for a long time there were only a scattering of translations in a few anthologies, and Buson has sadly been far from the recent vogue for haiku composition abroad. In 2013, however, perhaps the first English-language anthology devoted exclusively to Buson was published.

The translations are the fruit of a collaboration between W. S. Merwin (1927–2019)—an American poet who in addition to his own work translated many volumes of classical and modern poetry, East and West— and Takako Lento, a United States–based poet who has translated Tamura Ryūichi (1923–1998), Tanikawa Shuntarō (b. 1931), Ōoka Makoto (1931–

2017), and other Japanese poets. Their translations have been published in a beautiful two-hundred-fifty page book entitled *Collected Haiku of Yosa Buson* (2013). After the translations of 868 haiku, I was pleased to see translations of Buson's three long poems, including the elegy, which is entitled "In Mourning for Hokuju, the Elder Hermit."

Here are the opening lines of Buson's elegy for Hayami Shinga in the Merwin-Lento translation:

> You
> left this world in the morning
> now that it is evening
> why is my mind scattered
> wandering far away[2]

The first thing that stands out is the word "You" alone in the first line, strong and bold. This was a daring move on the part of the translators, and it succeeds. As I mentioned above, thoughts of *kimi*—the image of the old sage Hokuju, the generous mentor who supported his anxious, fragile self—consume the young poet's heart and his entire being. Hearing *kimi* addressed in English as "you" lends even greater intimacy to the figure of the departed.

Then comes the question of the subject of the inquiry "why so far?" Merwin and Lento clearly take it to mean that the poet's own mind has gone somewhere far away. This interpretation clarifies and tightens the connection between the lines. Yet at the same time, the sense that "you" are the one who is far away is undeniably present, and that implied meaning deepens and enriches the poem.

As I was pondering these things, I came upon an earlier translation of those same lines, dated nearly twenty years before the Merwin-Lento version, where the subject is definitely and unhesitatingly taken as *kimi*.

> You left in the morning. Tonight my heart is
> in a thousand pieces
> Why are you far away?
> —translated by Robert Hass[3]

Also, where Merwin and Lento have "You/left this world in the morning," Hass writes simply "You left in the morning," an interpretation that seems quite reasonable to me. You have not died, you have simply gone off somewhere for a while: the poet's mind is filled with the desire to think this, to refuse to believe that the sage is dead.

In this way, rereading Buson with a couple of English translations at my side gives me greater insight into the psychological nuances and the depth of the language of the original. The same is also true of course for the next few stanzas of this poem. What immediately stands out in the second and third stanzas are the expressions of boyishly frank and intense grief, captured with simplicity and clarity in both translations.

> *kimi o omōte okanobe ni yukitsu asobu*
> *okanobe nanzo kaku kanashiki*
>
> *tampopo no ki ni nazuna no shirō sakitaru*
> *miru hito zo naki*

Thinking of you I go to the hillside and wander.
The hillside—why is it so saddening?

Yellow of dandelions, the shepherd's purse blooming white.
There's no one to look at them.
　—translated by Robert Hass

You are on my mind
as I climb the hill and wander
why should the hill make me sad

You are no longer here
to see the dandelions open
yellow
and the shepherd's purse white
　—translated by Merwin and Lento

Reading these English translations, I am struck by how much they read like the sort of free-verse poems that adolescents would contribute to literary magazines in the late Meiji and Taishō eras (early 1900s to mid-1920s). The poem is straightforward in its expression of feelings and their accompanying gestures, things that the postwar generation in Japan would have found too embarrassing to send in to any publication. But the poem was written around 1745 by a young aspiring artist on the outskirts of the castle town of Yūki, in the hills by a branch of Tone River, and so we can only shake our heads in wonder at how very much ahead of his times this poet was.

The poem does not include a single Chinese character read in its Chinese (*on*) reading. The words are all *yamato kotoba*, soft and flowing native Japanese words that encourage and feelingly convey the outpouring of grief. These Japanese words suggest the lonely wandering of a young man burdened by sorrow. The translators have grasped this well, rendering the passage clearly and plainly:

> Thinking of you I go to the hillside and wander...
> You are on my mind/as I climb the hill and wander...

These lines read like something I myself might be able to write in English. And yet, in both an original work and a translation, such simplicity and clarity are in fact difficult to attain. When the poem was written, Chinese and Japanese classics exerted dominant influence over every genre of poetry in Japan, including poetry in Chinese, *waka*, and haiku. The influence had become oppressive, the banal use of classical references a stifling sludge that the thirty-year-old poet, Buson, escaped by deliberately returning to the artless frankness of a country youth. As early as the mid-eighteenth century, he was experimenting with ways to rejuvenate poetry, as Masaoka Shiki (1867–1902) later did by "sketching from life" (*shasei*).

The "you" in the lines above seems to be not an aged mentor forty-five years older than the poet but a slightly senior friend, male or female, perhaps even a first love. The hillside in Buson's poem echoes the image of the eastern hill in the famous Chinese poem "The Return" (*Guiqu laixi ci*) by Buson's all-time favorite poet, Tao Yuanming (365–427). In the elegy, the hill has the same psychological, dreamlike quality as in the following celebrated haiku by Buson, both dated the fourth month of 1774:

On climbing the eastern hill:
Wild roses—
how this resembles
the road at home!

Lost in reverie
I climb the hill—
wild roses

However, in the elegy Buson avoids the pedantry of the difficult Chinese compound for "eastern hill." In the second line, he further simplifies the native word for "hill," *okanobe*, by writing it all in *hiragana*. In the third stanza, the mention of yellow dandelions and white shepherd's purse emphasizes the idyllic, rural atmosphere. Both are wildflowers that Buson loved all his life. Their rusticity and simple colors and shapes make them far more apropos in this 1740s *shintaishi* than more brilliant flowers such as roses, peonies, or poppies. The young man, that is, the poet, sees the flowers blooming on the hillside, sits down among them, very likely hangs his head and murmurs, "There is no one to see them."

As the stanzas progress, the refrain-like repetition of similar-sounding or similarly constructed phrases gradually increases:

why so far $\longrightarrow$ why so sad
go to the hill $\longrightarrow$ why the hill
there is no one to see $\longrightarrow$ there was a friend

Then whole lines are repeated, in a style reminiscent of the pantoum:[4] "I had a friend. He lived on the other side of the stream" and "You left in the morning. In the evening my heart is in a thousand pieces." Buson's experiment with a new form of poetry was successful. Nearly three centuries later, its fresh, profound reverberations continue to echo.

I do not have the space to continue analyzing this poem line by line and word by word.[5] Ever since my first encounter with "Mourning the Old Sage Hokuju" some fifty years ago at Princeton University, I have wished that some composer in Japan or overseas would set to music this exquisite lyric poem from eighteenth-century Japan. Schubert, Schumann, and Wolf did so for poems of Goethe, Mörike, and Heine, creating lieder of haunting beauty. Duparc, Fauré, and Debussy set the poems of Baudelaire, Verlaine, and Apollinaire to music as *mélodies*, and the singers' voices and piano accompaniment continue to move us deeply.

If only someone would set this first modern lyric poem of Japan to music and let us hear it as a beautiful, heartrending art song in the style of Schumann or Debussy! Nobutoki Kiyoshi (1887–1965) and Takemitsu Tōru (1930–1996) both could have done it, but they are long gone. Yuasa Jōji (b. 1929) has written orchestral music for sections of Bashō's *Narrow Road to the Deep North*, but to me his work is overly difficult. Isn't there anyone who could give new life to "Mourning the Old Sage Hokuju" as a twenty-first-century elegy with music that has the plainness suited to Buson as well as a jaunty freshness, combining the solidity of classical poetry with the *intimité* of modern poetry?

Then one day I learned from a small article in the *Chūnichi Shimbun* that my dream was to become reality. On July 12, 2013, at six in the evening in Nagoya's Shirakawa Hall, the Central Aichi Symphony Orchestra was to debut for its 128th concert "Mourning the Old Sage Hokuju," composed by Hayashi Hikaru (1931–2012) and under the direction of Saitō Ichirō. I had just recovered from a rather serious illness, but I could not stay away.

According to the pamphlet, the work was a solo cantata for tenor that Hayashi began composing in the spring of 2009 and completed on December 4 of the same year, three years before his death. I was happy to learn that the work was not commissioned but grew out of Hayashi's own love of the poem. The tribute to the old sage Hokuju, sung eighteen months after the composer's death by tenor Chūbachi Satoshi with string and wind accompaniment, had a sonorous beauty. To my ears, however, it seemed a touch strident—probably because I had been anticipating something like Schubert's lieder "The Trout" and "Death and the Maiden" or one of the Schubert string quartets.

Hayashi's twenty-minute cantata was followed by a seventy-two-minute performance of Beethoven's Symphony No. 9. To keep Hayashi's music from being eclipsed by Beethoven, I left, with the tenor's voice echoing in my mind. I would very much like to listen to the cantata again sometime in quiet contemplation.

In 2013, some 270 years after Buson wrote the elegy and 230 years after he died, "Mourning the Old Sage Hokuju" attained new life in an unexpected venue, surprising and delighting us, introducing us once again to the fresh poetic sensibility of youth, and further enriching our lives. Reading and listening to a bit of Buson's work for the first time in a long while, I felt once again how deeply affecting and wondrous his poetry is.

---

1 AN: Ogata Tsutomu, "Kaisetsu" [Commentary], *Buson haikushū* [The collected haiku of Buson] (Iwanami shoten, 1989), 297-299.
2 Yosa Buson, *Collected Haiku of Yosa Buson*, W.S. Merwin and Takako Lento, trans. (Port Townsend, WA: Copper Canyon Press, 2013), 237.
3 AN: Robert Hass, ed. and trans., *The Essential Haiku: Versions of Bashō, Buson, and Issa* (Hopewell, NJ: Ecco Press, 1994), 129.
4 A pantoum is a poem composed of a series of quatrains with repeating lines; the second and fourth lines of each stanza become the first and third lines of the succeeding stanza.
5 For Haga's analysis of the full poem, see *Yosa Buson no chiisana sekai* [The small world of Yosa Buson] (Chūō Kōronsha, 1986), Chapter 1.

14 | WOMEN BECOMING
MORE AND MORE BEAUTIFUL:
BUSON AND HARUNOBU

In mid-eighteenth-century Japan, men of every status and occupation became absorbed in natural history and horticulture, or gave themselves up to the pleasures of music, artistic accomplishments, haiku, and *kyōka* (comic verse), but what were the women in their lives doing? They of course had amusements and occupations of their own. And above all else, they became ever more beautiful.

In a time of widespread peace and hedonism, women become more alluring, and also they gain status. This was as true in the Tanuma era and the later Taishō era as it is today. Women were at the heart of *fêtes galantes*, courtship parties with a delicately veiled eroticism, in mid-eighteenth-century Japan, a society that Sugita Gempaku described in *Dawn of Western Science in Japan* as "extraordinarily beautiful and splendid." Historian Tsuji Zennosuke (1877–1955) quotes men of the 1770s as exclaiming boldly, with sighs of admiration, "Never since the beginning of heaven and earth have women been as beautiful as they are now!"[1]

Such sentiments led to the formation of something like a cult of feminine beauty. At the same time, unlicensed prostitution, forbidden during the reign of the eighth shogun, Yoshimune, revived as soon as Yoshimune breathed his last. The Edo districts of Fukagawa and Shinagawa became thriving centers of prostitution, places where lower samurai and townsmen could pursue fleeting pleasure. Senior Counselor Tanuma Okitsugu then surprised everyone by subjecting all brothels to taxation.

That such things happened is a fact, although not a dishonorable, dark fact, as critics with a Confucian or Puritan streak later maintained. At the same time, Yoshiwara courtesans used "futon seven deep, pale gold satin on the back and crimson crepe on the front, dyed in the Tatsuta River design" (Hanaōgi of the Ōgiya brothel in Edo-chō) or "futon seven deep, with a scattered family crest design in gold thread on bright scarlet" (Nioteru, also of the Ōgiya),[2] describing a phenomenon that did not merely belong to the history of erotica but also was an indication of the cultural preferences and extravagance of the times.

The courtesans of the Yoshiwara district were highly educated in poetry and calligraphy as well as in music and dancing, and they prided themselves on their characters even more than their looks. Customers had to indulge the women's pride and dignity (*hari*) with lavish spending and *iki*, a spirit of quiet sophistication. People in that milieu cultivated the most unusual aesthetic of love since the one articulated in "Sleeping Alone" (*Hitorine*, 1724–1725) by the literati artist Yanagisawa Kien (1703–1758).[3] The An'ei-Temmei era (1722–1781) saw the emergence of the so-called "eighteen grand sophisticates," rice brokers in Asakusa Kuramae and other wealthy merchants who were playboys and had a glamorous, elaborate manner of amusing themselves with courtesans that fascinated contemporary society.

Yet of course not all women belonged to the demimonde. Those who most evoked men's admiring sighs and who stir our imagination today were ordinary townswomen going about their business. These women were reported to be truly lissome and lovely.

Patterns on kimono and obi fabric preferred by eighteenth-century Japanese women include *akebono shibori* (dawn tie-dye) and *kabeshijira* (rhythmic weave), whose very names are "like delicate music sweet and low" (from the Verlaine poem "My Familiar Dream" ["Mon rêve familier"], translated by Ueda Bin). Recalling the Buson haiku "the purple/ curtain of dawn—/spring breeze" are a kimono tie-dyed a faint bluish purple (*akebono shibori*) and an obi of white silk that in shifting light reveals a pattern of subtle grace (*kabeshijira*); the quiet, pleasing delicacy of an everyday kimono in a fine cross-striped weave of endless variety; the crisp, winning vitality of kimono dyed to a rich, deep indigo or a paler indigo hue. Endless ingenuity went into the designing of Edo *komon*, kimono for everyday wear. The origins of Japan as a design powerhouse can be seen in the kimono, obi, and ornaments worn by Edo women.

Fashions in women's hairstyles, too, changed year by year. Women in prints by Suzuki Harunobu (ca. 1724–1770) often have their hair done up in ways too complicated to describe, twisted, bound, combed out long in back and looped into buns (*mage*) that became ever more elaborate in style as the years went by. Fancy ornamental combs and hairpins added to the effect. The versatile Hiraga Gennai earned money toward the end of his life selling pretty combs of carved ivory and silver ornaments known as "Sugawara combs" or "Gennai combs."

This was, in short, a preference for graceful elegance that I call rococo taste—a far cry from the Baroque taste of the Genroku era with its preference for lavish display. Townswomen were the most faithful embodiment of the finely textured, light, supremely refined, and coquettish style that imbued nearly every aspect of mid-eighteenth-century culture.

The unknown author of the essay "The Humble Bobbin" (*Shizu no odamaki*, 1802)[4] looks back fondly on the manners of the time:

> Everyone, high and low, hummed these lines from a popular song—clove-brown parasols in checkerboard patterns, red lacquer combs, and floral hairpins—and ivory hair ornaments were all the rage, decorated with gold-sprinkled lacquer. It was all lovely and fine.

The clear mental picture evoked by this elegiac passage captures the author's nostalgia and longing.

Some of Buson's haiku also create a poetic visual image of women:

> The fragrance
> of a silk robe left unfolded
> in the spring twilight

> Young bamboo—
> the courtesan in Hashimoto,
> is she still there?

A woman's robe, cast aside in a languorous mood, lying like a fallen petal on the floor of the chamber in twilight; the seductive figure of a young courtesan glimpsed in a bamboo grove—Buson's haiku call these images, hazy in outline and oh so beautiful, vividly to mind.

Then what of his *shintaishi* "Spring Breeze on the Kema Embankment"? The poem celebrates the figure and heart of a "very attractive" young woman who is on her way home across the long Kema embankment by the Yodo River, having been granted three days' leave from her work as a servant in an Osaka merchant's house.

> Spring breeze—
> the riverbank is so long
> and home so far

The season is spring, and it is spring in the girl's heart, too, as the rare sensation of freedom lifts her spirits. When she stops to pick fragrant herbs growing down along the riverbank, thorns snag the hem of her pretty kimono and scratch her legs. She scolds the thorns: "You won't let me by? My, how jealous you are!" Continuing on her way, she pauses at a teahouse and blushes when the old woman, who knows her, praises the fashionable kimono the girl herself is also secretly proud of. She senses the admiring eyes of male customers as well. Enjoying the warm sunshine, she gathers dandelions, yellow and white, and continues along the embankment where willows are sprouting tender leaves. Finally, she sees her house in the twilight: in the doorway, waiting for her, stands her aged mother.

Where in Western poetry of this era is a coquettish, winsome young girl like this portrayed with such vivid beauty? Perhaps closest are several verses of "The Book of Suleika" in *West-Eastern Divan*, in which Goethe (1749–1832) pretends to be a Middle Eastern poet. This poem by Buson is the jewel of rococo literature in the Tanuma era.

The poem is not purely a product of Buson's imagination. In a letter to a pupil in the spring of 1777, he explained the poem, which is set in his own hometown (a village on the Kema Embankment by the lower reaches of the Yodo River):

When I was a child, on quiet spring days I would always climb up on the embankment and play with my friends. Boats went to and fro on the river, and travelers came and went on the embankment. Among them were country girls who went to work in Osaka as domestics and quickly imitated Osaka fashions, even doing their hair in the manner of geisha in brothels. Some were drawn to the Shigedayu *jōruri* love suicide story and grew envious of such a romantic death.

Indeed, the scene the poem portrays was quite common in real life on the outskirts of Osaka. The girl in the poem, returning home for the short annual visit she is allotted, is decked out in the spring style she spotted in Osaka. Like readers of women's weekly magazines today, no doubt she hung on news of the romances of popular actors and singers, admiring such celebrities and finding her country-bred relatives at home wanting in comparison; she looked down on them a bit even as she longed for home and made her way there, humming a popular song as she walked.

Even now, at the midsummer Bon vacation or at the end of the year, such scenes can often be seen on streets and in stations. This is the unchanging, endearing frivolity of young girls. But the slender figure of Buson's young woman is beautifully dressed in a kimono made of something like *akebono shibori*, with "red-lacquered combs and floral hairpins" in her hair as she walks along the spring pathway. Compared to the office workers of the early twenty-first century, I believe she cut a far more elegant figure in her finery.

The haiku poet Tan Taigi (1709–1771), seven years older than his friend Buson, lived in a hermitage in the precincts of the Kyoto pleasure quarters in Shimabara. Several of his finest haiku are about young women:

Seated on the swing
at the highest point of the arc
she smiles in greeting

Firefly light shines
in the hand passing it on—
between her fingers

Imagine these women as the principal characters in eighteenth-century Japan's *fêtes galantes*, and they are all the more alluring. Taigi's haiku on the swing is a famous poem that Hara Katsurō did not neglect to include in his essay "Thoughts on Swings."[5] Hara sees Taigi's haiku as an early example of the revival of *saijō* (colored ropes), an amusement that had been neglected since Heian times: in the spring, blossoming branches were hung with swings of beautifully colored ropes that girls in springtime attire would climb on and enjoy.

Just as her swing rose high into the sky, the girl saw the poet and gave him a big smile: "Oh, sensei!" The haiku scans 5-8-5 with an extra syllable in the middle, neatly capturing the effect of the swing momentarily freezing in midair at its highest point. Taigi's haiku ranks with and perhaps is even more graceful than any depiction of young girls on swings by European rococo painters of *fêtes galantes* from Watteau to Fragonard.

The firefly haiku, too, is a work of ineffable beauty and eroticism. Through the single image of pale greenish firefly light shining between plump, fair fingers, it evokes the feel of those fingers, the girl's slightly bent posture, the expression on her face glimpsed in the dark of evening, and even the faint scent of her hair as she approaches. The firefly light is similar to the shadowy glimmers in Buson's "On a slender wick/ it shines all night—/Doll's Festival light" and "Short spring night—/near my pillow/a silver screen" or the luster of seashells in "Spring rain—/just enough to moisten/little shells on the sand." It is a half-imagined light, the light of Japanese rococo.

When that light burns a little brighter in the twilight, we have haiku like these, filled with a trembling innocence that leads directly to the world of Harunobu's charming *nishiki-e* (multicolored woodblock prints):

The mosquito coil
suddenly flares up—

her shy face
　　—Buson

First love—
faces close together
by the stone lantern
　　—Taigi

The single-sheet or sets of woodblock prints by Suzuki Harunobu (1725–1770) often depict, with great delicacy, figures of two young people of indeterminate sex, their hair styles providing the only clue: a beautiful young boy and girl breaking off a branch of blossoming plum against the solid background of a lustrous black sky in Harunobu's unique style; a young male customer and female server at a riverside teahouse hung with red lanterns, taking in the scene and enjoying a cool breeze; or, on a veranda with bush clover in bloom nearby, a woman in a pale lavender kimono nestling her cheek by that of a young man and taking him by the hand as she whispers words of love.

Against a solid background of a neutral color like silver gray, dark blue-gray, or clove brown, colors that Harunobu was the first to brush across the entire surface of a painting, a young man and a young woman respond to the beauty of the season and the moment, barely displaying any emotion. They resemble flowers blossoming from garments, their bodies twisted in narrow S-shapes as if those garments were unbearably heavy. Their eyes are slits in the classical *hikime-kagihana* (lines for eyes, hook for nose) style, their lips are like plum blossoms, their hands and feet are impossibly tiny. This is the world of Harunobu.

Harunobu's world has the style and color tone of Japanese rococo, as different as it could possibly be from the women painted by contemporary French painters John Honoré Fragonard (1732–1806), François Boucher (1703–1770), and Jean-Baptiste Greuze (1725–1805); those richly fleshed, sensual women's bosoms are a shade of pink known as *cuisse-de-nymphe* (fairy's thigh) and their actual thighs can often be seen. Nagai Kafū (1879–1959) perfectly captures the atmosphere of Harunobu's woodblock prints, including the suggestion of classical taste in them:

Rather than merely beautiful or sensual, they inspire a faint pathos, like watching blossoms scatter with unquiet hearts at the sound of the evening bell. The simple beauty of Harunobu's women, like that I feel in the love poems of the *Kokinshū*, fills me with a pathos resembling smoke.[6]

Langueur monotone, a sentiment tinged with a certain fatigue, is the psychological state in which, drained of power to exercise the will, one accepts what one senses as reality and lingers, entranced, on the emotions that reality inspires. This state is deeply connected, it seems to me, with the essential emotions of Buson's poetry, "spring languor" and "spring sorrow."

> The fading spring
> lingers yet in
> late-blooming cherries

> Fading spring—
> the lute in my arms
> so heavy

> Spring evening—
> as the incense burns down
> I add more

> Spring rain
> the day ending
> I linger too

> Slow spring days
> piling up, so far away
> the past

Takahashi Seiichirō (1884–1982) said that Harunobu was an artist not of youth but of the end of spring, youth gone. I heartily concur with that elegant assessment.

Amid figures so delicate that even the adjective "fairylike" seems too robust, what gives Harunobu's works the atmosphere of an elegant Edo feast is their unique coloration. His polychrome prints represented a great leap forward from *benizuri-e*, the earliest form of colored woodblock prints. Harunobu's brilliant polychrome prints burst into flower in 1765, causing his ukiyo-e to be called *azuma nishiki-e* (brocade pictures of the East—that is, Edo). In Harunobu's color technique, colors were seldom used in their "pure" state but were mixed with white *gofun* pigment to keep them muted and opaque. Harunobu was central in introducing this and other sophisticated techniques such as *ji-tsubushi* (using a plain background of a single color), *karazuri* ("empty" or blind printing, without paint), and *kimekomi* (cutting into the wood)— groundbreaking contributions to the history of printmaking. (Notably, the now accepted theory, first introduced by Morishima Nakayoshi, is that Harunobu got the idea of trying polychrome printing from Hiraga Gennai, his friend and neighbor in Kanda Shirakabe-chō.)

The connoisseur Kikunoya Kiyosen, a shogunal retainer with a stipend of 1,600 *koku*, recognized Harunobu's genius and became his patron, ordering everything from *e-koyomi*, traditional calendars with pictures, to ukiyo-e. In Edo of the early 1760s there were also various associations of upper-class samurai and townsmen devoted to such luxurious amusements, vying to outdo one another in displays of taste and skill. We must also note the superior technical skills of the phalanx of artists, engravers, and printers supporting those associations, the steady improvement of skills, and the consolidation of the division of labor through major publishing houses that took place at this time.

The works of Harunobu soon left the associations and went on the general market at ten times the going rate, sold separately in thick sheets of color-printed wrapping paper or in sets encased in paulownia boxes. However high the price, demand was strong in Edo and beyond. Because these were polychrome prints, the woodblock had to be changed repeatedly, and each time, the paper had to be rubbed hard against the wood with a circular, pad-like tool called a *baren*. *Hoshōshi*, a sturdy, fine-quality paper made from mulberry wood, was capable of withstanding this process. In the mid-eighteenth century, *hoshōshi* production techniques improved dramatically in Takefu, Echizen province, and other papermaking localities, enabling mass production at reduced prices. At the same time, a distribution network evolved facilitating the spread of the paper to and within Edo. As Takahashi Seiichirō points out, these socioeconomic conditions lay behind the skyrocketing success of Harunobu's colorful woodblock prints.[7] All these factors, aided by the liberality of the Tokugawa shogunate in permitting such extravagance, made Harunobu's *azuma nishiki-e* the crystallization of Japan's rococo culture in the Tanuma era.

Even though the honeyed mood of a Harunobu *nishiki-e* cannot be conveyed in words, if I were to start expounding on their appeal one spring night or summer evening, I would go on and on. Women troubled by the slightest of breezes, scarcely able to bear the weight of their own clothing; couples in love, exchanging dulcet secrets through gestures, without need of words. Entrance to this world, a universal microcosm possessed of storybook charm, requires only the ability to allow oneself acutely attuned senses and feelings. More than the works of his contemporaries Kitagawa Utamaro (d. 1806) and Torii Kiyonaga (1752–1815), who also painted beautiful women; more than the paintings of Watteau in eighteenth-century France or Qiu Ying in Ming-dynasty China; and probably more than the genre paintings of Hyewon in Korea during the Joseon dynasty, Harunobu's woodblock prints deserve to be called a "microcosm."

In order to create that microcosm of love in medium-sized multicolor prints, Harunobu, far more than Hishikawa Moronobu (ca. 1618–1694), Okumura Masanobu (1686–1764), or any other of his predecessors, needed to be keenly sensitive to the psychology of curves. He deliberately and meticulously brought into his paintings what may be called the geometry of coquetry.

What do we see, for example, in *Whispering Lovers on the Veranda* (*Sasayaki*, Figure 51) from the late 1760s? On a veranda in the cool of a summer evening, a man (or woman?) holding a fan is romancing a young woman. The focus of this attention has kicked off a *geta* clog and is sitting with one knee drawn high, clinging to the wooden pillar on the veranda with her left hand to support her unstable position, expressing

Figure 48. Suzuki Harunobu, *Evening Chime of the Clock* (*Tokei no banshō*) from *Eight Parlor Views* (*Zashiki hakkei*). Hiraki Ukiyo-e Foundation.

Figure 49. Nishikawa Sukenobu, *Picture Book: Tamakazura* (*Ehon Tamakazura*), British Museum.

Figure 50. Suzuki Harunobu,
A Story of Love on the Veranda
(*Ensaki monogatari*).
Tokyo National Museum.

Figure 51. Suzuki Harunobu,
*Whispering Lovers on
the Veranda* (*Sasayaki*).
Tokyo National Museum.

bashfulness with every inch of her being. Her head, kimono, and obi combine to create various elongated C-, S-, and reverse C-curves, all contained in a pear-shaped oval. The curves perfectly express her feelings—her mingled uncertainty and consent, her unspoken, surging thoughts. The curving line that after much meandering drifts finally down to the hem of her kimono forms an isosceles triangle with the line of the kimono of the wooing man (or woman?) leaning over and against her. When you reexamine the print after reading Terada Torahiko's brilliant essay "Curves in Ukiyo-e," it becomes apparent that the crown of the young man's hair is the tip of the isosceles triangle, and the plumb line descending from that point merges with the line of the woman's sleeve.[8]

This style of feminine pose, especially in Harunobu's early works, is something the artist learned from Nishikawa Sukenobu, an ukiyo-e printmaker active in Kyoto in the Kyōho era. To be more precise, Harunobu plagiarized this technique.[9] However, a look at an early Harunobu print like *Evening Chime of the Clock* (*Tokei no banshō*, ca. 1766) from the series *Eight Parlor Views* (*Zashiki hakkei*, Figure 48), where the borrowing is blatant, shows that the women drawn by artists two generations apart have completely different body weights. The figure fresh from the bath in Sukenobu's *Picture Book: Tamakazura* (*Ehon Tamakazura*, 1726; Figure 49) is a mature woman of considerable presence, sitting lazily and solidly on the veranda, bosom bared. Harunobu's beauty just out of the bath, with no one watching, is wiping her right earlobe with her left hand tucked inside her *yukata* robe, a complex, coquettish gesture that further complicates the curving lines of her garment, under which the undulations of her pale body seem to disappear. Comparison with Sukenobu makes plain that Harunobu's interest lies in tracing the flow of delicate swirls even at the sacrifice of a realistic portrayal of the human physique.

In place of the healthy physicality of Sukenobu's earlier women, rendered in bold lines, Harunobu has a young girl glancing over her shoulder at a clock that has just begun to strike the hour, adding a slight psychological dimension to the scene. A striking clock is a common motif in Harunobu's works. Like the French spectroscope depicted in *The Jewel River of Kōya* (*Kōya no Tamagawa*), it shows Edoites' taste for imported gadgets in the 1760s, which was pointed out by Sugita Gempaku;[10] the clock also adds a definite emotional frisson.

This Japanese mannerism of the latter half of the eighteenth century weaves a still mellower and more refined pattern of the geometry of love in a masterpiece from Harunobu's late period entitled *A Story of Love on the Veranda* (*Ensaki monogatari*, Figure 50). The setting is an autumn afternoon on a veranda near flowering bush clover. Here the roles of the previous whispering lovers are reversed. An older woman leans in, laying her cheek alongside that of a young man, presses his hand, and puts her arm around his shoulders as she murmurs something into his ear. Is she herself in love with him and wooing him? Or is she the nurse of the young girl peeping out through the crack in the screen behind, telling the young man her charge's feelings for him? Or perhaps, in the course of conveying that message, did she fall for the handsome young man herself and begin to woo him, not realizing that the girl is watching? The scene presents a psychological drama rife with possibility.

In any case, close examination of this beautiful drawing will show a yet more complex, gracefully curved line running from the top of the woman's bun through her nape, shoulder, back, hips, and raised knee, down to the trailing skirt of her kimono. These are the mellow curves of a woman filled with love. Drawn toward the woman, the young man leans back with his hand under her tiny hand, toppled against her in an unstable pose with his left leg stretched out, while the long, narrow lines of his kimono ripple down to the hem and then flare.

The flowing lines of the figures tell the story of the psychological drama unfolding between the woman and the young man. As in *Whispering Lovers on the Veranda*, the lines simultaneously form a triangle of romance, one even more bewitching. Then there is the wonderful effect of the plumb line that starts from the woman's bun, the top of that equilateral triangle, and extends down her right sleeve. Harunobu's frequent use of plumb lines in his paintings of lovers shows that in addition to a "spirit of delicacy" he also had a "spirit of geometry," carefully planning the linear movement in his works to construct sweet melodic lines.

Here the romantic triangular shape formed by the two main figures is bookended by straight lines—the narrowly opened sliding doors, where the young woman peeps out through the crack, and the bamboo lattice in the window—as well as diagonal lines on the stepping stone under the veranda, further intensifying the sweetness of the whispered secrets. Comparison with works in the style of Harunobu by Suzuki Harushige (pseudonym of Shiba Kōkan, 1747–1818) and Isoda Koryūsai (active 1769–1790) shows plainly that Harunobu's geometry of love was far more subtle and carried far finer psychological shading.

The coquettish curves that created these "love nooks" of Harunobu would in the latter half of the nineteenth century travel to Europe, becoming part of the *fin de siècle* art that followed *japonisme*, then return to Taishō Japan in paintings of beautiful women by Takehisa Yumeji (1884–1934). Today these softly flowing feminine lines that seem to be disappearing in real life are perhaps best represented in archetypical form by the *onnagata* Bandō Tamasaburō.

---

1 AN: Tsuji Zennosuke, *Tanuma jidai* [The Tanuma era] (Iwanami shoten, 1980 [first published, 1915]), 94.

2 AN: Ibid., 111.

3 AN: See Abe Jirō, *Tokugawa jidai no geijutsu no shakai* [Tokugawa art and society], *Abe Jirō zenshū* [The complete works of Abe Jirō], vol. 8 (Kadokawa shoten, 1961).

4 Iwamoto Sashichi, ed., *Enseki jisshu* [Series of Edo folktales], vol. 1 (Kokusho kankokai, 1907), 201-236.

5 AN: Hara Katsurō, "Shūsenkō" [On swings], *Nihon chūseshi* [History of medieval Japan] (Kōdansha, 1978), 291-303.

6 AN: Nagai Kafū, "Suzuki Harunobu no nishiki-e" [The *nishiki-e* of Suzuki Harunobu], *Edo geijutsu ron* [On Edo art] (Iwanami shoten, 2000), 33.

7 AN: Takahashi Seiichirō, *Shin ukiyo-e nihyakugojūnen* [Two hundred fifty years of new ukiyo-e] (Chūō kōron bijutsu shuppan, 1961), 59.

8 AN: Terada Torahiko, "Ukiyo-e no kyokusen" [Curves in ukiyo-e], *Terada Torahiko zuihitsu shū* [Collected essays of Terada Torahiko], vol. 2 (Iwanami shoten, 1947), 92-97. Terada came up with mathematical analyses of ukiyo-e perhaps because he was a physicist as well as an author/essayist/poet.

9 AN: See Kobayashi Tadashi, *Harunobu* (Sansaisha, 1970).

10 See Chapter 10.

15 | COPING WITH THE LONG PEACE: YOUNG ROWDIES, ŌTA NAMPO

Among the writings of comparative literature scholar and Rilke specialist Fujikawa Hideo (1909–2003) is a masterful book entitled *Poets of the Later Edo Period*.[1] Fujikawa takes up the poems of Kan Chazan (1748–1827) and others who wrote in classical Chinese, works read today by only a handful of experts. His fluent explanations in a smooth narrative style bring to life a world of forgotten poetic beauty.

Like a picture scroll, the book depicts contemporary nature and society in detail, as captured by the sensibilities of a variety of poets. The writers' reactions and impressions are conveyed with surprising intimacy. No discussion of the Pax Tokugawana would be complete without mention of this book.

It's hard to know where to begin, but here is an interesting episode that deals with poets of the Chaos Club (Kontonsha). The stylish name suggests a group of early twentieth-century anarchist poets or socialist literati, but actually it was a late eighteenth-century association of Seishin School poets writing in Chinese, led by the Confucian poet Katayama Hokkai (1723–1790), a resident of Osaka. The salon of townsmen was representative of the bourgeois (*chōnin*) culture of Osaka. Members included Kimura Kenkadō (1736–1802), the well-known master of a sake shop and leading cultural enthusiast of the day; the owner of a hardware store; and the young master of a pharmacy, each with a love of reading and writing poetry. The group met once a month and vied in drinking and versification. Rai San'yō's father, Rai Shunsui (1746–1816), joined in 1766 at twenty, when he left Hiroshima to study in Osaka.

Fujikawa introduces an episode from Shunsui's recollections of his youth in Osaka in a book entitled *Record of a Stay in Settsu* (*Zaishin kiji*). The episode vividly recreates a trip down the Yodo River one autumn day in the peaceful age of Tokugawa. I have taken the liberty of paraphrasing the text as follows:

> One autumn, Shunsui went with his teacher, Chō Tōsai, a Confucian from Sakai, to see the fall leaves in Takao, outside Kyoto. After spending two nights in Kyoto, they returned from Fushimi by taking a boat along the Yodo River. Some of the passengers spoke in elegant, graceful Kyoto dialect, others had a rustic twang, but everyone chattered away, enjoying the boat trip.
>
> At Hirakata, half a dozen fellows on the bank shouted out to hail the boat and trooped on board. They were young rowdies in the garb of *komusō* monks. Their speech was coarse and so were the looks on their faces. As they carried on without the slightest regard for anyone else, the other passengers, until then so talkative, suddenly fell silent.
>
> Chō sat with his eyes closed and seemed at first to pay the young men no heed. After a time, however, he turned to them and said sternly, "Why are you making so much noise? Since you're here, how about playing a piece to entertain me?"
>
> When the other passengers heard this, they exchanged uneasy looks, afraid the young toughs would get violent. Instead, to everyone's surprise, they responded, "Since you wish it, old man, we'll play for you."
>
> Two of them promptly took out flutes from the bags they carried and started to play them, while another two sang along. One more imitated the sounds of a koto, and the remaining fellow mouthed an accompaniment, sounding like a *kokyū*.[2] The various performances harmonized perfectly, and the result was musically pleasing, with a fine melody. The *komusō* secretly prided themselves on their ability to do this; each young man was a virtuoso.
>
> The other passengers listened to the impromptu perfor-

mance with relief and delight. The boat glided slowly down the river, giving off music as it went along. Toward evening, the boat arrived at Gempachi Ferry Terminal, whereupon the young men straightened their kimono, disembarked, and went away.

Everyone turned to Chō, thanking him vociferously. "Because of what you said, not only did they settle down, they sang and played for us. Thanks to you, this was a wonderful trip."[3]

Rai Shunsui honors the way his first teacher, Chō Tōsai, put an end to the young men's horseplay with a single remark, a remarkable display of humanity and aplomb. Still more, he seems to recall with pleasure how much the musical artistry of the young *komusō* monks surprised him, a kid fresh from the country, and what an unexpected treat it was to share time on the riverboat with them.

Going from Fushimi in Kyoto to Temmabashi in Osaka takes less than an hour today by the Shinkansen or the Meishin Expressway, but in those days the trip upstream took all day or all night, twice as long as going downstream. Traveling up and down the river by boat is a luxury that modern Japanese can't dream of. People back then sat on reed matting in passenger boats called "30-*koku* boats"[4] and were slowly propelled along without the least impatience. Their sense of time was different from ours.

Hiroshige's woodblock print *Passenger Boat on the Yodo River* (*Yodogawa*) from the series *Famous Places in Kyoto* (*Kyoto meisho no uchi*), a much later work dating from the Tempō era (1830–1844), also portrays that boat trip with a beauty that inspires nostalgia for days gone by. A *hototogisu*[5] crosses the sky by a large, pale full moon—a moon of wonderful purity, like all of Hiroshige's moons. The captain, wearing only a loincloth, maneuvers the 30-*koku* boat with a pole, leaning far back as he looks up at the moon beyond the mist. Beneath the hovering darkness of early evening, the Yodo River is a chilly blue. The viewer can almost feel the cool of the breeze off the river. Inside the boat, under a thatched roof with braided-straw hats fastened on top, passengers seem to be enjoying the brief freedom afforded by the journey. Their expressions

Figure 52. Utagawa Hiroshige, *Passenger Boat on the Yodo River* (*Yodogawa*). Hiroshige Museum of Art, Ena.

are so carefree that just looking at them is soothing. One man, apparently a merchant, pours himself a drink while deep in conversation with his neighbor. Another buys supper from a skiff pulled up alongside. A fair-skinned woman nurses her baby. A monk gazes at the moon. Another man is stretched out, dozing. Two friends light each other's pipes. A box with a red *tengu* (long-nosed goblin) mask on the back was perhaps carried on the shoulders of an itinerant peddler.

The print seems to echo with the murmur of conversation, exactly like the scene Shunsui described in the passage above. The following five-character-quatrain, also by Shunsui, is thought to have been composed aboard the boat:

> Alone in the darkness on the boat I take in
> the conversations of different companions:
> men from the country, the world of mulberry leaves and hemp;
> people from the capital, the world of flowers and willows[6]

That warm, relaxed circle was invaded by a boisterous crowd of ill-behaved young men dressed as *komusō* monks. The passengers' alarm is easy to imagine. *Komusō* were generally regarded warily as strange creatures. Although originally attached to the Fuke school of Zen, they did not chant sutras, observe Buddhist precepts, or shave their heads, but simply went on pilgrimages, playing the shakuhachi and receiving alms. Knaves and ronin would often disguise themselves as *komusō*. Arai Hakuseki wrote in his autobiography about a story his father told of a young samurai who fled his domain after committing a grave offense. After the daimyo took his mother hostage and she died in prison, the bitter samurai became a *komusō*, vowing to take his former lord's life.

The Fuke school of Zen was formally recognized while Hakuseki's father was still a young man, very early in the Tokugawa period. The shogunate recognized *komusō* and used them as spies around the country. Only samurai were formally allowed to join the school, but how long that policy lasted is unclear. The group who boarded Shunsui's boat may have been the ill-natured second and third sons of impoverished samurai or unruly sons who had been disowned by their fathers, stern members of the old guard who remembered the bygone age of Yoshimune. Or they may simply have been idlers and vagabonds in temporary disguise.

Komusō were originally lone wolves who prowled life's back alleys and had a dark, antisocial aura. But after a century and a half of peace, like Tokugawa society in general, they had become softer and more urbane. The well-known *komusō* symbol, a deep hat of woven straw like an overturned bucket with a little window, was worn only until the mid-eighteenth century. From the Meiwa era (1764–1772) on, the hat had taken on a foppishly narrow, twisted shape; that must be what Shunsui's rowdies wore as they clattered aboard the riverboat. *Komusō* also wore silk kimono tied with padded obi where they tucked the brocade bag holding their shakuhachi, the tool of their trade. They undoubtedly took pains with their appearance in other ways as well, paying attention to color coordination and accessories.

Writer Ueda Akinari (who could well have become a *komusō* himself) wrote a collection of tongue-in-cheek, skeptical essays entitled *Chronicles of Audacity and Timidity* (*Tandai shōshinroku*) that were published in

1808, the year before he died. He slammed the state of the country: "Arts and accomplishments are rampant, springing up everywhere. This [pursuit of adulation and profit] is dust stirred up by the current reign." Under the influence of Senior Counselor Tanuma Okitsugu, the rigidly controlled government of Yoshimune gave way to a more liberal rule, and arts and amusements blossomed in every layer of society: the Way of Sencha Tea[7] that Akinari himself followed, in addition to (as already noted) natural history, horticulture, kabuki, *senryū* (satirical verse), music, *nishiki-e*, *gesaku*, *kyōka* (comic verse), haiku, and Chinese verse. Because the young monks were the spiritual descendants of *komusō* of the Fuke school of Zen, which took the shakuhachi as its trademark, they of course would have responded to Chō Tōsai's request with alacrity, vying to show off their musical skills.

Still, the picture seems to me emblematic of the Pax Tokugawana: young monks, doubtless sporting long, stylish sideburns, playing the flute, imitating other instruments, and singing for the entertainment of Shunsai, Chō Tōsai, and the other passengers listening raptly as the boat bore them all down the Yodo River one autumn evening. "They were all young rowdies," Shunsui wrote, "so-called *komusō* monks," but their having been "young rowdies" gives the story all the greater charm.

The long banks of the Yodo River, seen from the 30-*koku* boat, were the same as the embankment strewn with dandelions and willow trees in Buson's poem "Spring Breeze on the Kema Embankment," where in early spring of roughly the same time period that "very attractive" young woman headed home on a short vacation from her job in Osaka, dressed in a "fancy spring robe in Osaka style" and humming a popular tune as she walked along, light of heart. As such images show, during the Pax Tokugawana, the lives of young idlers and nursing mothers, Confucian scholars, and young women in domestic service seem to have all been imbued with a pervading sense of order, gentle yet unbreakable. Even though those times are long past, that impression seems unlikely to be a mere illusion.

Endless peace in the small community of an island nation with many people jammed in close quarters could of course be hard to bear, and some reacted by breaking into a run and shouting. This attitude was especially common among intellectuals of the samurai class, first and foremost among them Hiraga Gennai, who wrote in *On Farting, Part II*, feigning indifference:

> The ronin's idea of relaxation is a simple bowl of rice and soup, a thimbleful of sake. Though he lacks a fixed occupation and income, he also lacks a useless master, and with no stipend to stick to him like rice grains on the soles of his feet, he is free to run around as he pleases; if he doesn't want to go someplace, he just makes fun of it. He enjoys lifelong freedom, and that is his reward.

I don't intend to dwell further here on Mr. Penniless Poorman—as Gennai calls himself in the above-quoted essay—but in fact, after running hither and yon without pause, contributing his ideas and abilities to myriad projects all over Japan, Gennai was engulfed by a whirlpool of his own making and died in prison.

The pioneers Yamagata Daini (1725–1767), who wrote the political treatise *Master Ryū's New Thesis* (*Ryūshi shinron*,1759); Hayashi Shihei (1738–1793), who wrote *Military Defense of a Maritime Nation* (*Kaikoku heidan*, 1786–1791); Honda Toshiaki (1743–1821), who wrote *Tales of the West* (*Saiiki monogatari*, 1798); and even Sugita Gempaku, who translated *A New Book of Anatomy* (*Kaitai shinsho*, 1774), all were contemporaries and kindred spirits who, unable to wait for society to change, broke into a run to spur its transformation. But Daini was executed on charges of lèse-majesté; Shihei died in a fit of anger, his book banned; and Toshiaki vanished, leaving little trace of his personal life. The only one who lived on to a ripe old age, having witnessed the light and dark of the age of peace, was Gempaku, the stubborn realist.

At the same time, there were many more of the sort of people who bore some resemblance to these pioneers and could understand their intentions and their exasperation, but lacked the spirit to run and shout out along with them. Then there were people who had a lively curiosity about the reality of life around them in city streets and were widely accepting of it but whose education was a barrier to their finding peace therein. As with Japan's thinkers today, this latter miserable type seems to have been more common by far.

Some men didn't know what to do with themselves and spent their lives coping with the monster of the Pax Tokugawana in a tricky in-between state, at times making fun of it and at times letting it get the best of them, finally becoming one with it. Ōta Nampo (1749–1823), who also wrote under the name Shokusanjin, is a prime example.

Nampo was a man of enormous talent left dangling and disconsolate; he was a samurai warrior who lived in the springtime of a too-long peace, his primary *raison d'être* lost, and despite his ability he had no prospects. Knowing this, he and his cohorts made themselves into caricatures, the butts of their own jokes; Nampo called himself Neboke Sensei, "Master Groggy." Laughter was his sole means of consolation and of saving face. Through wit and irony, he managed, just barely, to escape his own fecklessness and rise above his scruffy reality, skimming its surface to gain a reputation in the world.

> Have you seen Edo on New Year's Day?
> Such an auspicious time, brief glory like a dream
> Master is groggy and wants to go out somewhere
> His formal *kamishimo* costume is threadbare, his swords scruffy
> Last night's calculations are useless,[8] but
> "a samurai, even when he has not eaten, uses a toothpick like a lord"
> This morning, without having drunk a drop of spiced sake,
> he floats happily out the front gate by the pine-and-bamboo decoration
> Together we say, "Happy New Year," "May peace last forever"
>   —"New Year's Day"[9]

This celebrated comic Chinese poem (*kyōshi*) is from Nampo's debut work, *Master Groggy's Literary Collection* (*Neboke sensei bunshū*), which he published in 1767 at age eighteen with an introduction by his older mentor, Hiraga Gennai. The caricature of a hapless salaried samurai, flurried and vain, resonated with downhearted samurai and townsfolk alike, propelling the talented author to citywide popularity.

Nampo's comic Chinese poetry, comic prose, and comic *waka* (*kyōshi*, *kyōbun*, and *kyōka*) certainly do not have the qualities of the *gesaku* by his mentor, Hiraga Gennai: explosive, exuberant eloquence; barbed satire and jokes; *allegro con brio* exhilaration; and shadows of exasperation and despair. Compared to the works of Gennai, a ronin from Shido in Sanuki province on the island of Shikoku, the Chinese writings of the urbanite from Ushigome in Edo have a clipped, slighter humor, and the air of a faint wry smile. As a result, they enjoyed a wider readership. Rather than launch a furious attack on the lazy heaviness of society during the great peace, Nampo showed people how to work with it, play with it, live with it. Although a shogunal retainer, he belonged to the lowest rank of vassals and was impoverished, earning a stipend of seventy bales of rice and rations for five; we should remember that behind the playfulness and jokiness of his writing lay an anguish with no other outlet.

In a Chinese poem written around the same time as *Master Groggy's Literary Collection*, young Nampo, a newly-appointed vassal, told of this feeling: "a cup of unrefined sake, a koto piece; with one cup and one piece I seek to forget my melancholy." Fifteen or so years later, self-mockery over his own fecklessness casts an even darker shadow in his writings, as if it is all he can do to bring a bitter smile to his lips.

His residence, which he grandly named "House of Rest" in Chinese, was actually one of a row of dilapidated houses for low-ranking vassals in Naka-Okachimachi Ushigome. One day in the eleventh month of 1871, when he was in his mid-thirties, Nampo lay in his futon suffering from a cold and looked out on the withered, squalid garden. He wrote this short passage in Chinese:

> The desolate garden is full of fallen leaves, unswept by any broom. Beyond the garden, gaps in the wooden fence of the house next door have been repaired with what seems to be rush matting, and when smoke from the noon cooking fire seeps through, it looks just like a rush-thatched boat.
>
> Shabby though it is, the garden has an apricot tree, and they

say Confucius' house had one, too, so I look on it with pride, confident that in this one respect my garden is the equal of the master's. But alas!—stretching from the treetop to a nearby pillar is a long cord where, of all things, my infant son's diapers hang to dry.

The weeping peach tree, peonies, chrysanthemums, and bamboo have all withered in the cold, and since the garden is neglected and never tidied, tissues that someone blew their nose on and threw away lie there, and dog dung too.

It's all quite desolate, and yet, wondering if the plum tree has marked the return of spring by putting out buds as it should, I look up from my pillow, but the calligraphy practice sheets of my pupils hanging in the window flap in the wind and the child's futon airing on a pole under the eaves reeks. I close the sliding doors by my pillow and go back to sleep.

Caught the flu and now
here I am
no thoroughfare
If you have no business here
you're not getting through
　　—"No Thoroughfare" (*Kurumadome*) from *Yomo no aka*[10]

The wretchedness of his life hits home to us today. On a weekday morning when normally he would be out, the invalid takes time off work with a cold. He lifts his tired, feverish head and looks around the house and the garden outside, struck afresh by how depressingly shabby it all is. The sad lot of petty officials and low-paid office workers hasn't changed a bit, Nampo reminds us, making us feel the pitifulness of our own circumstances all the more keenly.

Yosa Buson's Kyoto home at Bukkōji Karasuma Nishi-iru may have been no different from the "House of Rest" in Ushigome in Edo. But Buson wrote about his home in haiku like these: "Narrow alleyway/leading to Peach Blossom Spring[11]/winter confinement"; "Buried embers/my hermitage too/buried in snow." With his unique poetic imagination focusing on the inside of his home, he was able to transform it into a warm, pleasant, and intimate space perfectly suitable to his curled-up body. He seems to be saying that the smaller, narrower, and more dimly lit his house is, the more surely it shuts out the world, creating a cozy, peaceful space where not even the wind can get in through the cracks. From that poetic perspective, indolence, slovenliness, and neglect are states of repose in which a person can set aside all social conventions, return to himself, and breathe easy. In that sense, tedium, negligence, uncertainty, scarcity, loss, and other negative phenomena in human affairs and nature are, for Buson, tinged with a fresh and deeper poetic significance.

Ōta Nampo was not a poet with the ability to find that sort of imaginative dimension. He was a good-natured, sociable Edo samurai whose *kyōka* colleagues were fond of him, as is shown in the following tribute, which involves an affectionate play on the characters in his name.

> Master Ōta, your name
> can be read *daita ko*
> "a child held close"
> I look back with great affection
> on how young and sweet you were

He was also a brilliant student of Confucianism, talented in worldly matters and a conscientious worker. He was a man of common sense, with no tolerance for things that struck him as not the way they were supposed to be. His own life story was too dismal, too pathetic for him to poeticize loneliness and wretchedness. He could only tame those aspects of his life through self-derision.

In summer 1782, Nampo suffered a recurrence of scabies in his legs and was forced to lie still in bed. He wrote humorously about the experience:

> These days
> the sores on my shins
> fester so
> all I do is put on plasters
> and lie in bed, that's all

My hair is so shaggy that I look like a demon in an *Ōtsu-e* folk painting. There's dirt under my fingernails because I scratch everything in sight. I'm filthy, smelly, and miserable beyond belief. One of the neighbors must be burning *okera* root to get rid of the damp from the endless rains; the smoke drifts in and mingles with the stench of diapers in the hamper. Truly wretched.

In the back of the house, my old mother, wearing a bamboo hat, peers in the neighbor's kitchen window while scooping water from the well. They complain to each other:

"This weather is awful, isn't it? It's as if the bottom of the heavens fell out. Leaving the house is so much trouble."

"Yes, and the humidity is something else! I can never get the fire to light in the morning. Now, what shall I put in tomorrow's miso soup?"

In a guard's house, next door in the other direction, a girl about four years older than our daughter, told by her mother to practice her singing, is playing the shamisen and screeching out the lyrics. Our daughter started imitating her. When my wife said, "Stop that noise," our son, who turns two this year, imitated his mother and scolded his sister by growling at her.

My wife grabbed him. "You haven't gone wee-wee yet, have you? Come here."

"No!" he shouted and ran off. When she finally caught him and felt him, he was soaking wet. Off to the hamper with the offending item. Life here truly stinks.

—"Summer Grass" (*Natsukusa*) from *Yomo no aka*[12]

A hectic, noisy evening when, after a sultry day of solid rain, Nampo, his parents, his wife, and their two children are stuck in a house that feels even more cramped than usual. It is a scene of quotidian Japanese life that today's readers have seen and know well, and that they look back on with mingled nostalgia and horror. What is most appalling is the dirty, scabies-infested figure of the master of the house lying in bed amid the bedlam. The only relief comes from the pathos of Nampo's portrayal of the lives of low-ranking vassals and the Edo petty bourgeoisie, himself included.

This type of writing, known as *kyōbun* or comic prose, has definite affinities with the poetry and prose of Buson, Rai Shunsui, and Kan Chazan, as well as the short fiction of Gogol, Chekhov, Natsume Sōseki (1867–1916), Yasuoka Shōtarō (1920–2013), and Nosaka Akiyuki (1930–2015), This is not to say it is of high literary merit. However, such writing evokes, with palpable clarity, the life and mood of a man who lived two hundred years ago in the Yamanote section of Edo, gasping for air amid the great peace of Tokugawa. As a prose essay, it is sometimes more to be admired than *kyōka*, comic verses, which are often little more than plays on words.

Known throughout Edo by his pen names Shokusanjin and Yomo no Akara as the writer of comic verse in Chinese and Japanese, Ōta Nampo, as much as any Edo commoner, endured poverty and dreadful illnesses, and lamented his failure to get ahead. There were times when he hit rock bottom and could only get his daily bread through the intervention of friends. Yet, neither making a show of his circumstances nor concealing them, he made them the seeds, or fertilizer, of his poetry and prose, and displayed sparkling talent in every genre of light literature of the age. That surely made his name even more familiar and beloved among ordinary people, further cementing his popularity.

Here are some of the most famous of Nampo's innumerable *kyōka*:

> Lacking money
> how boring it is
> at the end of the year—
> playing a game of shogi
> unable to make a move

> The season greeter
> tipsy with toasts
> weaves unsteadily
> down the avenue—
> lo, the New Year has come!
>   —translated by Burton Watson

New bracken sprouts
their small fists
flailing against
the mountain face
as spring breezes blow

Unfailing optimism and humor amid the most impoverished and straitened of circumstances was characteristic of old Edo residents during the Great Peace, and it was surely what enabled them to carry on.

Nampo's fellow *kyōka* poets included people of all occupations and stations in life: the shogun retainers Karagoromo Kisshū and Akera Kankō; Kankō's wife, Fushimatsu no Kaka; Hezutsu Tōsaku, the owner of a tobacco shop in Shinjuku, Edo; Ōne Futoki, a for-hire sentry; Motono Mokuami, the proprietor of a bathhouse in Kyōbashi, and his wife Chieno Naishi. These people were comparable to the wealthy Osaka merchants of the Chaos Club, but were a more chaotic group of petty bourgeois who vied to excel in jokes, puns, plays on words, parodies, and twists, combining humor and charm and creating an unprecedented craze for *kyōka*. Since they took as their theme the everyday life in the streets of Edo, they never ran out of ideas. They held bring-your-own-lunch poetry parties that cost no money and were doubtless an agreeable pastime, one that helped to erase the dreary monotony of the seemingly endless peace. However, *kyōka* was far too minor of a genre to be called a literature of the growing capital, and perhaps too delicate a flower as well.

In 1786, Senior Counselor Tanuma Okitsugu was ousted from power and a new shogun took over. The following year, Matsudaira Sadanobu (1758–1828) became senior counselor, touting a policy of encouraging literary and military arts. Before anyone else, Nampo then gave up writing *kyōka* and *gesaku*, and he also gave up his old circle of friends. He presumably had various reasons for this. In any case, the swiftness and discipline of the change are remarkable. It was perhaps a kind of *tenkō*, an ideological about-face. Nampo's keen sense of balance, developed during his time in limbo as a shogunal retainer who was also an intellectual, enabled him to react more swiftly than others. Immersed since his teens in the bawdy world of *kyōbungaku* (crazy literature), he had enjoyed himself in constant high spirits, and it seems likely that as he approached forty, he experienced a growing distaste for that world and reflected on his participation in it. Also, he had recently taken a former Yoshiwara courtesan as his mistress, putting an added strain on his already hard-pressed finances, and no doubt acted to protect his domestic affairs. After years of entertaining society with *kyōka* and *gesaku*, he must have felt relief at being able to return to his original dream of becoming a scholar of poetry and prose in Chinese.

Men like Hōseidō Kisanji (1735–1813), a retainer of the Akita domain; Koikawa Harumachi (1744–1789), a retainer of the Ojima domain in Suruga province; and Santō Kyōden (1761–1816) of Edo, among other *gesaku* writers, kept on writing political satire during the Kansei Reforms of 1787–1793, which were aimed at shoring up the lax financial and moral condition of Tokugawa government. Those men did so even when ordered to cease and desist; some were driven to suicide. Nevertheless, I cannot bring myself to blame Nampo for lacking the backbone to follow their example. Having backbone, putting up resistance, and sticking to one's principles would all have been out of character for writers of *kyōka* and *gesaku*, and would probably even have been impediments to success.

The word for Confucianism in Japanese is *jugaku*, and one theory holds that 儒, the character for *ju*, means basically to crawl like an earthworm, moving forward on one's path by a series of peristaltic waves.[13] In that sense, Confucian teachings offered an ideal means of accommodating the slippery monster of the Pax Tokugawana, flexibly adapting to its undulations and prolonging its life. Even if the Pax Tokugawana seemed wobbly, at least the peace that was seen in everyday life could be maintained. And if everyone focused on their own peristaltic movements, peace might be restored to the nation as a whole.

There were surely countless ways of managing the long peace, from hanging around dressed as a *komusō* monk to taking up pastimes like gardening, music, and literature, raising ennui itself to an art, or even (though I wasn't able to touch on it here) spending one's life setting off small explosions, getting into fight after fight the way Katsu Kaishū's father, Kokichi, did. But the anti-fundamentalist lesson that Ōta Nampo demonstrated through his actions may have been the most typical of Tokugawa Japan, or of Japan in general, and the most important of all.

> Twisted though it be
> a ladle serves to
> scoop things up
> Straight though it may seem
> a wooden pestle crushes

---

1 AN: Fujikawa Hideo, *Edo kōki no shijintachi* [Poets of the later Edo period] (Chikuma sōsho, 1972; Heibonsha Tōyō bunko no. 816, 2012).

2 A stringed instrument played with a bow.

3 AN: Fujikawa, op cit., 31–32.

4 These boats were large enough to hold as many as 30 *koku* of rice. A *koku* was a unit of rice equivalent to about 180 liters (5 bushels).

5 The *hototogisu*, or little cuckoo (*Cuculus poliocephalus*), is a bird appreciated for its early summer call.

6 AN: Fujikawa, op cit., 31. JWC: "Flowers and willows" suggests graceful urbanity, in contrast to the rusticity of mulberry leaves and hemp.

7 Chinese-influenced tea ceremony using leaf tea rather than powdered tea.

8 It was customary to settle all debts before the New Year. Master Groggy, however, lacks the wherewithal to do this.

9 AN: Nakano Mitsutoshi, Hino Tatsuo, and Ibi Takashi, eds., *Neboke sensei bunshū* [Master Groggy's literary collection], *Shin Nihon koten bungaku taikei* [New compendium of Japanese classical literature], vol. 84 (Iwanami shoten, 1993), 15–16.

10 AN: Nakano Mitsutoshi, et al., op cit., 263–265. JWC: Translated from Haga's rendition of the Chinese.

11 A reference to the ancient fable *Peach Blossom Spring* [*Taohua yuan ji*] by Tao Yuangming (ca. 365–427), in which a fisherman stumbles on a hidden utopia where people lead an ideal existence in peace and harmony.

12 AN: Nakano Mitsutoshi, et al., op. cit., 263–265. JWC: Based on Haga's translation from the Chinese.

13 AN: From a statement by novelist Takeda Taijun (1912–1976) at a roundtable discussion.

16 | THE FRENCH REVOLUTION AND JAPAN: MILD SPRING WEATHER IN A "LITTLE ICE AGE"

Jean Starobinski (1920–2019), the Swiss scholar of the eighteenth century whose interpretation of Jean-Jacques Rousseau set a new standard, wrote a fascinating book entitled *1789, The Emblems of Reason* (*1789, les emblèmes de la raison*, 1988).[1] He studied a cross-section of synchronistic artistic activities in Europe, in and around the year of the French Revolution, reading therein a system of emblems to explain how the peoples of Europe sensed and interpreted the historic changes of that time. In the book, Starobinski looks at a succession of artists including the Venetian painters Francesco Guardi (1712–1793) and Giovanni Battista Tiepolo (1696–1770); Francisco Goya (1746–1828), William Blake (1757–1827), and Jacques-Louis David (1748–1825); a variety of architects and urban planners; and Mozart and his *Magic Flute* (1791). While delving into the intricacies of each man's work, he offers a brilliant analysis of how the feelings that blazed up in search of *lumière*, revolution, and renaissance ended, after all, in the return of darkness.

I will forego a detailed discussion of Starobinski's analysis and focus on an early chapter in the book entitled "Cold Wave" ("*Vague froide*").

The winter of 1788–89 was bitter throughout Europe. Even the Venetian Lagoon in southern Europe froze over, and the Seine was chockablock with chunks of ice. The weather had been unsettled from summer on, and all across France the harvest was meager. As people struggled to make a living, unrest broke out, with widespread riots and looting. As many historians have pointed out, this *mentalité collective* was directly connected to the revolution that began six months later.

Starobinski uses *Winter* (*La Nevada*), a Goya painting from around 1786, to explain the privations of the harsh winter (Figure 53). Five farmers trudge across a dark wilderness, buffeted by a cold wind laced with snow. They are bent forward, their heads covered in sackcloth. Behind them is a donkey with a pig draped across its back. The painting is a vivid portrayal, says Starobinski, of life as penance. Even so, the peasants warm themselves with their internal fires, huddling close together as they brave the wind and snow to press on. In Starobinski's view, the painting shows the moving solidarity of people determined to live.

After that horrendous winter, spring was long in coming. Starobinski next cites a short passage from *Wishes of a Solitary Man* (*Voeux d'un solitaire*) by Jacques-Henri Bernardin de Saint-Pierre (1737–1814), written in May 1789, not long after *Winter* was painted and just six weeks before Bastille Day. He uses the painting to analyze how the inclement weather was seen as emblematic of the times. Bernardin de Saint-Pierre was living on the outskirts of Paris, fresh from a resounding success with the 1788 novel *Paul and Virginia*, a sweet pastoral set on Île de France (present-day Mauritius), an island then under French rule. This is what he wrote:[2]

> This year, on May 1, 1789, I went to the garden as the sun rose and took a look around. I wanted to check the status of my garden after the awful winter, because on December 31, for example, the temperature fell to 19 degrees below zero. On the way there, I recalled the dreadful damage from a hailstorm that had attacked the whole country on July 13 the year before. When I went into the garden, the cabbage, artichoke, white jasmine, and daffodils were gone. The carnations and hyacinths were all but wiped out. The fig tree and the linden viburnum, which always used to flower in January, were withered. Still-young ivy tendrils were dried out, the leaves rust-colored.
>
> Although their growth was behind by about three weeks, the

Figure 53. Goya, *Winter*. Museo del Prado.

other plants were all right. . . . The rows of grape, apple, pear, peach, plum, cherry, and apricot trees were all in bloom; the grape buds had just begun to open, while the apricot trees and others were already starting to bear fruit.

Is this spectacle of botanical life and death simply a natural phenomenon following the eternal order of nature, and is Bernardin de Saint-Pierre's appreciation of that microcosm a means for his cowering soul to flee the harshness of history? No, says Starobinski. As becomes even clearer in the passage after the one quoted above, Bernardin de Saint-Pierre understood that the dark shadow of contemporary history was mirrored in abnormalities in the natural world. The phenomena he observed were sensory images reflecting, in the material dimension, the collapse of state finances, the laxity of the establishment, and the misery of the people. They were badges of mourning, indications that the body politic was on its last legs. The above account is by no means a bit of extraneous scene-setting inserted into the text. Signs of spring in the garden, too, he took as prophetic signs of hope for the regeneration of all things. Starobinski goes on to argue that Bernardin de Saint-Pierre's associative interpretation of nature and history, coming at a time when the naive piety that read in all things an expression of divine will or Providence had lost currency, is all the more deeply revealing of the European state of mind in the spring of 1789.

This, however, is not the place to introduce Starobinski's thinking in full. And, having read this far, our minds are already turning to the distant Eastern Hemisphere where, on the western rim of the Pacific Ocean, lie the islands of Japan.

During the Pax Tokugawana, at precisely the same time as prerevolutionary France and Europe, Japan, too, was assailed by a succession of extraordinary natural disasters. Year in and year out, storms and fires in Japan are too frequent to enumerate, but in the winter of 1774 something unheard-of happened: a bitter cold wave caused the Sumida River to freeze over. In 1779 and 1780, volcanic eruptions shook the islands of Izu Ōshima, off the Izu Peninsula, and Sakurajima, in Kyushu, while heavy summer rains overwhelmed rivers in the Kanto area, causing disastrous floods. The year 1782 had unstable weather and frequent earthquakes; oceanic waters, too, were evidently affected, for that year no Dutch ships came calling. The next summer, the eruption of Mount Asama in central Honshu and a cold spell led to a nationwide famine.

And in Japan, too, someone observed these natural disasters that seemed to portend the end of the world and recorded, year by year, the poverty, unrest, and rioting with as much detail and sociopsychological insight as Bernardin de Saint-Pierre, Goya, or Hogarth, seeing in it the upheaval and deadlock of the establishment. That man was one of the translators of *A New Book of Anatomy*, the Dutch-style physician Sugita Gempaku. The record he kept, entitled *Looking Back* (*Nochimigusa*),[3] covers the years from 1760 to 1786. At times more impetuous than Bernardin de Saint-Pierre, Gempaku not only interpreted natural disturbances as emblems of the death and rebirth of the establishment but sometimes adopted a harsh tone, accusing the authorities of incompetence and corruption. Even so, his writings are more objective and even more scientific than those of Bernardin de Saint-Pierre, who also wrote *Studies of Nature*. Gempaku faithfully recorded disasters like those mentioned above, both natural and man-made, and gave graphic descriptions of the damage from the cold weather and famine of 1783–1785 that hit the northeastern Tōhoku area particularly hard, using the wide network of information available to him as a physician.

For example, in the final year of the record, 1786, Gempaku described the latest series of disasters as follows:

> In this year of the fire horse, from midway through the first month to the end of the second month, Kanto experienced day after day of high, destructive winds and abnormal dryness, so that in Edo great fires sprang up every few days; people's hearts were full of terror, wild rumors flew, and prices soared. In the fourth month there was a sudden change, and in the fifth and sixth months the weather was abnormally cold, with long rainy spells. As a result, from the twelfth day of the seventh month, storms grew particularly violent, and finally on the eighteenth, there was unprecedented flooding in the Kanto area. Damage was especially heavy in Edo.
>
> Of floods in places near the city limits, there were many after Tōshōgu shrine was moved to Kanto,[4] but the worst was in 1742. This year, the flooding has been incomparably more severe. From the middle of the fourth month, there was such incessant rain that the ground became exhausted, or perhaps a water vein burst, so that in Aoyama and Ushigome, located in the elevated Yamanote part of the city, roads split open and water gushed out in all directions. In some places, people traveled by boat. . . . Worse still, floodwaters in lowland areas like Honjō and Fukagawa were more than 1.2 meters above the average for the Kampō era [1741–1744]. Bridges across the Sumida River in Eitai, Ryōgoku, and Shin-Ōhashi were swept away. As far as I could see, the damage was terrible, and I can only imagine how bad it may have

been farther on. As if that weren't enough, since this year's rice crop and other harvests were poor, and every little thing was swept away and lost, people were in desperate straits with nowhere to buy enough vegetables for even a day or two. The water did not recede and remained for a month or two, leaving roads in Dewa and Mutsu[5] provinces impassable and increasing food shortages. It was a flood disaster of rare proportions, and everyone was terrified.[6]

Gempaku's account of this record-breaking flood allows us to imagine the faces of the Edo populace, people with literally nowhere to turn. Amid fears that the annual recurrence of these major disasters might portend upheaval in human affairs as well, Senior Counselor Tanuma Okitsugu, who had long wielded central power in the shogunate, was suddenly ousted in the middle of the flooding, in summer 1786. A month later, the tenth shogun, Ieharu, died. "Tanuma culture," whose splendor and uncertainty exactly matches the description Starobinski gave rococo culture under the old establishment—a "style of extravagance"—rapidly lost its sheen.

Heavy rain continued to fall even after the government was taken over by Ienari, the eleventh shogun, and Senior Counselor Matsudaira Sadanobu. Revolts and riots continued to break out, but Gempaku now interpreted them according to the saying *ame futte chi katamaru* ("rain strengthens the ground" or "adversity strengthens the foundations"). He ends his singular, critical account of contemporary history on a note of faint hope for calm after the storm.

On the one hand, a cold wave that struck Europe on the eve of the French Revolution and the semiotic interpretation assigned to it by a contemporary writer; on the other, a succession of natural disasters at the exact same time in 1780s Japan, and a Dutch-style physician's historical diagnosis: a comparison of these two, taking into account their remarkable commonality and slight difference (Gempaku took the Asian approach that "the path of righteousness is to submit to the dictates of nature") may be enough to establish a comparative cultural history of the eighteenth century. I think to a certain extent it is enough. Such synchronistic comparisons are far more interesting, wholesome, and intellectually challenging than, say, comparing the rational thought of the Confucian thinker Ogyū Sorai (1666–1728) with theological thought in medieval and Renaissance Europe and arguing over how relatively advanced or behind his European counterparts he may have been. However, the synchronicity of abnormal weather conditions in East and West might be coincidental, and so perhaps no such overview could escape the charge of arbitrariness.

Fortunately, a powerful suggestion from meteorologist Yamamoto Takeo erases that apprehension. Yamamoto's research[7] indicates that from the latter half of the eighteenth century through the first half of the nineteenth century, the North Pacific region and the North Atlantic region both went through a "little ice age." The high-pressure system in each region was part of a larger high-pressure system encircling the globe at the middle latitudes and moving the same way in the long term. In the time period in question, that zone moved south, sending the distribution of low-pressure zones farther south and disrupting wind patterns. Yamamoto refers to two hundred and sometimes four hundred years' worth of data from Europe, including such categories as the frequency of southwest winds in the London area and the average monthly temperature in the Netherlands. Since comparable data on the Japanese side is scant, he graphed the frequency of long rainfall, floods, famine, and the annual average number of village riots in the Tokugawa period as recorded in the *Chronology of Calamities in Iwate Prefecture* (*Iwate-ken saii nempyō*). He found a clear correlation in climate irregularities in East and West and also demonstrated plainly that they caused social upheaval.

In Japan, the worst of the ice age fell in the half century from 1783 to 1837, bookended by the Temmei famine (1783–1786) and the Tempō famine (1833–1837). The same holds true for Europe, where the time span covered by Bernardin de Saint-Pierre's observations was bookended by the French Revolution (1789–1799), and the long Napoleonic Wars (1803–15). The harsh winter of 1812–1813, when Napoleon's Moscow expedition ended in failure, was also a time of extreme cold in Japan: not only the Sumida River in Edo but also the Yodo and other rivers in the Kansai region froze over. Concerning the Great Kanto Flood of 1786, Yamamoto also cites the above passage from Sugita Gempaku's *Looking Back*, pointing out that such floods do not take place by chance, but "occur in concentration at the apex of long-term climatic upheaval."[8]

In this way, Bernardin de Saint-Pierre and Sugita Gempaku, although separated by tens of thousands of kilometers and of course having no connection whatever, both observed the little ice age that befell the middle latitudes of the northern hemisphere in the late eighteenth century and recorded its abnormal consequences. Each interpreted it according to his culture and personality. I must also mention Gilbert White (1720–1793), a natural historian in Selborne, England, who carefully recorded the severe cold of 1768 and 1776 as well as the unusually severe summer heat and natural disasters of 1781 and 1783. I would venture to say that the reason all of these men left detailed records had less to do with an interest in natural science or indignation at people's suffering than with the abnormal cold of which they were to some extent aware. The eschatology which all three shared was certainly influenced by long spells of cold and rain. (It is also interesting to note that the previous little ice age to affect both East and West was in the mid-fifteenth century, or right around the time of Kyoto's dreadfully destructive Ōnin War of 1467–1477.)

But, to shift our focus from climate history to international relations, the French Revolution that took place during the abnormal cold of the little ice age ended up assuring that Japan, which was also affected by the same little ice age of the northern hemisphere, would enjoy, if not decades more of the Pax Tokugawana, at least a sociopolitical Indian summer. That is the strongest direct impact of the French Revolution on Japan. In other words, for thirty years after 1789, while Tokugawa Japan may have experienced some friction in its foreign relations, it was able to preserve an "Indian summer" of peace unlike the turmoil that followed the Tempō era precisely because of the commotion that preoccupied Europe after the French Revolution.

From the Western perspective, Japan was a tiny island nation in the Far East, farther off even than China, and in the minds of many a troublesome country that had put up a protective wall around itself through a stubborn policy of national isolation. But if the Western powers had not been plunged into continuing chaos and upheaval by the French Revolutionary Wars (1789–1799) and Napoleonic Wars (1799–1814), they would certainly have used their energies to compete in attacking Japan from the north and the southwest, easily wrecking Japan's daydream of Great Peace. That, it seems to me, was the greatest political influence the French Revolution had on Japan.

Actually, in the latter half of the eighteenth century, the "calm of the four seas" encircling the islands of Japan was not necessarily as great as the occupants of those islands imagined. An expedition led by British naval captain James Cook surveyed the North Pacific from 1776 to 1779. A few years later, Frenchman Jean François de Galaup, comte de La Pérouse, acting on orders from Louis XVI, led a fleet on a grand voyage of exploration (1785–1788) in the course of which, completely unbeknownst to the Japanese, he circled the archipelago, mapped the coastline, and discovered La Pérouse Strait (present-day Sōya Strait) between Sakhalin and Hokkaido before moving on to the South Pacific.

Even more than Britain and France, Russia, of course, had long held great interest in its neighbor, Japan. Already in 1739, in accordance with the dying instructions of Peter the Great, the naval lieutenant Martin Spangberg had led a squadron south from Okhotsk to survey the Japanese coastline, stirring a brief sensation over "the Black Ships of Gembun" (a reference to the era name). After that, there were periodic tangles with Russia in Ezochi (present-day Hokkaido). In 1771, the Hungarian military officer Maurice Benyovsky (or Hambengoro, as he became known in Japan) escaped from prison on Kamchatka, and when he landed on Amami-Ōshima, an island between Kyushu and Okinawa, he notified the Dutch in Nagasaki of a planned Russian invasion of Ezochi. This, however, turned out to be a false rumor of uncertain motivation. Years later, when Kudō Heisuke and Hayashi Shihei of the Sendai domain heard of this report, they were astonished; Kudō wrote *Thoughts on the Russia Rumor* (*Aka Ezo fūsetsu kō*, 1783) and Hayashi wrote *Military Defense of a Maritime Nation* (*Kaikō heidan*, 1786).

By the time Kudō and Hayashi began sounding warnings and criticizing the shogunate's stance, Benyovsky's information was no longer a false rumor. In 1792, Adam Kirillovich Laxman landed at Nemuro in Hokkaido on orders from Catherine II, accompanied by Daikokuya Kōdayū and another Japanese castaway. Laxman was the first representative of a nation other than the Netherlands or China to seek a trade agreement with the shogunate, and he paved the way for formal negotiations.

Since various countries had begun to take action vis-à-vis Japan, why did they not go on to mount strong enough attacks to tear down the vulnerable wall of isolationism that surrounded the country? One likely reason is the abnormally concentric eddies of change that arose on the European continent after the French Revolution. Across the channel from France, Britain was putting up tenacious resistance to the revolution and Napoleon, while also using its strikingly modern industrial and naval power to defeat France in a series of conflicts over French colonies in India and Canada. When the Netherlands came under French domination, Britain promptly took over Dutch colonial interests and consolidated its standing in Southeast Asia, achieving absolute supremacy even in Canton trade by the 1790s. At least for the time being, Britain was too deeply engaged elsewhere to make a move on Japan and had no need to do so.

But what of Russia, the country closest to Japan? Even if dispatching Laxman as envoy had been simply an adventure designed to test Japanese mettle, after he returned with documents from Senior Counselor Matsudaira Sadanobu granting Russia access to Nagasaki harbor, no sustained effort was made to put them to good use. In her final years, Catherine II's attention was absorbed rather by great issues of Western diplomacy, including the Franco-Russian Alliance of 1793, suppression of the anti-Russian movement in Poland, and the final partition of Poland in 1794—all while she was enacting repressive measures against malcontents at home. Even after hearing Laxman's report on his mission, she no doubt lacked the leisure to pursue Russian interests in the Far East.

Finally in 1804, some ten years after Laxman, the Russian minister plenipotentiary Nikolai Petrovich Rezanov arrived in Nagasaki bearing the trade documents his predecessor had been granted and a personal request from Alexander I to open the country. He and his party stayed in Nagasaki for nearly a year, striving to achieve their goal. Although they did greatly unsettle the Japanese, in the end they were forced to withdraw with nothing to show for their efforts. Stress ran high in Japan at the time, however. Kobayashi Issa (1763–1827), a farmer-poet living hand to mouth on the outskirts of Edo, was moved to write a haiku praying for continued peace in the land.

> Be more like
> the land of spring breezes,
> Russian ships

Issa's prayer notwithstanding, Rezanov and his Russian fleet took revenge for their diplomatic failure by committing various outrages in Hokkaido before returning home. Due to Russia's domestic weakness and the burden of the Napoleonic Wars, which were then unfolding with increasing intensity, Russia was unable to force Japan to open by applying powerful, planned, continuous pressure.

Four years after Rezanov's visit to Japan, in 1808, the British frigate HMS *Phaeton* entered Nagasaki harbor, bowing to pressure from Napoleon to seize the last rights and interests of the Netherlands, which had come under French domination. This incident, which shook Japanese people more profoundly than any of the previous ones, was the most direct effect of international events on Japan in the wake of the French Revolution. However, unlike the mutual restraints European nations imposed on one another, which gave Japan a major reprieve in having to open the country, the *Phaeton* incident had no lingering impact.

After 1808, Dutch ships ceased calling, and Hendrik Doeff (1777–1835), the director of the Dutch trading post in Nagasaki, was isolated without word from his home country and without butter or wine. Britain, having won naval supremacy in Asia, took over the Dutch colony of Java in 1811. Doeff, who stuck it out on Dejima for nine years before a ship flying the Dutch flag at long last came for him, was perhaps the person who suffered the most in Japan during the Napoleonic Wars.

But during that time, unmolested by "foreign devils," Japanese people enjoyed their last days of halcyon peace in the Pax Tokugawana.

And yet—

> From this day on
> geese of Japan
> sleep in peace

> Cherries bloom away
> in Great Nippon—
> in Nippon, hurrah!

> These end-times—
> everywhere you look
> cherry blossoms!

> Butterfly flits
> as if without a hope
> in this world

> In blossoms' shade
> no sleep for me
> for fear of what may come

The haiku poet Kobayashi Issa came to emphasize Japan in his works, and to reveal intimations of a coming end, perhaps because even he, intrepid nationalist that he was, had begun to feel a remote sense of uncertainty concerning the world, both in and out of Japan. Indeed, once the European mainland had begun to stabilize (and the little ice age was nearly over), in the 1820s and 1830s, warships of the Western powers, with Britain in the lead, began to frequent the seas around Japan. The Pax Tokugawana that had filled the archipelago over the past two hundred and more years would soon end, and people would experience the opening of the country and the Meiji Restoration— changes not necessarily for the better.

1 AN: Jean Starobinski, 1789: *The Emblems of Reason*, Barbara Bray, trans. (Cambridge: MIT Press, 1988).

2 AN: Henri-Jacques Bernardin de Saint-Pierre, *Les Voeux d'un solitaire* [*Wishes of a solitary man*] (Paris: Didot, 1789), 1–2. JWC: Translated from Haga's translation of the French. https://books.google.co.jp/books?id=lfo9AAAAcAAJ&printsec=frontcover&source=gbs_ge_summary_r&cad=0#v=onepage&q&f =false

3 AN: Iwamoto Katoshi, ed., op. cit., vol. 2, 408–462. https://dl.ndl.go.jp/info:ndl-jp/pid/991268

4 Tokugawa Ieyasu (1543–1616), founder of the Tokugawa shogunate, was first buried on Mt. Kuno in Shizuoka. His remains were moved to Nikkō in 1617.

5 The Tōhoku region, consisting of present-day Yamagata, Akita, Fukushima, Miyagi, Iwate, and Aomori prefectures.

6 Iwamoto Katōshi, ed., op. cit., 447. JWC: This passage was summarized in modern Japanese.

7 AN: Yamamoto Takeo, *Kikō no kataru Nihon no rekishi* [Climate and Japanese history] (Soshiete bunko, 1976), 134.

8 Ibid., 136.

Part

V

17 | TOWARD THE END OF THE PAX TOKUGAWANA

Shimazaki Tōson's Recollections from Paris

Shimazaki Tōson sailed to Paris on a French ship in mid-April 1913, at age forty-one. The next summer, when World War I broke out and France joined the fighting, he evacuated temporarily to Limoges in central France, but in mid-November he moved back into his *pension* on Rue de Port-Royal, near the Luxembourg Gardens in Paris. He continued living there until the end of April 1916, as the city came under direct attack from German airplanes and airships. He returned to Japan in July.

During his first two years in Paris (August 1913–August 1915), Tōson faithfully wrote up news of the city mixed with cross-cultural observations. These pieces appeared intermittently in the *Tokyo Asahi Shimbun* newspaper. In 1915, while he was still in Paris, they were published in book form under the titles *Paris at Peace* (*Heiwa no Pari*) for the first half and *War and Paris* (*Sensō to Pari*) for the second. Later Shinchōsha published them in two volumes under the title *Tidings from France* (*Furansudayori*). Volume I appeared in September 1924, preceded by Volume II in June 1922. The fee and royalties for these works paid Tōson's living expenses in Paris.

I bring up Tōson's *Tidings from France* here because a passage in *War and Paris* is surprisingly rich in implications about Japanese cultural and intellectual history in the latter half of the Tokugawa period. The fourth of eleven essays gathered under the title *Awaiting Spring* (*Haru o machitsutsu*), it was written in Paris on March 13, 1915, and published on May 5 of that year in the *Tokyo Asahi*. Though the season was early spring, Parisian skies offered only "a glimmer of pale yellow light" or "clusters of pink clouds"; the city remained enveloped in a deep dark fog. From his *pension* window Tōson could look down at the street below lined with plane trees, where a unit of French infantry often came to relax.

Here is the passage:

> If only someone would write a study of nineteenth century Japan! I would read it with great pleasure. The division between the Meiji era and the Tokugawa period is often pointed out, but when one thinks of the past century as a whole, a different perspective arises. First I would like to read a study beginning with the death of Motoori Norinaga. Studies of the *Man'yōshū*, the revival of the spirit of classical poetry, love and respect for the Japanese language—I would like to read about the effect such developments had on the rise of classicism in the nineteenth century. I would like to read about whether that was in any degree the foundation for the awakening of national consciousness that took place around then. I would also like to read about how at the start of that era, with the deaths of Kitagawa Utamaro, Minakawa Kien, and Ueda Akinari, characteristic eighteenth-century arts gradually gave way to the naturalist tendencies of Santō Kyōden, Shikitei Samba, Jippensha Ikku, Tamenaga Shunsui, and the Utagawa school of painters.
>
> While on the one hand, literary arts, pastimes, and morals were overlaid with a longing for China, with Yushima Seidō[1] as the center of learning, at the same time Dutch studies were progressing with great momentum. In the early nineteenth century, old and new co-existed chaotically. I would like to read about that in detail. Some say that the Japan of today was formed in the short space of forty or fifty years after the first systematic attempts to introduce Western things, but I find that way of thinking altogether too self-deprecating. One must look at least

a century further back. The first half of the nineteenth century has to be seen as a time of preparation. I want to read all about how men like Maeno Ryōtaku, Katsuragawa Hosan, Sugita Gempaku, and Ōtsuki Genkan, as well as Adachi Sanai, Takahashi Sakuzaemon, Itō Keisuke, and Adachi Chōshun laid the foundations for the coming age.

Rai San'yō is someone else from that era who cannot be overlooked. His writings are a mixed bag, but there is no doubt that they charmed the minds of people of that generation. And yet he retains a distinctly nineteenth-century flavor. Watanabe Kazan, Takano Chōei, and Yoshida Shōin introduce a new mold of samurai. They are more fervent in their passions, more practical in their ideology, fresher in their learning. Their rebellious, angry natures, taken together with their tragic willingness to sacrifice themselves, reveal a violent agitation and a sensitivity unique to the nineteenth century and are tinged with hues of the new age. If only there were a book explaining all that in detail, I would love to read it.

The nineteenth century was a time when the old was being gradually abandoned and the new had not yet fully materialized. All things were crying out for consolidation. At the same time, the great intellectual class of samurai was disappearing. This surely gave rise to many tragedies. I want to read about them. I want to read something that demonstrates how the *gembun itchi* movement[2] begun by Hasegawa Futabatei, Yamada Bimyō, Ozaki Kōyō, and others contributed to the consolidation of the Japanese language. New forms of poetry also began to appear on the scene finally at the end of the nineteenth century.[3]

After the leisurely examination of the Pax Tokugawana we have undertaken in this book, I cannot think of a more fitting or more insightful passage to cite as we turn now to the approaching end of that time. When I read the bulky work *The Crisis of the European Conscience 1680–1715* (*La crise de la conscience europeénne*, 1935) by Paul Hazard, the French pioneer of comparative literature, I wondered when a similar *crise* of sensibility and conscience might have arisen in modern Japan, and while groping for an answer I happened to come across Tōson's *Tidings from France*. My eyes opened in shock and admiration.

This fascinating passage, so full of repeated assertions that if Tōson had books containing studies of nineteenth-century Japan, he would gladly read them, gives the impression that he is pouring out thoughts he has been cogitating on ever since arriving in France. The essays before and after this one contain observations on civilian life in wartime Paris or touch on the patriotic manifestos of politicians and men of letters, which makes this sudden riff on modern Japanese history all the more notable. The style, moreover, conveys a sense of exhilaration. After nearly two years of viewing Japan from afar in Paris, Tōson has acquired a broad outlook on Japanese history, the history of modern Japan in particular. His bird's-eye view affords him the right perspective for a reappraisal. Amid the crisis of world war, the words and conduct of European intellectuals as they begin to seek a path of escape and renewal put him in mind of how in the nineteenth century Japan, beset by a host of domestic troubles and external threats, turned toward unification as a modern nation-state. He must have entertained new ideas about that historical narrative.

The opening line is arresting: "The division between the Meiji era and the Tokugawa period is often pointed out, but when one thinks of the past century as a whole, a different perspective arises." The suggestion sounds fresh even today. Now at the start of the twenty-first century, one hundred years after Tōson wrote these words, history books that view the cultural and intellectual history of Meiji and Tokugawa as a whole remain scarce.

Tōson calls the accumulation of studies by Motoori Norinaga (1730–1801) and others of Japanese classics like the *Kojiki* and *Man'yōshū* "the effect of classicism." He says he wants to know how such nativist studies led to the awakening of a "national consciousness" or national identity in nineteenth-century Japanese people. These words presage his own attempt to portray early modern Japan a dozen years later in the novel

Before the Dawn. He does not overlook the trend toward realism and the increasingly colorful popularization of Tokugawa culture by writers of *sharebon* (gay-quarter novelettes), *ninjōbon* (sentimental fiction), and *gesaku* (light fiction) such as Jippensha Ikku (1765–1831) and Tamenaga Shunsui (1790–1843), or by ukiyo-e masters such as Kunisada (1786–1864), Kuniyoshi (1797–1861), and Hiroshige (1797–1858). This shows the ambition of Tōson the novelist to fully capture the changes in nineteenth-century Japanese culture and society without dividing it into intellectual history, literary history, and art history.

What stands out above all in this passage is that while acknowledging the power of Confucian studies and Chinese classics, the mainstays of Tokugawa scholarship, Tōson emphasizes the historic significance of the dual threat to traditional Confucian and classical Chinese scholarship posed by *rangaku* and *yōgaku* on the one hand, and by nativist studies on the other.

Perhaps Tōson had in mind a famous lecture that Natsume Sōseki gave in 1911, entitled "The Civilization of Modern-Day Japan" (*Gendai Nihon no kaika*), in which Sōseki said: "If the Westerners, whose mental and physical powers far surpass ours, took a hundred years to get where they are now, and we were able to reach that point in less than half that time (forgetting for the moment the difficulties they faced as pioneers), then we could certainly boast of an astounding intellectual accomplishment, but we would also succumb to an incurable nervous breakdown."[4] Tōson is dismissive of the accepted wisdom that, as Sōseki implies, Japan had only been engaged in systematically accepting Western civilization for the forty or fifty years since the Restoration, finding "that way of thinking altogether too self-deprecating." He asserts that to understand Japan's history of studying and absorbing Western civilization "one must look at least a century further back," and he sees in that history a source of intellectual and cultural continuity from Tokugawa to Meiji.

Tōson's choice of pioneers in Western learning is interesting. Maeno Ryōtaku and Sugita Gempaku are there, naturally. Tōson also includes in his list a Katsuragawa Hosan whose given name is written with the characters 甫粲. I believe that Tōson is mistaken here and actually meant the Katsuragawa Hosan (1730–1783; also Kuninori) whose given name is written with the characters 甫三. This latter Hosan was a third-generation physician of the highest order who attended the shogun.* An able guide, Hosan would take Ryōtaku and Gempaku, as well as Hiraga Gennai and others, with him to call on the Dutch consul in the Nagasakiya inn in Koku-cho, Edo, and engage in dialogue. When his son Hoshū (1751–1809) translated *A New Book of Anatomy* along with Ryōtaku, Gempaku, and Nakagawa Jun'an, it was the father's idea to present a copy to the shogun to avoid censure from the shogunate. If Tōson was going to include the father, he should also have included the son, who edited the Russian reminiscences of the castaway Daikokuya Kodayū, *A Brief Account of a Northern Drift* (*Hokusa bunryaku*, 1794).

By the same token, if Tōson had mentioned Ōtsuki Genkan (1785–1837), who worked at the shogunate's Office for Translation of Barbarian Books (Bansho Wage Goyō Kyoku), then he should also have mentioned Genkan's father, Ōtsuki Gentaku (1757–1827), a *rangaku* scholar in a direct line from Ryōtaku and Gempaku who headed the Shirandō Academy in Edo and taught many distinguished pupils. Tōson's list would be even more impressive if it included Hiraga Gennai, Shiba Kōkan, and Honda Toshiaki, men at the end of the eighteenth century who possessed "unquiet spirits."[5]

Tōson's list of those who "laid the foundations for the coming age" further includes Takahashi Kageyasu (1785–1829), head of the shogunate's Astronomy Institute (Temmongata), who was jailed for his involvement in the Siebold incident[6] and died in prison, and Itō Keisuke (1803–1901),

---

* AN: When I first wrote these remarks, I was unfamiliar with the name Katsuragawa Hosan 甫粲, whom Tōson ranks alongside Maeno Ryōtaku and Sugita Gempaku. That name does not appear in either the history of the Katsuragawa family by Imaizumi Genkichi (1891–1969), who was himself a Katsuragawa descendent, or a biographical dictionary of students of Western studies. I later discovered that Katsuragawa Hosan 甫粲 was the birth name of Morishima Chūryō (1756–1810), the son of Hosan 甫三 , younger brother of Hoshū (mentioned below), and junior colleague of Hiraga Gennai. I am struck anew by how well informed Tōson was.

who studied with Siebold and introduced the Linnaean plant classification system to Japan, choices that are easy to understand. Other names are less familiar to us: Adachi Sanai (1769–1845), Takahashi Kageyasu's assistant in calendar study, later learned Russian in Matsumae, Hokkaido, and became one of the first Japanese to master the language; Adachi Chōshun (1776–1836) introduced Western-style obstetrics to Japan. What materials on Japanese scholars of Western studies Tōson may have had access to in Paris is unknown, but certainly his interest in the field was both wide-ranging and deep.[7]

Rangaku began in the eighteenth century with the study of surgical anatomy and broadened to include various fields of Western medicine. In the nineteenth century, it expanded swiftly to embrace geography, languages, astronomy, and natural history. As Gempaku noted with joy at the end of his vivid memoir *Dawn of Western Science in Japan*, "If a drop of oil is put into a pond, it will spread and cover the entire pond." The original of Gempaku's book was lost until Kanda Kōhei, a friend of *rangaku*, found it in a stall behind Yushima Seidō in 1867. When Fukuzawa Yukichi (1834–1901) heard this, realizing the magnitude of the discovery, he arranged for the book to be published in 1869 as a block book.

Fukuzawa had a discerning eye for the fundamental trends of history. Seven years after the republication of Sugita Gempaku's *Dawn of Western Science in Japan*, on September 28, 1876, there was a memorial service held at the Ōtsuki home in Hongō Kinsuke-chō to commemorate the forty-ninth anniversary of the passing of Ōtsuki Gentaku. Fukuzawa, on behalf of all Gentaku's successors, read a tribute to the *rangaku* pioneer. His remarks contained the following superb commentary on the significance of Tokugawa *rangaku* in Japan's intellectual history.

Historical change, he maintained, is effected neither by revolution nor by war nor by government policy. Rather,

> All such change is part of human affairs, deriving fundamentally from changes in the human heart and tracing back without exception to intangible circumstances. A century before us, our

predecessor in Western studies had already nurtured the elements of such changes in the human heart, passing them on as a legacy that lives today, and so clearing the brambles from the path of civilization. . . . Our predecessor's achievement is great, and the grace he has bestowed on us is a thing of beauty.[8]

Could it be that Shimazaki Tōson had read this famous passage and remembered it while he was in Paris? The likelihood of that seems slim, yet one part of *Tidings from France* echoes Fukuzawa's words.

More than a dozen years after his memorial address, Fukuzawa wrote a long introduction to a new edition of *Dawn of Western Science in Japan*, dated April 1, 1890, in which he further emphasizes the significance of early Western studies in Japan.

> The republication of *Dawn of Western Science in Japan* should not merely enhance recognition of our predecessor's achievements throughout Japan but also demonstrate to people of every nation that nearly 120 years ago in the Asian nation of Japan, Western civilization had already begun taking root in the community of scholars, and that present progress is no coincidence.[9]

Rereading these words now, I realize that while living in Paris, Tōson likely felt the same way as Fukuzawa. In speaking with his Parisian friends and acquaintances, both Japanese and French, he must have found that among intellectuals of both nationalities, the belief was widespread that Japan had begun the study of Western civilization only after the Meiji Restoration, and hence its understanding of the West and its modernization were still extremely shallow. This discovery must have mortified him. With the private intention of refuting that popular belief, surely he set out, like Fukuzawa, to "demonstrate to people of every nation" that Japan's "present progress" was "no coincidence." His words seem to show indignation on behalf of the pioneer scholars in Tokugawa Japan and pride in his country's modern history. The vigorous style of the passage, as if it were dashed off in one sitting, helps to convey that impression.

As I touched on briefly before, in the nineteenth century, Western studies in Japan expanded beyond medicine to embrace the fields of natural science, the humanities, and social science. In the first half of the 1800s, as foreign vessels began to appear with increasing frequency off the Japanese coast, Western studies proliferated to include domestic and foreign politics, society, and military affairs. This development marked the shift from *rangaku* (Dutch studies) to *yōgaku* (Western studies) and was sharply influenced by criticism of the Tokugawa system, which was then being shaken by domestic troubles and external threats, and a sense that the two-hundred-year-long Pax Tokugawana was in danger.

At the end of the passage quoted above, Tōson declares Rai San'yō (1780–1832), the author of *An Unofficial History of Japan* (*Nihon gaishi*, 1829) and a strong supporter of the emperor, to be less representative of the nineteenth-century "new mold of samurai" than Watanabe Kazan (1793–1841), Takano Chōei (1804–1850), and Yoshida Shōin (1830–1859). This is a fascinating and completely accurate assessment.

When Tōson recalled those new samurai intellectuals of nineteenth-century Japan in his Paris lodgings, he surely visualized them in action and entered into their feelings with greater intimacy and immediacy than when he was in Japan. His comments, though brief, are very empathetic and amazingly true to life. To quote him again, "Their rebellious, angry natures, taken together with their tragic willingness to sacrifice themselves, reveal a violent agitation and a sensitivity unique to the nineteenth century and are tinged with hues of the new age."

Tōson immediately continues, "If only there were a book explaining all that in detail, I would love to read it." What he longed for was not the sort of book that treats the political, intellectual, or diplomatic history of nineteenth-century Japan, or the history of Western learning, in isolation. He was hoping for a new kind of history book, one containing a history of the spirit unique to nineteenth-century Japan underlying all those other fields—a history in particular of the psychological and emotional paroxysms that drove samurai elite. This was a view of history that remains fresh today and demonstrates keen and instinctive understanding, as one might well expect from the future author of *Before the Dawn*, that epic novel of the final years of the shogunate and the first two decades of the new era.

Takano Chōei, a Western scholar who studied under Siebold and became friends with Watanabe Kazan, was an indomitable fighter, judged later to have been "preposterous, outrageous, obstinate...utterly willful."[10] Sakuma Shōzan (1811–1864), another *yōgaku* scholar and a gunner, described himself as he had been while in prison: "My will was resolutely opposed and indignant, my mind set and increasingly concerned."[11] At his encouragement, his pupil Yoshida Shōin, a *shishi* or "man of high purpose," set out at the age of twenty-four to learn about the world. Intending to "use the foreigner to defeat the foreigner," late at night on the twenty-seventh of the third month, 1854, Shōin climbed aboard the flagship *Powhatan* in Perry's fleet anchored off Shimoda, bearing a piece of paper that said, "I want to go to America."

Those men's associates and successors in Western studies include Egawa Tarōzaemon (1801–1855), Kawaji Toshiakira (1801–1868), Takashima Shūhan (1798–1866), Sano Tsunetami (1823–1902), and Fukuzawa Yukichi, as well as Sakamoto Ryōma (1836–1867), Katsu Kaishū (1823–1899), and Nakaoka Shintarō (1838–1867). But their lineage knows no end. Of the three intellectual samurai named by Tōson, Watanabe Kazan had the greatest understanding of the lives of the general populace in the Pax Tokugawana. He also foresaw the end of that time of peace, groped toward a reform of the Tokugawa establishment by learning about the West, and ultimately, due to his criticisms of the establishment, took his own life. Kazan was also perhaps the most cultured samurai of his day, a painter as well as a scholar of Western studies. I will close with a consideration of his portraits, which in themselves form a psychohistorical record of that era.

Watanabe Kazan and the Pax Tokugawana

Right now, I have before me a thin exhibition catalogue entitled only *Watanabe Kazan*. It is just thirty pages long. The last page is inscribed, "Sponsored by Nihon Keizai Shimbunsha. Supported by the Cultural Properties Protection Committee. August 15–20 at Nihombashi Mitsukoshi."

The year of the exhibition, however, is nowhere to be found. Marveling that exhibition catalogues used to be so abbreviated, I thumbed through the book and found at the very end of the chronology of Kazan's life the notation, "Shōwa 36 (1961): Exhibition of Kazan's Greatest Works." Then I finally understood. Elsewhere, I found a column mentioning: "This year marks the one hundred twentieth anniversary of Kazan's death."

Then it all made sense. After the crackdown known as the "Suppression of the Barbarian Studies Group" (*Bansha no goku*), Watanabe Kazan, along with Takano Chōei and others, escaped the death penalty and was sentenced to house arrest in Tahara. However, on the eleventh day of the tenth month of 1841, at age forty-eight, he took his own life by *seppuku* (ritual disembowelment), just 120 years before the 1961 exhibition commemorating him.

In 1961, I was unemployed, having just returned from France to the doctoral course at my university. I lived on a stipend of twenty thousand yen a month (then equivalent to USD55.55) from a public institution as support of my research on "The Crisis of Awareness in Early-Modern Japan." In the course of that research, I happened to read *The Iwakura Embassy, 1871–73: A True Account of the Ambassador Extraordinary & Plenipotentiary's Journey of Observation through the United States of America and Europe* (*Tokumei zenken taishi Bei-Ō kairan jikki*), the five-volume report by Kume Kunitake published in 1878. I found the account fascinating and had just finished writing an article on it.

The members of the mission were leaders of the new government, former shogunate diplomats and samurai who had become elite government officials. The keenness of their intellect in grasping the overall picture and the particulars of Western civilization, and the strength of their courage and sense of mission, amazed me. To learn more about the intellectual environment that had nurtured them, I began to shift my attention from the Meiji Restoration to the waning days of the Tokugawa period and further back, intending to examine in my own way the development of Dutch studies and Western studies in eighteenth- and nineteenth-century Japan. I must have set off for Mitsukoshi Department Store eager to find out more about Watanabe Kazan, one of the premier samurai intellectuals of nineteenth-century Japan. The exhibition of his art surprised me by showing his soft side, the richness of his inner life.

Of course, I took a close look at the National Treasure *Portrait of Takami Senseki* (*Takami Senseki zō*, 1837), which shows that Kazan had already mastered the principle of shading through his study of Western art, masterfully incorporating it into the traditional painting style to portray the dashing appearance of Takami Senseki (1785–1858), an early *rangaku* scholar and a chief retainer of the Koga domain (present-day Ibaraki prefecture). The black-and-white ink portrait of the Confucian scholar Tachihara Suiken (1744–1823, Figure 54), whose son Kyōsho was Kazan's friend and a fellow pupil of the painter Tani Bunchō, I also found striking. Perhaps because Kazan had met Suiken as a young man, he portrayed his face with keen brushstrokes, emphasizing the eyes and nose, the tightly drawn lips and unshaven jaw, and bringing to vivid life the spirit of the aged scholar of *soraigaku*, Ogyū Sorai's Mito school of Neo-Confucianism. The exhibition also featured portraits of Kazan's teacher, the Confucian scholar Satō Issai (1772–1859), who taught at the Shōheikō Academy, and of the celebrated calligrapher Ichikawa Beian (1779–1858), including both the finished portraits and preliminary sketches. In both cases, the sketches are more penetrating in style than the finished work, giving their subjects a look of harsh repugnance. Later on, when I learned that at the time of Kazan's persecution, those two men, unlike others in Kazan's circle, had made no effort to spare his life, I recalled the harshness of the sketches with new understanding.

In addition to these portraits tracing one line of Japanese intellectual history of the nineteenth century, the exhibition also included a large number of paintings from Kazan's later years on Chinese-style themes. Perhaps because of my youth, they didn't much interest me at the time. What I learned about for the first time, and stared at in endless fascination inside its glass display case, was *Clean Sweep: Myriad Aspects* (*Issō hyakutai*), sketches of life in Edo that Kazan completed in 1818, when he was twenty-five. I was equally drawn to his other travel accounts, from *True Views of Four Provinces* (*Shishū shinkei*), an illustrated journal

Figure 54. Watanabe Kazan, *Portrait of Takami Senseki*
(*Takami Senseki zō*), Tokyo National Museum.

Figure 55. Sketch of Edo street life. Watanabe Kazan, *Clean Sweep: Myriad Aspects* (*Issō hyakutai*). Tahara Municipal Museum.

he kept in 1825 during his travels on foot through Musashi, Shimousa, Hitachi, and Kazusa, to the 1833 observation report (*Sankai zasshi*) on the Tahara domain possessions of Atsumi Peninsula and, just off Cape Irago, Kamishima. (A facsimile of the latter work was on display, the original having been destroyed in a fire after the Great Kanto Earthquake of 1923.) These personal documents and records made me aware that even this distinguished samurai intellectual experienced, as of course he must have, emotional ups and downs over life's daily joys and sorrows and an irrepressible curiosity concerning trifling matters. Knowing this gave me a sense of relief and further deepened my fond respect for the man.

In 1974, thirteen years after the Mitsukoshi exhibition, I published a book entitled *Watanabe Kazan, Gentle Traveler* (*Watanabe Kazan, yasashii tabibito*) examining Kazan's later illustrated travel diaries.[12] I will take this opportunity to reexamine a few old-Edo street scenes from *Clean Sweep*.

Human faces are rendered in light brown. For example, sitting cross-legged at the side of the road, pipe in mouth, is a man peddling goldfish and killifish in a shallow wooden bucket. A little boy holding a bowl supplied by the stall is eagerly ordering some fish from him. Standing next to the boy is a dignified samurai, apparently his father, wearing *hakama* and two swords, while a pipe holder dangles from his obi. The father holds a paper umbrella in his left hand and is reaching to pat his son's shoulder with his right; the look on his face is indulgent yet a bit wry, as if to say, "Here we go again!" The peddler is holding a triangular net and, nostrils flared, seems to ask, "All right, sonny, how many will it be?" Beyond him is another peddler with a big bamboo basket and a couple of baby turtles fastened to it that are half standing as they strain against the threads that tie them. A baby delightedly watching the turtles is being dandled by a young boy who, although enjoying the moment, seems a bit overwhelmed by his charge.

I well remember taking my small sons to the festival at Fuji Shrine near our house and having the very same experiences.

On the top of the next page is a Kompira pilgrim dressed in white, carrying on his back a box containing a big mask of the god Sarutahiko. As he rings a handbell, a refined-looking old couple yields the right of way. The way the old woman's head is turned to one side, as if to bury her face in her husband's shoulder in embarrassment, is most agreeable. But why is she doing that? Perhaps the long nose on the mask had a lewd meaning. In the lower part of the picture is a scene of Edo *yose*, comic storytelling. The raconteur is seated on a platform, his head scrunched into his collar as he talks, while a couple of men sitting with bad manners on the ground are laughing, nostrils flared, while another pair of men in the back row look away, focused on their pipes. The scene is representative of the Pax Tokugawana in its final years.

On the page to the left, a man practicing *kouta* singing has made a mistake and cowers as the woman on the shamisen scolds him. Next to him, a woman and two men are seated around a large square hibachi, chatting. In front of the hibachi is a man reaching behind him to pour hot water into a teapot, and another man with time on his hands, poking his teeth with a toothpick while listening absently to the chitchat.

How was a twenty-five-year-old samurai able to observe and reproduce with such liveliness and familiarity the daily activities and facial expressions of his contemporaries? The only reason can be that, while aware of his elite status as a samurai, at the same time Kazan lived on the same level as the common people and shared their feelings about life. In contrast, *Hokusai's Sketches* (*Hokusai manga*) by the printmaker Hokusai (1760–1849), published in a series of volumes beginning in 1814, show men and women going about their business in an intentionally comic style, as if the artist were laughing at them; Kazan's sketches suggest rather that he looked on his characters' worry-free expressions with a sympathetic smile.

Finally, a well-known scene in two facing pages of a *terakoya*, a public school where children of commoners could learn to read and write. On the right side, a dozen naughty boys are wrestling, getting up to mischief, or yawning, while on the left, a small pupil sits before the teacher, earnestly attempting to read aloud from a Chinese classic as a middle-aged couple, evidently his parents, cheer him on: a truly delightful scene.

Soon after enjoying that scene, at a lecture in Komaba by the Rilke scholar Fujikawa Hideo (1909–2003), I came across a poem in Chinese that Rai Shumpū (1753–1825), the uncle of the Confucian scholar, artist, and poet Rai San'yō, composed on a visit to Edo. Here it is, following Fujikawa's interpretation:

> Outside town, a fragrant wind blows from a dozen leagues off
> Noon cock's crow sounding near, I enter a pastoral place
> Children are gathered, what class is this?
> The teacher leans on his desk as they copy out the textbook.[13]

The "noon cock" refers to the fable *Peach Blossom Spring* (*Taohua yuan ji*) by Tao Yuanming (ca. 365–427), in which a rooster in the hidden village crows in the afternoon like a ninny. The poem describes a scene very similar to the one in Kazan's sketch.

Actually, it was after my encounter in the mid-1960s with the poems and paintings or sketches of Watanabe Kazan, Rai Shumpū, and Kan Chazan (1748–1828), about whom Fujikawa also spoke enthusiastically, that my image of the Pax Tokugawana began to take clear shape.

Kazan's later travel writings frequently contain the phrase "just like

Peach Blossom Spring." Perhaps that is because, writing in the Tempō era, Kazan sensed that halcyon scenes of the Pax Tokugawana, so resembling the idyllic Peach Blossom Spring for which he longed, would soon disappear. As Japan faced pressing troubles at home and abroad, Kazan used his knowledge of Western-style maritime defense to speak out in favor of defending the peace of his beloved country and compatriots, starting down the road that would lead him finally to take his own life.

"A Most Secret and Eternal Farewell": Watanabe Kazan, the Intellectual Who Explored the World

The painter Watanabe Kazan, retainer of the Tawara domain in Mikawa province, first came into contact with things Western in the 1820s. Like Shiba Kōkan, Hiraga Gennai, and Tani Bunchō, artists of the preceding generation, he developed an interest in Western painting techniques after coming across Dutch lithographs and copperplate illustrations in books. That interest led him to Kaempfer's *History of Japan* and an encounter with Koseki San'ei (1787–1839), a scholar of Dutch studies through whom he met and befriended talented pupils of Siebold such as Takano Chōei. From this progression we may infer that the pace of the times had picked up, and that after *Dawn of Western Science in Japan*, *rangaku* had evolved into a broader and more substantial study of the West.

Kazan himself did not know the Dutch language, but he was flanked by his friends San'ei and Chōei, top *rangaku* scholars of the day. With the aid of these men, Kazan's interest in studying the West intensified from around 1832, when he became a domain elder and also worked to improve the domain's coastal defenses. Some idea of the vigor with which he approached his studies can be gained from the titles of Dutch books of all kinds, and his notes on their contents, in the essays "Record from the Guest Seat" (*Kyakuzaroku*, 1837) and "Brief Account from the Guest Seat" (*Kyakuza shōki*, 1837–1839). His 1838 essay "Dialogue with a Shrike's Tongue" (*Gekizetsu wakumon*), a set of questions and answers to the speaker of a language as unintelligible as the cries of a shrike, gives the clearest picture of the direction of his interest in the

West, the shrewdness of his investigations, and the sophistication and unconventionality of his prior knowledge, as well as the urgency of his criticisms of Japan's status quo. This was Kazan's account of his dialogues (mediated by an interpreter, of course) with Johannes Erdewin Niemann (1796–1850), director of the Dutch factory in Nagasaki, in the third month of 1838.

Despite Kazan's reference to a shrike, Niemann was actually seven foot three, as physically imposing as a Higo ox. At forty-two, four years Kazan's junior, he had seen much of the world; his field, moreover, was *aardrijkskunde* (geography). He was so studious, according to Kazan, that he always had a book in his hand, even when he was in a palanquin or using the toilet. The director of the Dutch factory on Dejima also earned Kazan's trust and admiration by his fondness for Kaempfer's *History of Japan*; he was apparently unusually well read.[14] Kazan's record of his question-and-answer session with the Dutch scholar falls midway between *Tidings of the West*, Arai Hakuseki's account of his 1709 dialogue with the Italian missionary Sidotti, and the 1864 *Pencil Record* (*Empitsu kibun*) by Kurimoto Joun (1822–1897), who studied in Hakodate with the French missionary Eugène-Emmanuel Mermet-Cochon (1838–1889). Like the other two, it is a masterful first-person contribution to studies of the West.

"Now is not the past." The world around Japan was in flux. It was crucial to "have a clear understanding of the world's ordinary state to know how it is changing...If we know this, our way will go smoothly."[15] Adopting this lively stance of temporal and spatial relativism, Kazan showered Niemann with all his pent-up questions, coming at him from all directions and getting closer to a true picture of the world beyond the sea. For example, in response to Kazan's first question, Niemann said, "Dutch scholars keep up with the vanguard of learning through books written in German and French. If we waited for Dutch translations, our progress would be delayed by three or four years."[16] Japanese people then involved in Dutch studies were insufficiently aware of basic facts like this. (Some thirty years later, Matsumoto Kōan, Fukuzawa Yukichi, Mitsukuri Shūhei, and others sent to Europe as part of the shogunate's embassy of 1862 would be struck by the truth of this when they stopped by book stores in Amsterdam and elsewhere.)

The barrage of questions continued:

> Q: Then what country in Europe is the most advanced in learning now?
>
> A: Germany and France, as I said, but lately Britain has made enormous strides in the field of industrial technology. Ever since the invention of the *stoommachine* (steam engine) in particular, London has flourished as the center of industry in the West, and they are working now on the invention of a ship with a *vuurmachine* (thermal power engine).[17]
>
> Q: Why is it that Europe makes such steady progress in learning and technology?
>
> A: That is because our public school system is developed in mathematics, the humanities, and engineering, and steady achievements are being made in those fields. Those who show ability in their studies receive governmental support. Their achievements are publicly evaluated by academicians and the relevant government office; people are also allowed to sell their discoveries to capitalists and reap the profits. Often their discoveries are published, extending the benefit of new knowledge to every corner of the world. In short, throughout society, people with talent are nurtured and selected for high office, for the common good. No one stays buried in baseless prejudices. This is utterly different from a certain country that is closed off and self-sufficient, full of "self-conceit and contempt for others, the ears and eyes closed, in a narrow view like that of the frog in the well."[18]
>
> . . . The scale of scholars is grand. They excel at listening to others and at expounding their own opinions; concerning things they have no knowledge of, they say nothing. For this reason, practical learning flourishes. Day by day, more and more people turn to study. Just as sunshine and rain nurture plants, those who aspire to learning lack for nothing in their daily lives.[19]

From the earliest days of Dutch studies in Japan, the modern principles of social fluidity and openness in education and learning seen in Europe attracted the strong interest of men like Maeno Ryōtaku, Sugita Gempaku, and Honda Toshiaki, who discussed such things with envy. Similar discussions would be repeated among students of the West all the way into the Meiji era.[20] Kazan was doubtless the first to turn his knowledge into such cutting criticism of the Tokugawa establishment.

> Q: What is the Japanese character like?
> A: The Japanese character resembles that of the Turks. "They revere higher learning, but do not learn from matters close at hand. Therefore men of ability slide into arrogance, and ordinary men become indolent. They are extremely quick to imitate any marvelous device they see, but because they are not stable by nature, they are unable to invent anything. In my country, we call such people *lichthoofd* [light-headed]."[21]

Reading such harsh criticism of the Japanese, one begins to suspect that Kazan put words in Niemann's mouth to express his own long-standing opinions. That may be true in part; Kazan was perceptive and undoubtedly quick to connect a hint from Niemann with his experience, his domain, his teachers and friends, and the whole of Tokugawa society.

I do not have space here to introduce all the questions and answers Kazan records, but he conducted a piercing probe with his many queries. He asked about recent political developments in various countries, including France after the Napoleonic Wars, the German Confederation, Russia, Britain, Italy, Denmark, Poland, Belgium, and Spain, and new trends in international relations. He asked in detail about recent acts of colonization by the Western powers, chiefly Britain, in Africa, North America, Canada, and Australia. Then he turned the tables and asked Niemann's view of Japanese culture; the policy of national seclusion ("There is no other country so peaceful. In the West, one cannot sleep or eat in peace even a single day. As a result, the value placed on good government and the level of devotion to the country also cannot be matched."[22]); the nation's relative wealth; and Niemann's impression of Edo ("Japan must be first in the world in the number of beggars and fires"[23]). Kazan also asked about medical education in Europe, physicians' accreditation and place in society, dissection of cadavers, trends in medicine, and more, each question highly pertinent and rising out of his own keen interest.

Through these exchanges, we can ascertain the three-dimensional, dynamic political geography unfolding in Kazan's mind: his image of the post-Napoleonic Western world consisting of Britain, then leading the Industrial Revolution, and other countries which, while jousting within themselves and with each other in vigorous pursuit of modernization, already dominated four-fifths of the globe and were rapidly closing in on Japan. This was an image many times deeper than the ecstatic visions of the West Kazan had had aboard a ship bound for the island of Enoshima and on a cliff on the island of Kamishima in the morning, when he imagined with yearning and vague unrest what might lie beyond the sea.[24] From a generous, gentle samurai-painter content to idly observe women of Kamishima going peacefully about their business on that idyllic island, he was transformed into a daring explorer of a West riddled with dangers and threats, penetrating farther and deeper into that world than anyone else of his generation in Japan.

Kazan used the rich store of knowledge he acquired to survey the West and Asia together, with mounting apprehension over what lay ahead for the islands of Japan that were presently "surrounded on all sides by peaceful seas."[25] His sense of peril was further heightened by the rumor that in summer 1838, the American ship *Morrison* had approached Japan and been fired upon in accordance with the 1825 Edict to Repel Foreign Vessels. This turn of events led him to pick up his pen. Thus Watanabe Kazan the gentle traveler, the broad-minded, democratic painter, became an anti-establishment intellectual who possessed, in the words of Shimazaki Tōson, a "rebellious, angry nature. . . [and] a tragic willingness to sacrifice" himself. Or he allowed that side of himself to come to the fore. He showed himself to be a samurai who possessed "a violent agitation and a sensitivity unique to the nineteenth century." His sense of imminent crisis is vividly conveyed in two of his final essays,

"Arguments for Restraint in a Critical Situation" (*Shinkiron*, 1838) and "Affairs in the West" (*Seiyō jijōsho*, 1839).

What was the state of Japan's domestic politics, which would have to adjust to the approach of "rank-smelling Westerners"?[26] What were the attitudes, awareness, and abilities of those in power? While the people suffered from famine and were sick with fear of the uncertain future, officers of the state "left the great and took the small, in a world of utter indifference," quite as if they intended to destroy the country ("Arguments").[27] When one knew about the state of the enemy, that is, the West, the state of Japan was certainly cause for unease. To remain uninformed, however, was to be content to be a frog in a well or a wren on a branch ("Affairs").[28] Under the circumstances, what could one do but fold one's arms and wait for an invasion ("Arguments")?[29]

In the two essays, Kazan expressed in biting tones his intense sense of crisis and his distrust of and anxiety concerning the government, conveyed with all the trembling sensitivity of his *True Views of Four Provinces* and the sharp delineation of his portraits of Tachihara Suiken and Takami Senseki. Inevitably, the essays contributed to the crackdown on *rangaku* (Suppression of the Barbarian Studies Group) in the fifth month of 1839.

Finally, at New Year's 1840, Kazan was sentenced to house arrest in Tahara, where on the eleventh day of the tenth month of that year he would take his own life.

On the tenth day of the tenth month 1841, the night before he killed himself, Kazan wrote a letter to his disciple Tsubaki Chinzan. Here is the letter in full:

> I am writing you a few lines. Hoping that I would be better able to look after my mother, I made the mistake of agreeing to Hankō's proposal for an exhibition.[30] I finished the works commissioned up to the third month, but the rest I have left incomplete. Lately there are rumors and groundless gossip about me that have come to the attention of the authorities, and I fear it is going to end in calamity. The peace of his lordship

[the daimyo of the Tahara domain] has been imperiled. Under the circumstances, I intend to kill myself tonight. People are sure to say I criticized the government and then failed to act prudently. Without a doubt, this calamity is the result of my carelessness and lack of self-examination, which led to a mismatch between my words and my actions. This is not the fault of heaven but something I brought on myself, beyond question. If things continue as they are now, my mother, my wife, and my children will surely suffer great hardship, and even his lordship is not likely to escape unscathed. That is why I made the decision mentioned above.

No doubt I will be a laughingstock, and reports of my infamy will seethe like a cauldron. Please endure this for the sake of our deep friendship. If, a few years from now, a great change takes place, will there be anyone to mourn?

This is a most secret and eternal farewell. I bow my head in respect.

The tenth day of the tenth month

P.S. I have destroyed all my letters from you.[31]

As Kazan finished writing, surely the far-off sound of the sea came to his ears: the ceaseless pounding of waves in Mikawa Bay, surrounding Atsumi Peninsula, and the crash of Pacific Ocean breakers.

In a sense, it was the sea that drove Kazan to his tragic end. Listening to its distant roar at night, he wrote, "If, a few years from now, a great change takes place, will there be anyone to mourn?" What was the true meaning of those poignant words? They may have ranged surprisingly far. Did they foretell the end of the policy of national isolation? The collapse of the shogunate? As a Tokugawa samurai, his thoughts probably did not go so far, so what sort of "great change" did he envision at age forty-eight, his faculties as keen and sensitive as ever?

In that year, 1841, Senior Counselor Mizuno Tadakuni was just about to institute the Tempō Reforms. In China, meanwhile, although Kazan had no way of knowing it, the Opium War had been underway since the previous year. The merciless invasion of East Asia by European powers, particularly Britain, lay at hand. This was twelve years before the American squadron led by Commodore Perry would arrive in the waters of Uraga.

> The Dutch chief too
> lies prostrate before him—
> springtime of the shogun's reign

> Spring sea—
> all day long the waves
> gently rise and fall

The balmy, halcyon Pax Tokugawana described in such haiku was at long last drawing to an end. In 1868, just twenty-some years after Watanabe Kazan's suicide, the Meiji Restoration took place—the great "about-face" precipitated by men like Sakuma Shōzan, Yoshida Shōin, Yokoi Shōnan, Hashimoto Sanai, Abe Masahiro, Iwase Tadanari, Kawaji Toshiakira, Oguri Tadamasa, Katsu Kaishū, Sakamoto Ryōma, Nakaoka Shintarō, Enomoto Takeaki, Ōkubo Toshimichi, and Saigō Takamori, samurai intellectuals whom Tōson called "nineteenth-century-style" men of action, as well as by Fukuzawa Yukichi, Tsuda Mamichi, Nishi Amane, Kurimoto Joun, and other samurai scholars of the late-Tokugawa enlightenment movement.

Needless to say, these men and their comrades were all born and bred in Tokugawa Japan. They themselves were the greatest legacy of the Tokugawa period, investing the new Meiji era with Tokugawa civilization and spirit, revitalizing that civilization and spirit and preparing Japan to face a new international environment.

Led by Iwakura Tomomi (1825–1883), the Iwakura Embassy set sail from Yokohama on December 23, 1871, seen off by Chancellor of the Realm Sanjō Sanetomi (1837–1891) with a gallant poem instructing them:

> Go! Cross the sea on wheels of fire
> the land on a train
> dash ten thousand leagues
> proclaim our brilliance far and wide!

Over the course of a year and nine months, they conducted a thoroughgoing, firsthand survey and study of American and European civilization and history, returning to Japan in September 1873. The dispatch of that band of fifty or so, as well as the fifty or so young men and women who went along to study abroad, was simultaneously the triumphal arch of Tokugawa civilization and the starting-point of Meiji Japan. That is my view, but a description of that grand adventure will have to wait for another book.

---

1 A Confucian temple in Tokyo established during the Genroku era. It was made into an important state-run school in 1797 and closed in 1871 after the Meiji Restoration.

2 "Unification of writing and speech": a reform movement of the Meiji era aimed at the creation of a form of prose closer to the spoken language.

3 AN: *Sensō to Pari* [War and Paris], vol. 6, *Tōson zenshū* [The complete works of Shimazaki Tōson] (Chikuma shobō, 1967), 391–392.

4 Natsume Sōseki, "The Civilization of Modern-Day Japan," *Kokoro: A Novel and Selected Essays*, Edwin McClellan and Jay Rubin, trans. (Seattle: Madison Books, 1992), 257-283.

5 Haga quotes the philosopher Ōnishi Hajime (1864–1900) as writing in a 1894 essay published in *Kokumin no tomo* [Friend of the people], "Unquiet spirits sought quietude," a comment that Haga sees as linking him philosophically to Schopenhauer and Shiba Kōkan. See Haga's essay "Nihon bungaku ni okeru 'kindai' to 'kinsei': Tokugawa kara Meiji e" ["*Kindai*" and "*kinsei*": from Tokugawa to Meiji], vol. 25, *Nihon kindai bungaku* [Early Modern Japanese Literature]. https://amjls.jp/zasshi/025.pdf

6 Philipp Franz von Siebold was accused of spying for Russia and deported in 1829 after he was found to possess detailed maps of Japan and Korea that Takahashi Kageyasu had given him.

7 *Yōgaku nempyō* [Chronology of Western studies] by Ōtsuki Joden was published in 1877, and *Shinsen yōgaku nempyō* [Newly compiled chronology of Western studies] came out fifty years later, in 1927.

8 AN: *Fukuzawa Yukichi senshū* [Selected works of Fukuzawa Yukichi], vol. 12 (Iwanami shoten, 1980).

9 AN: "*Kaisetsu*" [Commentary], Sugita Gempaku, *Rangaku kotohajime* [Dawn of Western Science in Japan], Ogata Tomio, ed. (Iwanami shoten, 1959), 121–122.

10 AN: Mayama Seika, "Gemboku to Chōei" [Gemboku and Chōei], *Gemboku to Chōei hoka sampan* [Gemboku and Chōei, and three other works] (Iwanami shoten, 1952), 13.

11 AN: Sakuma Shōzan, *Seikenroku* [Record of conscience] (Juenrō: 1871).

12 AN: Haga Tōru, *Watanabe Kazan, yasashii tabibito* [Watanabe Kazan, Gentle traveler], Nihon no tabibito [Travelers in Japan], vol. 13 (Tankōsha, 1974).

13 AN: Fujikawa, op. cit., 60.

14 AN: Watanabe Kazan, "Gekizetsu shoki" [Brief account of the shrike's tongue], Watanabe Kazan, Takano Chōei, Sakuma Shōzan, Yokoi Shōnan, Hashimoto Sanai, Satō Shōsuke, ed., *Nihon shisō taikei* [Philosophical thought in Japan], vol. 55 (Iwanami shoten, 1971), 74–75.

15 Ibid., 79.

16 Ibid., 81.

17 Ibid., 82.

18 Ibid., 83.

19 Ibid.

20 AN: See, for example, the record of the Iwakura Embassy of 1871–1873, especially vol. 3, "Britain": *The Iwakura Embassy, 1871-73: A true account of the Ambassador Extraordinary & Plenipotentiary's journeys of observation through the United States and Europe* [*Tokumei zenken taishi Bei-Ōō kairan jikki*] (Japan Documents and Princeton University Press, 2002).

21 Ibid., 88.

22 Ibid.

23 Ibid., 87–88

24 In *Visit to Sagami* (Yūsōki, 1821), his earliest travel account, Kazan records his excited shouts on the island of Enoshima: "How wonderful! How marvelous! From here to the southeast is what the Westerners call the Pacific Ocean and the American states! They must be very close!" Donald Keene, *Frog in the Well: Portraits of Japan by Watanabe Kazan, 1793–1841* (Columbia University Press, 2002), 74.

25 AN: Watanabe, op cit., 72.

26 Ibid.

27 Ibid.

28 The latter analogy is a reference to the Chinese classic *Zhuangzi*: "When a wren builds its nest, although the woods may be deep it uses no more than one branch." Watanabe Kazan, "Seiyō jijōsho" [Affairs in the West], Satō Shōsuke, ed., op.cit., 61. https://terebess.hu/english/Zhuangzi-Eno.pdf

29 AN: Watanabe Kazan, "Shinkiron" [Arguments for restraint in a critical situation], Satō Shōsuke, ed., op. cit., 72.

30 Kazan's disciple Fukuda Hankō held a benefit exhibition in Edo in an attempt to shore up Kazan's straitened circumstances.

31 AN: Watanabe Kazan, "Isho" [Death note], Satō Shōsuke, ed., op. cit., 156.

Awakening to Indigo Blue

> Morning glories—
> one the color of
> a deep pool

Upon reading this haiku by Yosa Buson, Japanese people of a certain age will be overcome by a refreshing sensation. What will Westerners feel, I wonder? Perhaps it will only seem mysterious to them.

Yosa Buson, the finest Japanese poet of the eighteenth century, was the contemporary of Thomas Grey and Jean-Jacques Rousseau. Along with Matsuo Bashō, who came before him, and Kobayashi Issa, who came after him, he was one of the trio of poetic geniuses of Tokugawa Japan who created the seventeen-syllable haiku, the world's shortest poetic form.

The morning glory, true to its name, blooms at dawn, and when the sun is high, its flowers fade. It blooms from summer to early autumn, and in haiku it is a season-word for autumn. The reason it represents autumn even though it mostly blooms in summer is because its flowers come out in the coolest part of a summer day, the early morning. Its lovely, trumpet-shaped flowers bloom in all sorts of colors. After morning glory seeds were introduced from China in the early tenth century for medicinal purposes, the flowers won the hearts of the Japanese people for their shape, simpler even than the tulip, and their fresh, bright colors. By Buson's time, morning glories were widely cultivated as ornamental flowers.

It is easy to create new varieties of morning glories in various shapes and colors. In the eighteenth century, Japan's "century of natural history," morning glory enthusiasts, along with goldfish enthusiasts, researched rare varieties, and all sorts of instruction books on horticulture were published. In the early nineteenth century, an early-morning fair specializing in morning glories began to be held at Iriya Kishimojin (Shingenji temple) in Edo. That summer fair continues even now and always receives heavy coverage in the newspapers and on television. Fishmongers and greengrocers, carpenters, schoolteachers, and policemen all go to the fair to buy two or three pots of morning glories and take them home to decorate their front step, veranda, or windowsill. Those who are more devoted will save seeds of flowers whose color or shape they particularly like, plant them the following year, and enjoy the same flowers all over again. Even more than tulips to the Dutch in spring, morning glories have long been an inexpensive, modest pleasure of summer for the nameless common folk of Japan, who traditionally sought in them a bit of needed relief from summer heat.

At the end of slender tendrils that wind around bamboo supports, the morning glory puts out bright green leaves and trumpet-shaped flowers of light pink or pale reddish purple. Sometimes the flowers are white with streaks of red or blue. Gardeners also came up with variegated flowers. Unlike tulips, morning glories do not have brilliant colors, but come in fresh and delicate hues, as if someone had brushed the thin petals with watercolors. The flowers have a pure beauty perfectly suited to summer and early-autumn mornings in Japan.

The color that best represents the morning glory, however, is surely indigo. It is, as Buson wrote, "the color of a deep pool," as when a fast-flowing mountain stream is separated by rocks and forms slow swirls of deep blue. Because the flowers are the shape of a trumpet or a tapering glass, when you peer inside, the indigo seems to deepen progressively. This creates the image of a deep pool in a mountain stream, as captured in Buson's haiku.

One morning in summer or early fall, Buson must have gazed on the morning glories blooming perhaps on a hedge in the tiny garden of his home in Kyoto. Drawn particularly to one flower, he looked inside it and seemed to see the cool still water of a pool in a mountain stream, spreading until he could almost feel a cool gust of wind arise from deep within. Haiku poets have a vivid imagination that enables them to glimpse in tiny things a vast world of a different dimension, and this haiku is a superb example of that imagination at work.

Indigo Summer

The color indigo (*ai*), "the color of a deep pool," becomes, as it lightens, blue (*ao*) or light blue (*mizuiro*). Those are the colors of a clear sky in early summer or early autumn, and of the shallow streams and lakes that reflect the sky. When indigo darkens, it becomes navy blue (*kon*). Sometimes the color absorbs all the strong light and takes on a purplish cast, becoming bluish purple (*murasaki kon*). This is the color of the midsummer sky with cumulus clouds afloat over the archipelago, and of the billowing sea reflecting that sky, and of Mt. Fuji, soaring into the sky beside the sea, and of ripe eggplants beneath that sky. Morning glory flowers naturally come in all these gradations. Japanese people have always associated the flower with water and sky and mountains, and savored the bit of cool it imparts.

Indigo, which seems to contain all the vitality of the Japanese islands, is, along with crimson and purple and green, one of the colors that Japanese people love best. Indigo dye comes from the leaves of the indigo plant *Persicaria tinctoria*, in the knotweed family, and indigo dyeing has been carried on in Japan since the ninth century, using both domestic plants and those imported from China. However, it wasn't until the Tokugawa period, and the eighteenth century in particular, that indigo balls began to be produced in large numbers as a specialty crop of the province of Awa in Shikoku and the color indigo permeated all aspects of people's lives in Japan. Looking back, we can see that indigo, along with brown, gray, and green, was so deeply connected with Edo culture that we may call it an "Edo color."

Indigo dye works equally well on silk, hemp, cotton, and even paper, with the power to enhance the beauty of any fiber. Silk takes on luster, hemp emits a stiff sheen, and cotton, while it does not shine, acquires a soft, deep texture pleasing to the hand and the eye. Cotton in particular, as noted in a 1924 essay by the ethnologist Yanagita Kunio[1] (1875–1962), was cultivated throughout the land in Tokugawa Japan, and as it became widely available it greatly changed people's lives. According to Yanagita, people loved cotton fabric and took to it quickly not only because it was new and inexpensive, but also because it made comfortable work clothes that felt good next to the skin, and it was easy to dye however one pleased.

In the beginning, cotton was dyed in solid colors, but as the number of dyers began to increase in villages everywhere, cotton thread was dyed in a variety of colors, and farming women would then vie to weave those colorful threads into unusual striped patterns. Houses made "stripe notebooks" containing samples of striped patterns to use as reference. Each house and each individual dyer exercised inventiveness and creativity, with constant refinements of taste and skill. In some areas, weaving on a loom provided farming families with an important secondary source of income. Whether the finished product was a solid color or striped, and whether the stripes were horizontal, vertical, latticed, or some more unusual design, indigo, along with yellow and brown, was always a basic and very popular color. Between the extremes of navy and light blue, there were all sorts of intermediate indigo hues, such as *hanada-iro*, a medium blue tinged with red that came in varying shades, or *onando-iro*, blue with a grayish cast. Sometimes the blue approached black, and sometimes it was brightened to a reddish purple. An infinite variety of intermediate indigo-based shades was used as solid colors or woven into stripes of every imaginable geometric design, lending color and warmth to the lives of Japanese people during the time of national isolation.

Farmers and fisherfolk preferred to work in garments dyed with long-lasting, stable indigo. In Edo, Osaka, and other castle towns, most merchant houses used navy-blue indigo for the heavy shop curtains that hung at the entrance, as well as for the aprons and livery coats worn by shopkeepers and apprentices. Work coats, jackets, and waistcoats worn by carpenters, plasterers, artisans, firefighters, and other workers were all made of thick, sturdy navy cotton that had a pleasant texture. Freshly made items boasted a beautiful, "fragrant" indigo, and the slightly faded blue of well-worn items was also much admired. Merchant livery coats always had the shop symbol or name writ large on the back in white, undyed on a field of indigo; for firefighters, it was the name of the guild they belonged to. This would be matched skillfully with the geometrical design along the bottom of the coat, to fine effect.

Men who wore such garments while they worked not only took pride in the shop or guild they belonged to but also naturally strove to maintain a bearing and spirit consistent with the aesthetics of *iki*—a Tokugawa ideal of simplicity, nonchalant refinement, and originality—represented in the pattern, color, and shape of those garments. Crisply smart and supple: this was the everyday aesthetic of the Edo populace and the standard for behavior.

After the day's work, men and women would bathe and then relax on a summer evening in *yukata*. A simple kimono designed for relaxation, in its shape and colors the *yukata* was the simplest expression of the clean beauty that Edoites liked. It had a completely different aesthetic from the nightgown or negligee. Cut in straight lines like all kimono, the *yukata* was, and is, always made of unlined cotton. Cotton takes starch well, and when a freshly starched *yukata* is unfolded and put on, the lines of the shoulders, sleeves, and hem stay straight, for a cool-looking appearance even in hot weather.

Traditionally, the patterns on *yukata* were dyed in navy indigo, for men and woman alike. All sorts of stripes, lattice designs, and small motifs of birds, waves, and plants were used, as well as *kanji* and *hiragana* lettering; such elements, both concrete and abstract, were combined inventively and dyed in navy on a white ground, or left undyed on a field of indigo. Patterns favored by popular kabuki actors often determined the prevailing taste. *Yukata* worn by Edo men and women constituted in themselves a kind of multiform "stripe notebook" and made Japan into a design powerhouse.

The *yukata* I am wearing as I write these words has, in fact, a variation of a Tokugawa design dyed in indigo (probably the dye is synthetic rather than natural, however).

A freshly starched *yukata*, dyed with the colors of the seas and mountains of Japan, went on directly over just-bathed skin and was tied smartly with an obi. The silhouette of a man in a *yukata* had a kind of geometrical precision. A woman—any woman—who wore a *yukata* acquired an air of sophistication, with glimpses of curves affording a fresh eroticism. Not only in Tokugawa Japan but even a generation ago, the most appropriate and welcome attire on sultry summer nights was a *yukata*. Wearing one was a joy. *Yukata* make the wearer feel cool and refreshed, and onlookers, too, find the sight as refreshing as a cold drink.

Two of Japan's finest modern haiku poets wrote in praise of *yukata*:

> The breasts of a girl
> in a *yukata*
> lie smooth
> —Takahama Kyoshi (1874–1959)

> Silhouetted against the red of sunset
> relaxing in *yukata*:
> Japanese people
> —Nakamura Kusatao (1901–1983)

As they relaxed in *yukata*, Japanese people would always have in hand a round fan with which to create a cool breeze or brush away a mosquito. The picture or design painted in indigo on a fan also had a cooling effect. Fan designs, as well as the way of holding or using a fan, inevitably differed according to gender and age. Perhaps in the haiku below, the person holding a fan with a painting of the famous kabuki hero and heroine is a lovely young girl whose budding breasts "lie smooth," securely wrapped by the folds of her *yukata*:

> A round fan
> with a picture of, no less,

Seijūrō and Onatsu
　　—Buson

Or, one might see a woman sitting pensively on the far edge of the veranda in the twilight, fan in hand, leaving the lights unlit:

The widow
her face shadowed at dusk
wields her fan
　　—Buson

As recently as forty or fifty years ago, sleeping inside a mosquito net in summer was normal for Japanese people, even on sultry nights. Whether cotton or hemp, such nets were generally dyed in indigo of various shades. One would stretch out inside the net, wait for a slight breeze to come in through the open door, and now and then fan oneself before finally drifting off. The blue-green tint of the netting created the illusion of coolness, and sometimes in the midst of poverty it was possible to exercise a little ingenuity:

With my mosquito net
I made a light green mountain
inside the house
　　—Buson

Releasing fireflies
inside the mosquito net—
oh what fun!
　　—Buson

The genre of haiku is rare in the world for its ability to capture in this way the smallest details of people's lives, and the feelings invested in them.

Then in the morning people would get up, wash their faces while admiring the morning glories in the garden, and dry themselves not with a thick, Western-style towel, but with a thin hand towel called a *tenugui*. Like *yukata*, *tenugui* are made of cotton with stripes or lettering dyed in indigo on a field of white.

The morning glory
objects to the indigo
edging the *tenugui*
    —Buson

This morning glory is of course the one that is "the color of a deep pool." Seeing an indigo-dyed *tenugui*, the flower complains, "That's the same color as me! How will people tell us apart?"

As with *yukata*, round fans, and *furoshiki* wrapping cloths, no one knows who invented the *tenugui*, but from the mid-Tokugawa period until just recently, it was an indispensable part of daily life in Japan. People used it to mop their sweat, wash their faces, and bathe. The *tenugui* was an article of practical use that could serve as handkerchief or towel, but it could also be folded or twisted with dexterity and shaped into a headband, head wrap, or face covering. The way a *tenugui* was worn signaled the wearer's occupation and even mood, and was instantly understood.

Twisting a *tenugui* smartly and wrapping it around the crown of the head with the knot raised on one side was the mark of a dashing fishmonger. Folding it in a triangle and setting it on top of the head was for newspaper vendors. Wrap it around your head and tie it under your nose, and you were a thief. If you pulled your hair back, wrapped it in a *tenugui* and then piled it on your head, spreading it across your forehead, you were a babysitter. If a woman wore a *tenugui* draped lightly over her head with one corner between her lips, she looked alluring; the handsome fellow eloping with her would cover his head with his *tenugui* and tuck in the ends below his right ear. Folded vertically, worn around the forehead and tied tightly in back, a *tenugui* was an expression of samurai fighting spirit. Kamikaze pilots drove their planes into American aircraft carriers often wearing headbands of white *tenugui* with the rising sun motif in the center. Nowadays students plugging away to pass college entrance exams do the same while they study. Union demonstrators used to like to sport that style too.

Many of these *tenugui* styles were invented by kabuki actors onstage, and they often show sophistication. *Rakugo* artists (traditional storytellers) can indicate almost every prop and mannerism used by Japanese people in daily life, armed only with a folding fan and a *tenugui*. And ordinary people in Tokugawa Japan, no matter how they may have used *tenugui* to cover their heads, faces, or shoulders, unconsciously made sure to do so in such a way that the indigo picture, lettering, or stripes dyed into the cloth showed off to the best effect.

Japan's Tricolored Flag

Having come this far, mixing haiku in with our study, it begins to seem as if in Tokugawa Japan, at least in summer, everyone's days began and ended with the color blue. Certainly indigo blue was especially popular in the summertime, but it was of course used in other seasons as well. Shop employees and workers wore indigo-dyed livery coats and work clothes year round, showing off the beauty of the dyed fabric in every season and situation.

Lafcadio Hearn (1850–1954) arrived in Japan from the United States by way of Canada in early April 1890, on a beautiful spring day affording him a view of snow-capped Fuji in the distance—but Hearn's first impression was of indigo blue:

> Elfish everything seems, for everything as well as everybody is small, and queer, and mysterious; the little houses under their blue roofs, the little shop-fronts hung with blue, and the smiling little people in their blue costumes.[2]

The very air above the town possessed a faint suggestion of blue, contained in an atmosphere of extraordinary clarity. The rickshaw runner he employed wore a "short blue wide-sleeved jacket" and matching "blue drawers" and worked tirelessly, mopping the sweat from his face with "a small sky-blue towel with figures of bamboo-sprays and sparrows in white upon it." Looking out from his perch in the rickshaw, Hearn saw "an interminable flutter of flags and swaying of dark blue drapery, all made beautiful and mysterious with Japanese or Chinese lettering" and observed that "the same rich dark blue which dominates in popular costume rules also in shop draperies."[3]

Lafcadio Hearn seemed to feel he had wandered into a little kingdom of indigo and dark blue. Toward the end of the nineteenth century, nearly forty years after the opening of the country, the people's deep-rooted sense of color remained unchanged.

However, immediately after the passage quoted above, Hearn writes, "though there is a sprinkling of other tints—bright blue and white and red." And indeed, the various shades of indigo were not all that lent color to life in eighteenth- and nineteenth-century Japan. Year round, green, brown, gray, and black, as well as silver, gold, red, and white were used widely both in practical, daily necessities of food, clothing, and shelter and in a variety of ornaments and implements. However, and this is true also for indigo, apart from festivals and other public events, it was rare for any color to be used brightly on its own. In daily life, a single kimono, fan, book cover, or card combined all sorts of colors in a quietly rich and luxuriant harmony. Moreover, colors were almost always tinged with gray or indigo, red or brown for a subtle, understated effect summed up in the word "*shibui*." As I mentioned earlier, such neutral hues could, by the slightest difference in tone, expand in an infinite panoply of color. Herein lies the secret of the aesthetics of Edo taste, I believe.

The various lines of colors then in use, often named for vegetable pigments, are now indistinguishable to all but the most dedicated historians of color and customs. But when we see and handle Edo materials designed with colors that are at once *shibui* and *iki*, we feel our innermost, secret sensuality awaken and be drawn to them.

In closing off their country to all but a few Dutchmen in Nagasaki and a few Chinese traders each year, constructing an absolute peace that lasted two hundred fifty years, Tokugawa Japanese allowed their culture to ripen like sweet fruit, and at the core of that culture they created this little cosmos of neutral colors. On seeing the Tricolor or the Stars and Stripes, then beginning to wave over France and the United States, people accustomed to the colors of Edo, with their remarkably fine wavelengths, would surely have been unable to appreciate the foreign flags or would have found them too bright to look at. In fact, in

1853, after Tokugawa Japan was finally forced to open the country, one shogunate official said of the flags on foreign ships in Japan's harbors, "They hurt my eyes."[4]

However, just around the time that the French Tricolor came into use in the French republic, Japan had its own tricolor flag. That flag of course had nothing to do with any formal ideology like *Liberté, Égalité, Fraternité*, nor was it an expression of *yamatodamashii*, the Japanese spirit. It was the tricolor flag of the world of pleasure, the world of the arts. I am speaking of the curtain used on the kabuki stage with vertical stripes of *moegi, kaki*, and *kuro*, or dark green, persimmon, and black. Those colors came to symbolize kabuki, the theater that dominated the culture of Tokugawa Japan. They are the ultimate example of the neutral colors favored in Edo, and therefore extremely difficult to explain in words. *Moegi* refers to the yellowish green of onion sprouts, but on the kabuki curtain, that color is tinged with gray and deepened into the shade of strongly brewed fine green tea. *Kaki* refers to the persimmon, an autumn fruit that Japanese people love; the color is ferric oxide touched with black for a deep brown hue. Finally, the *kuro* of the curtain is by no means a simple black, but a blackish navy overlaid with a bit of the brightness of purple.

When Japanese people then and now see stripes in those three neutral colors, they immediately feel like returning to Edo to watch kabuki while wearing kimono and eating sushi. Look carefully and even in Tokyo today you will find those same beautiful, deeply meaningful colors on essential things in essential places. Some day when the Hinomaru, Japan's national flag of a red sun on a white ground, becomes unbearably offensive to peoples of other countries, Japan should exchange it for a *shibui* Edo tricolor flag. That, however, might cause trouble for printers and dyers around the world, who would have to struggle to reproduce that trio of complex colors.

Arts, Crafts, and Daily Life

Just as colors produced by nameless artisans over the course of many generations eventually became symbolic of the kabuki stage, in the same way colors favored by kabuki actors quickly became popular in Edo and the countryside, an interesting cultural phenomenon in the isolated island nation. The earliest example of such a trending color is thought to be a shade of brown liked by the *onnagata* Segawa Kikunojō (1741–1773; also known by his haiku name, Rokō), a contemporary of Yosa Buson who was active in Edo in the 1760s and 1770s. That complicated color, a subtle shade with hints of dark green, was popular throughout Japan until the 1820s under the name Rokō-cha, "Rokō brown." Then for the generations leading up to the end of the Tokugawa period, blues and browns that popular kabuki actors liked, as well as striped, linked (*tsunagi*) and small-scale repeated patterns (*komon*) of actors' devising, permeated the lives of Japanese people everywhere, in every social stratum. The effect was concentrated on but not limited to clothing, extending gradually also to the color and design of daily utensils, ornaments, and even toys.

The trends in taste shared by kabuki and daily life were a rich and colorful assortment of painting and literature, both of which became steadily more popularized with each passing generation. The writings of novelist Ihara Saikaku (1642–1693) and dramatist Chikamatsu Monzaemon (1653–1725) and the art of Ogata Kōrin and others spurred the development and increasing sophistication of Kamigata *jōruri* (dramatic narrative sung to shamisen accompaniment in the Osaka-Kyoto area) as bourgeois theater in the Genroku era, while ukiyo-e and *gesaku* light fiction of the late eighteenth century through the mid nineteenth century played a great role in spreading the costumes, lines of dialogue, and even gestures of kabuki among the populace.

Nishiki-e, full-color woodblock prints by artists such as Harunobu, Kiyonaga, Utamaro, and Sharaku, as well as Hokusai, Hiroshige, Kuniyoshi, and Eisen, boosted the popularity of contemporary actors by showing them in stage costumes featuring their favorite colors and designs. The color prints also portrayed famous courtesans of the pleasure quarters as well as the ordinary townsfolk, men and women, who lost no time decking themselves out in the latest fashion. And of course, apart from lionized celebrities, the prints showed the normal daily life of people of all social strata—merchants, artisans, and peasants going busily and cheerfully about their business or enjoying trips and excursions—as well as scenes of the city and the four seasons as the background of their activities. All this was vividly and beautifully depicted utilizing shades of Edo indigo, crimson, green, and brown.

Art collectors and avant-garde artists in late nineteenth century Europe went into raptures over the beauty and appeal of ukiyo-e, as is well known. Their passion for ukiyo-e gradually led them to explore the totality of Japanese art. In so doing, they discovered fresh ways of handling color and space and also recognized with deep excitement the open, robust interplay between life and art that continued to exist in Japan. Japan's natural features, painting, poetry, crafts, and architecture, as well as its design, theater, and the life of its people, were all interwoven in the rich circle of a unique civilization: this is what those *fin de siècle* Japanophiles realized. That remains, I would submit, a fundamentally correct understanding of the culture of Tokugawa Japan.

Rutherford Alcock, the first British ambassador to Japan, arrived soon after the opening of the country and, writing from his own experiences, gave a vivid and faithful account of that civilization in his book *The Capital of the Tycoon: A Narrative of a Three Years' Residence in Japan* (1863). Vincent Van Gogh, living in Arles in 1888, saw in the clear blue of the sky and in sun-dappled streams the exoticism of the "beautiful country" of Japan. At the same time, he thought of Japanese artists as philosophers able through the humble study of a single blade of grass to comprehend flora and fauna, the seasons, pastoral scenery, and even human beings. This was also just around the time that Lafcadio Hearn was beginning to think of traveling to Japan.

Van Gogh's view of Japanese aesthetics was probably inspired by articles he read in the Parisian magazine *Artistic Japan*. Siegfried Bing, the German-born Frenchman who edited the deluxe magazine, was an art dealer and the leading promoter of *japonisme*. In the magazine's first issue (May 1888), he wrote the following observations under the title "*Programme*":

The Japanese is drawn towards this pure ideal by a twofold characteristic of his temperament. He is at once an enthusiastic poet, moved by the spectacles of Nature, and an attentive and minute observer of the intricate mysteries which lurk in the infinitely little. It is in the spider's web that he loves to study geometry: the marks of a bird's claw upon the snow furnish him with a design for ornamentation: and when he wants to depict the curves of a sinuous line he will certainly resort for inspiration to the capricious ripples which the breeze draws upon the surface of the waters. In a word, he is convinced that Nature contains the primordial elements of all things, and, according to him, nothing exists in creation, be it only a blade of grass, that is not worthy of a place in the loftiest conceptions of Art. This, if I do not err, is the great and salutary lesson that we may derive from the examples which he sets before us.[5]

In the second issue (June 1888), the art historian Louis Gonse wrote a flowery encomium on the "Japanese genius for decoration," and thereafter a dazzling array of people contributed articles in French, English, and German on Japanese architecture, swords, and ceramics; the art of Hokusai, Hiroshige, and Kōrin; the art and traditions of Japanese poetry and theater; and even assorted *objets* such as combs and netsuke, making the magazine an outstanding general repository of research on Japanese culture. The authors' analysis of Tokugawa arts, crafts, and life was by no means mistaken, as I trust the reader of this essay will agree, after our examination of a morning-glory haiku followed by glimpses of indigo-dyed work clothes and *yukata*, fans, and *tenugui*, and the use of color and design in kabuki and ukiyo-e.

Achieving the same sort of harmony among nature, the arts, and life in twenty-first-century Japan will of course not come as easily as before. However, the fruit of this past national experience has not disappeared but lives on in Japanese modes of feeling and thinking and in the Japanese art of living. As long as the nation retains those core attributes, the graphic designs of contemporary Japan will, in the boldness of their composition, the clarity of their form, and the delicacy of their colors, go on displaying beautiful "Japaneseness" to the world just as Japanese automobiles and cameras will in their compactness and efficiency.

---

1 AN: Yanagita Kunio, *Momen izen no koto* [Before cotton], *Yanagita Kunio zenshū* [Complete works of Yanagita Kunio], vol. 17 (Chikuma shobō, 1990), 12–20.

2 Lafcadio Hearn, "On My First Day in the Orient," *Glimpses of Unfamiliar Japan*, vol. 1. https://english.pratilipi.com/read/glimpses-of-unfamiliar-japan-vol-1-chapter-1-on-my-first-day-in-the-orient-js0jzxnsb2wh-2e710n591045278

3 Ibid.

4 AN: Ivan Goncharov, *Nihon dokōki* [Record of a voyage to Japan; Russian: *Fregat "Pallada"*], Inoue Mitsuru, trans. (Iwanami shoten, 1941), 128.

5 Siegfried Bing, "Artistic Japan: Illustrations and essays" ("*Le Japon artistique*"), 6. https://archive.org/details/artisticjapanill01bing/page/6/mode/2up

AFTERWORD

This book came into being by a slow, roundabout process. It started out as a Foreword of some one hundred pages that I wrote for a long book with the same title: *Tokugawa Japan as a Civilization* (*Bummei toshite no Tokugawa Nihon*). That Foreword, entitled "Notes on Tokugawa Peace: A Study in Comparative Culture" (*Tokugawa no heiwa shōron: Hikaku-bunkashiteki ikkōsatsu*), contains the main thrust of the present book and several of its main points.

That huge earlier book was published by Chūō Kōronsha in 1993 as Volume I of a series on comparative literature and culture. The design was stylish, the contents intriguing. On the cover, the title was set horizontally in a white box below a color sketch of Hiraga Gennai's *erekiteru*, with designs of exotic-looking flowers and leaves on the lid and sides. As editor, I looked on that cover with great satisfaction, as it was just the sort of image I'd had in mind.

The idea for the series grew out of the impending retirements in 1992 of Hirakawa Sukehiro and myself, the first alumni of the Graduate School of Comparative Literature and Comparative Culture at the University of Tokyo's Komaba campus (Japan's first and still only graduate school dedicated to comparative literature and culture), to be followed in short order by our slightly younger colleagues Kamei Shunsuke and Kobori Keiichirō. Starting with the program founder Shimada Kinji, it had long been the custom for students to honor a retiring professor with a Festschrift. However, that many retirements crowded so close together would have posed a burden for both the writers and the publisher. We decided to change course and instead have each retiree edit a collection of writings on topics of interest to him. That way, we could demonstrate to the academic world and the general reading public the progress that had been made since the university's publication twenty years earlier of a series entitled *Lectures on Comparative Literature* (*Kōza hikaku bungaku*, 1973–1976); we could also invite feedback. Kawamoto Kōji and Ōsawa Yoshihiro, whose retirements were still a ways off, ended up joining in the project as well.

When we presented this plan to my friend Hirabayashi Toshio, then editor in chief at Chūō Kōronsha, he quickly approved it and offered to do all the copy editing himself. There are six volumes in the series, starting with the one I edited. Each takes up an important issue that had been debated and developed on the Komaba campus ever since the graduate school was established in 1953: links between literature of East and West; the migration of patterns of thought; people's comings and goings; links between Japan's antiquity, middle ages, and early modern period; and prospects for a comparative cultural history of East and West. These are the other five volumes:

> Hirakawa Sukehiro, ed., *Ibunka o ikita hitobito*
> (*People Who Have Lived in Other Cultures*), 1993.
> Kamei Shunsuke, ed., *Kindai Nihon no hon'yaku bunka*
> (*Translation Culture of Early-Modern Japan*), 1994.
> Kobori Keiichirō, ed., *Tōzai no shisō tōsō*
> (*East-West Ideological Struggles*), 1994.
> Kawamoto Kōji, ed., *Uta to shi no keifu*
> (*Genealogy of* Uta *and* Shi), 1994.
> Ōsawa Yoshihiro, ed., *Tekusuto no hakken*
> (*Discovery of the Text*), 1994.

Some twenty scholars contributed to each volume, including students and professors of the university, international students, researchers from overseas, and assorted colleagues and friends in and out of the university. With an outstanding array of themes and contributors, the series is to this day a compelling read, full of the intellectual vigor of the "Komaba School," pioneers in the burgeoning academic field of comparative literature and comparative culture.

The volume I edited contains contributions from nineteen gifted young (at the time) scholars who wrote in a free-flowing, readable style about their discoveries: Endō Yasuo, Kasaya Kazuhiro (Nichibunken— International Research Center for Japanese Studies), Kim Tae-Joon (Korea), Yamauchi Masayuki, Kanō Takayo, Sugita Hideaki, Tanaka Yūko, Choi Park-Kwang (Korea), Komiya Akira, Koyano Atsushi, Shirahata Yōzaburō (Nichibunken), Yamashita Mayumi, Saeki Junko, Ikeda Mikiko, Fukuda Mahito, Nobuhiro Shinji, Ida Shin'ya, Yomota Inuhiko, and Imahashi Eiko. The list includes the first-ever Korean exchange students in the Society of Comparative Literature at Komaba, Kim and Choi; up-and-coming students of Arabic and Persian like Yamada and Sugita; and my new colleagues Kasaya and Shirahata on the faculty of Nichibunken in Kyoto, which I joined in 1992, a year before my scheduled retirement from the university. The book turned out to be an exhilarating and intense experience even for me, the editor, and remains a monument in the history of studies of Tokugawa Japan.

That book provoked an unexpected response that led directly to the present volume. I sent a complimentary copy to Kawakatsu Heita, who was then a professor at Waseda University, and he indicated that he had read my Foreword with great pleasure. In writing the essay, I wanted to reject outright the standard left-wing dismissal of the Tokugawa period as the dark ages and to present Tokugawa Japan as an independent, peaceful civilization different from the later Westernized Japan of Meiji and beyond. This approach resonated with Kawakatsu and earned his approval. He also liked the topics I discussed and their manner of presentation. Kawakatsu urged Yuhara Norifumi, an editor at Chikumashobo whom he knew well, to consider publishing the lengthy Foreword as a stand-alone book.

Yuhara negotiated with Hirabayashi Toshio of Chūō Kōronsha and was granted publication rights to the Foreword. Sometime around the end of the 1990s or the beginning of this century, the first galley proofs were delivered to me. That is now some fifteen or twenty years ago. In 1999, following my stint at Nichibunken, I became president of an art college in Kyoto, a position that proved so interesting and kept me so busy that those proofs lay neglected for a long time in a paper bag next to my desk.

In 2010, I stepped down as president of Kyoto University of the Arts and director of Okazaki Mindscape Museum to become director of the Shizuoka Prefectural Museum of Art. The invitation to head the Shizuoka museum came from none other than my old friend Kawakatsu Heita, who had left Waseda to become first a professor at Nichibunken, then the second president of the Shizuoka University of Art and Culture, and finally, in a leap, the governor of Shizuoka prefecture.

My move to Shizuoka came just as the city and the prefecture were preparing for the four hundredth anniversary of the death of Ieyasu, the first Tokugawa shogun, who died in Sumpu Castle in Suruga province (present-day Shizuoka prefecture) in 1616. I became chair of the Tokugawa Mirai Gakkai (Tokugawa Future Society), with Tokugawa Tsunenari, the eighteenth-generation head of the Tokugawa family, as honorary chair. I was then drawn into the activities of the prefecture's Chamber of Commerce and Industry (whose president was then Gotō Yasuo, chairman and co-CEO of Hagoromo Foods Corp.). I learned a great deal, but at the same time, as a very old student living on my own, I became quite exhausted.

Under my direction, the Shizuoka Prefectural Museum of Art naturally joined in this chain of activities promoting a reconsideration of the Tokugawa period. We decided to hold a large-scale special exhibition entitled "Pax Tokugawana: 250 Years of Beauty and Wisdom," to run for over six weeks, from September to November 2016. As museum director, I would draw up the basic design of the planned exhibition, and the work of collecting and displaying the works involved would fall to Izumi Mari, the head of the Fine Arts Division, and curator Noda Asami. Preparations got underway some two years before the exhibition was to open.

In the course of planning, I remembered my old essay on the Pax

Tokugawana and had Chūō Kōron provide two copies, which I gave to Izumi and Noda so that they would understand my longstanding approach to the Tokugawa period.

Both women, especially Izumi Mari, responded with enthusiasm, which naturally made this aged student happy. Izumi specializes in the study of medieval and early modern screen paintings of all sorts, and she has written several splendid works including *Medieval Paintings Clothed in Light* (*Hikari o matō chūsei kaiga*, 2007) and *Studies of Medieval Screen Paintings* (*Chūsei byōbu-e kenkyū*, 2013). In both of those books, she examines *yamato-e* screens of the Heian and Muromachi periods, providing detailed interpretations bolstered by meticulous research and observation as well as her rich sensitivity and imagination; she also offers solid explanations of social mores and views of nature reflected in the paintings. Her approach: is marked by breadth and precision, something unusual among recent Japanese art historians, and her writing is pleasantly supple; I thought the expression "clothed in light" was particularly felicitous. In autumn 2014, the year I recruited her for the Shizuoka museum, *Studies of Medieval Screen Paintings* was awarded the Kokka Prize, the highest honor in the field of Japanese art history.

When I let on to Izumi and Noda that Chikumashobo had expressed interest in publishing a revised edition of my Foreword, they urged me to bring it out in time for the upcoming exhibition in 2016—switching from their usual stern tone with me to offer warm encouragement. And so the work I had begun with Yuhara all those years ago was revived. However, my declining efficiency delayed publication until autumn 2017.

In this way, this study of Tokugawa peace has a significant bond with Shizuoka prefecture, from Governor Kawakatsu Heita and Fine Arts Director Izumi Mari to the various events commemorating the four hundredth anniversary of Ieyasu's death. But as I have been at pains to point out in this book, in the chapter on Buson and elsewhere, the idea of reimagining the civilization of Tokugawa Japan as the Pax Tokugawana has been with me ever since my days as an international student at Princeton University in the mid-1960s. Over the years, that vision has been steadily corroborated and developed. The term "Pax Tokugawana" appears frequently in essays and articles I wrote after returning from Princeton.

In 1975, I became the first Japanese researcher at the Woodrow Wilson International Center for Scholars in Washington, D.C., and the following autumn, in my final presentation, entitled "Eighteenth-century Japan and the World of Western Europe," I offered fervent praise of the peace of the Japanese islands afloat on the sea, so elegantly depicted in the *seigaiha* pattern of layered concentric circles representing calm waves; people had lived there surrounded by art, far removed from a West preoccupied by enlightenment and social upheaval, revolution and war. I closed my talk by touching on the end of that time of peace with a quotation from *The History of the Decline and Fall of the Roman Empire* by Edward Gibbons (1776–1788), which had just been the subject of a symposium at the Wilson Center marking the book's two hundredth anniversary.

In the mid-1980s, at the invitation of Umehara Takeshi, I joined the preparatory committee for the establishment of Nichibunken in Kyoto. We met in the National Museum of Ethnology in Senri, Osaka. There was discussion about what themes for collaborative research the proposed center should pursue, and various suggestions were made. I hastened to suggest the Pax Tokugawana and explained the concept. The committee chair Umesao Tadao then revealed that he had once proposed that very theme, long ago. That was the beginning of a battle over what to prioritize. In support of my idea, I presented the results of research I had been carrying on since my days at Princeton, and I believe my view carried the day. Around that same time, I was tasked with explaining the purpose of Nichibunken to members of the Diet Committee on Literature in Tokyo, headed by Santō Akiko, and I brought up the Pax Tokugawana there as well. Umehara, the prospective director of the center, cautioned me, "If you go around talking about peace all the time, people may suspect you of being left-wing, so watch out." That, too, is a fond memory unique to that era.

A bit before those events, from April through September of 1983, every Thursday evening I gave a forty-five-minute lecture for the NHK Citizen University. This was a new experience for me, involving the hard labor of both writing the textbook and recording videos for broadcast. With my theme, "A Comparative Cultural History of Edo," I fleshed out ideas that I have included in this book, supplementing my talks with artistic images and literary passages that I read aloud. I must take this opportunity to fondly recall and sincerely thank Yamamoto Sanshirō, the director of that highly enjoyable long-run program.

This Afterword has stretched on, but I must also offer deep thanks to the many fellow students and friends, old and new, who encouraged, aided, and accompanied me on the journey to bring about the publication of this book.

It has been my longstanding habit to compose my articles and essays in my study, starting late at night and working until dawn. That is why my room is called Shokōsai, "Dawn Study." In the mornings, when I had almost finished writing a manuscript, my late wife Tomoko used to come down from the second floor, look into my study, and say, "You still haven't gone to bed, have you?" Then she would make me a soft-boiled egg or two and bring it in, along with a pot of freshly-brewed tea. It tasted wonderful. I can never forget her patience and kindness, and I dedicate this book, in which much of my personal history is entwined, to her.

Shokōsai
Komagome, Tokyo
May 2017

REFERENCES

Abe Jirō. *Tokugawa jidai no geijutsu to shakai*. In *Abe Jirō zenshū*, vol. 8. Kadokawa shoten, 1961.

Bing, Siegfried, ed. *Le Japon artistique*. The Society for the Study of Japonaiserie, trans. Bijutsu kōronsha, 1981.

Bitō Masahide. *Edo jidai to wa nanika: Nihon shijō no kinsei to kindai*. Iwanami shoten, 1992.

Craig, Albert M., ed. *Japan: A Comparative View*. Princeton: Princeton University Press, 1979.

Fujikawa Hideo. *Edo kōki no shijintachi*. Heibonsha Tōyō bunko, 2012.

———. *Kan Chazan to Rai Sanyō*. Heibonsha Tōyō bunko, 1971.

Fujioka Sakutarō. *Kinsei kaiga shi*. Perikansha, 1983.

Haga Kōshirō. *Kinsei bunka no keisei to dentō*. Kawade shobō, 1948.

Haga Tōru, ed. *Sugita Gempaku, Hiraga Gennai, Shiba Kōkan*. In *Nihon no meicho*, vol. 22. Chūō kōronsha, 1971.

———. *Hiraga Gennai*. Asahi sensho, 1989.

———. *Midaregami no keifu*. Kōdansha gakujutsu bunko, 1988.

———. *Shi no kuni, shijin no kuni*. Chikuma shobō, 1997.

———. *Watanabe Kazan, yasashii tabibito*. Tankōsha, 1974.

———. *Yosa Buson no chiisana sekai*. Chūkō bunko, 1988.

Hall, John W. and Marius B. Jansen, eds. *Tokugawa shakai to kindaika*. Miyamoto Mataji and Shimbo Hiroshi, eds. and trans. Minerva shobō, 1973.

Hamada Giichirō. *Ōta Nampo*. Yoshikawa kōbunkan jimbutsu sōsho, 1963.

Hara Katsurō. *Nihon chūseishi*. Kōdansha gakujutsu bunko, 1978.

Hass, Robert, ed. and trans. *The Essential Haiku: Versions of Bashō, Buson, and Issa*. Hopewell, NJ: Ecco Press, 1994.

Hattori Yukio. *Kabuki seiritsu no kenkyū*. Kazama shobō, 1980.

Hayakawa Monda. *Yashoku Rōdaizu: Onore ga jinsei no hyōshō*. In *E wa kataru*, vol. 12. Heibonsha, 1994.

Hayashi Susumu. *Sōtatsu kaiga no kaishakugaku: "Fūjin Raijin-zu byōbu" no Raijin wa naze shiroi no ka*. Keibunsha, 2016.

Hiraga Gennai. *Fūrai Sanjin shū.* Nakamura Yukihiko, ed. In *Nihon koten bungaku taikei,* vol. 44. Iwanami shoten, 1961.

Hirakawa Arata. "Zen kindai no gaikō to kokka: Kokka no yakuwari o kangaeru." In *Nihon shigaku no furontia 1: Rekishi no jikū o toinaosu.* Hōsei daigaku shuppankai, 2015.

Huizinga, Johan. *Homo rūdensu.* Takahashi Hideo, trans. Chūō kōronsha, 1973.

Iijima Isamu and Suzuki Susumu. *Taiga Buson.* In *Suiboku bijutsu taikei,* vol. 12. Kōdansha, 1977.

Inoue Tadashi. *Kaibara Ekiken.* Yoshikawa kōbunkan jimbutsu sōsho, 1963.

Ishikawa Eisuke. *Edo kūkan: 100 man toshi no genkei.* Hyōronsha, 1993.

Ishikawa Jun. *Watanabe Kazan.* Chikuma sōsho, 1964.

Iwamoto Sashichi, ed. "Shizu no odamaki." In *Ensaki jisshu,* vol. 1. Kokusho kankōkai, 1907.

Jansen, Marius B., ed. *Nihon ni okeru kindaika no mondai.* Hosoya Chihiro, ed. and trans. Iwanami shoten, 1968.

Kaempfer, Engelbert. *Edo sampu ryokō nikki.* Saitō Makoto, ed. and trans. Heibonsha Tōyō bunko, 1977.

———. *Kemperu Edo sampu kikō.* Kure Shūzō, ed. and trans. 2 vols. Yūshōdō, 1966.

———. *Kemperu no mita Tokugawa Japan.* Josef Kreiner, ed. and trans. Rokkō shuppan, 1992,

———. *Kaempfer's Japan: Tokugawa Culture Observed.* Beatrice Bodart-Bailey, ed. and trans. Honolulu: University of Hawaii Press, 1999.

———. *Nihonshi.* Imai Tadashi, ed. and trans. 2 vols. Kasumigaseki shuppan, 1973.

Kaibara Ekiken. *Ekiken zenshū.* Ekikenkai, ed. Kyoto: Ekiken zenshū kankōbu, 1910–1911.

Kawakatsu Heita. *Nihon bummei to kindai Seiyō: Sakoku saikō.* NHK Books, 1991.

Kawatake Toshio. *Kabuki.* Tokyo daigaku shuppankai, 2001.

Keene, Donald. *Nihonjin no Seiyō hakken.* Haga Tōru, trans. Chūkō bunko, 1992.

———. *Watanabe Kazan.* Kakuchi Yukio, trans. Shinchōsha, 2007.

Kimura Yōjirō. *Nachurarisuto no keifu: Kindai seibutsugaku no seiritsushi.* Chūkō shinsho, 1983.

———. *Nihon hakubutsushi no seiritsu: Rangaku to honzōgaku.* Chūō kōronsha, 1974.

Kira Sueo, Yamashita Kazumi, Maruyama Kazuhiko, and Matsuo Yasuaki, eds. and trans. *Kinsei haiku haibun shū.* In *Shimpen Nihon koten bungaku zenshū,* vol. 72. Shōgakukan, 2001.

Kobayashi Tadashi. *Edo kaigashi ron.* Ruri shobō, 1983.

———. *Harunobu.* Sanseisha Tōyō bijutsu sensho, 1970.

Kobori Keiichirō. *Sakoku no shisō: Kemperu no sekaishiteki shimei.* Chūkō shinsho, 1974.

Kojima Michihiro. *Rakuchū rakugai-zu byōbu: Tsukurareta 'Kyoto' o yomitoku.* Yoshikawa kōbunkan, 2016.

Kōno Motoaki. *Rimpa: Hibikiau bi.* Kyoto: Shibunkaku shuppan, 2015.

Kuki Shūzō. *Iki no kōzō.* Iwanami bunko, 1979.

Kumakura Isao. *Go-Mizunoo-in.* Asahi shimbunsha, 1982.

————. *Rimpa meihin hyakusen*. Nihon keizai shimbunsha, 1996.

Yamashita Kazumi, et al. *Temmei haikai shū*. In *Shin Nihon koten bungaku taikei*, vol. 73. Iwanami shoten, 1998.

Yosa Buson. *Buson haiku shū*. Ogata Tsutomu, ed. Iwanami bunko, 1989.

————. *Buson zenku shū*. Fujita Shin'ichi and Kiyoto Noriko, eds. Ōfū, 2000.

————. *Collected Haiku of Yosa Buson*. W.S. Merwin and Takako Lento, trans. Port Townsend, WA: Copper Canyon Press, 2013.

————. *Yosa Buson shū*. Shimizu Takayuki, ed. In *Shinchō Nihon koten shūsei*. Shinchōsha, 1979.

————. *Yosa Buson zenshū*. In *Nihon koten zensho*, Ebara Taizō and Shimizu Takayuki, eds. Asahi shimbunsha, 1957.

Yoshino Sakuzō. *Arai Hakuseki to Yowan Shirōte*. Bunka seikatsu kenkyūkai, 1924.

CHRONOLOGY

1521	Machida version, *Scenes in and around Kyoto* (*Rakuchū rakugai zu*), oldest extant example of the genre, completed around this time.
1543	Portuguese arrive on Tanegashima and introduce muskets to Japan.
1550	Francisco Xavier propagates Christianity in Yamaguchi.
1552	Residents of Kamigyō and Shimogyō (upper and lower) Kyoto perform *kanjin sarugaku*, a form of temple solicitation, at Hokkedō Hall ruins (Minamoto Yoritomo's grave).
1560	Oda Nobunaga defeats Imagawa Yoshimoto in battle of Okehazama.
1565	Uesugi version, *Scenes in and around Kyoto* by Kanō Eito, completed around this time.
1571	Nobunaga burns down Enryakuji temple on Mt. Hiei in Kyoto.
1573	Nobunaga drives Ashikaga Yoshiaki from Kyoto. Muromachi shogunate ends.
1574	Nobunaga presents Kanō Eitoku's screen paintings to Uesugi Kenshin.
1575	Combined forces of Nobunaga and Tokugawa Ieyasu defeat Takeda Katsuyori at Nagashino.
1582	Nobunaga (b. 1534) commits suicide at Honnōji temple in Kyoto.
1587	Toyotomi Hideyoshi holds Grand Kitano Tea Ceremony at Kitano Tenjin Shrine. Jurakudai Palace completed.
1590	Hideyoshi subdues northeast Japan, unifies the country.
1591	Sen no Rikyū (b. 1522) commits suicide at Jurakudai Palace, at Hideyoshi's command.

1595	Great Buddha Hall at Hōkōji temple virtually completed.
1598	Hideyoshi (b. 1536) dies in Fushimi Castle.
1600	English navigator William Adams (1564–1620) of the *Liefde*, part of a fleet owned by the precursor of the Dutch East India Company, meets with Ieyasu; later, as "Miura Anjin," becomes his diplomatic advisor. Ieyasu's Eastern Army defeats Ishida Mitsunari's Western Army at Sekigahara.
1603	Ieyasu becomes *seii taishōgun* (barbarian-quelling generalissimo); establishes Tokugawa shogunate in Edo. Okuni of Izumo performs "kabuki dance" in Kyoto.
1604	Kyoto townsfolk dance *furyū odori* (circle dancing) at a special festival in memory of Hideyoshi.
1605	Ieyasu abdicates and moves to Sumpu as retired shogun or Ōgosho. His third son, Hidetada (1579–1632), takes over as second Tokugawa shogun.
1606	Suminokura Ryōi (1544–1614) opens Ōi River west of Kyoto for navigation.
1607	Korean mission meets with Hidetada in Edo, Ieyasu in Sumpu.
1610	Ieyasu sends Kyoto merchant Tanaka Shōsuke and others to Mexico, making them first Japanese to cross the Pacific.
1611	Suminokura Ryōi applies to shogunate for permission to construct a canal in Kyoto, known as Takase River.
1614	Ieyasu orders winter siege of Osaka.
1615	In summer siege, Osaka Castle falls; Toyotomi clan is wiped out, ending opposition to Tokugawa regime. Ieyasu grants Takagamine, land northwest of Kyoto, to Hon'ami Kōetsu, who uses it to construct an artists' community.
1616	Funaki version, *Scenes in and around Kyoto* completed around this time. Ieyasu (b. 1543) dies in Sumpu and is buried in Kunō-zan Tōshōgu Shrine.
1617	Korean mission meets with Hidetada in Fushimi Castle.
1620	Hidetada's daughter Kazuko becomes empress consort of Emperor Go-Mizunoo (1596–1680). Construction of Katsura Detached Palace starts in summer, completed in 1624.
1622	In Nagasaki, fifty-five Japanese Christians executed in Great Genna Martyrdom.
1623	Hidetada abdicates. His second son, Iemitsu (1604–1651), becomes third shogun. Britain closes Hirado trading post and withdraws from Japan.

1626	Kanō Tan'yū (1602–1674) paints sliding partitions in Nijō Castle, Kyoto.

1626 Kanō Tan'yū (1602–1674) paints sliding partitions in Nijō Castle, Kyoto.

1629 Daitoku-ji monk Takuan Sōhō and others are exiled in Purple Robes Incident, as shogunate asserts authority over court and clergy. Shogunate forbids female participation in dancing and kabuki.

1630 Tawaraya Sōtatsu copies imperial scroll set *Life of Saigyō* (*Saigyō hōshi gyōjō ekotoba*). Screen paintings *Famous spots in Edo* (*Edo meisho-zu byōbu*) completed.

1635 Shogunate forbids Japanese people to go abroad or return. Laws for Military Houses (*buke shohattō*) are revised. System of alternate attendance in Edo (*sankin kōtai*) established for all daimyo.

1636 First Korean embassy comes to Japan and has an audience with Iemitsu.

1637 Hon'ami Kōetsu (b. 1558) dies in Kyoto. Shimabara Rebellion takes place in present-day Nagasaki prefecture.

1639 Shogunate forbids Portuguese ships to call, completing official policy of national seclusion.

1641 Shogunate forbids *furyū odori*. Dutch trading post moves from Hirado to Dejima, in Nagasaki.

1643 Second Korean embassy has an audience with Iemitsu.

1651 Coup attempt by Yui Shōsetsu and other ronin (Keian Uprising). Iemitsu's eldest son, Ietsuna (1641–1680), becomes fourth shogun.

1652 Shogunate forbids "young-man" kabuki (*wakashū kabuki*).

1653 Shogunate authorizes resumption of kabuki using adult male actors (*yarō kabuki*).

1655 Third Korean embassy offers congratulations on Ietsuna's succession.

1657 Great Fire of Meireki destroys much of Edo, including towers on Edo Castle.

1662 Confucian educator Itō Jinsai founds a private school, Kogidō, by Hori River in Kyoto.

1671 Kawamura Zuiken opens the Eastern Circuit, a coastal shipping route, followed by the Western Circuit in 1672.

1680 Iemitsu's fourth son, Tsunayoshi (1646–1709), lord of Tatebayashi domain in Ueno province (150,000 *koku*), becomes fifth shogun. Establishes state-run school Yushima Seidō and promotes government by law and reason. Laws of Compassion (*Shōrui awaremi no rei*) mandate protection of animals.

1681	Artists' community in Takagamine disbands.
1682	Fourth Korean embassy offers congratulations on Tsunayoshi's succession.
1684	Jōkyō lunisolar calendar is developed and will be adopted in 1685.
1688	Genroku era begins.
1689	Matsuo Bashō sets out on "narrow road to deep north," returning to Ōgaki six months later.
1690	German naturalist Engelbert Kaempfer (1651–1716) arrives in Nagasaki as physician for Dutch factory; visits Edo in spring 1691 and 1692.
1692	Kaempfer sets sail from Nagasaki, returning home after a ten-year absence.
1694	Kamo Aoi Festival is revived. Bashō (b. 1644) dies in Osaka.
1702	Revenge of forty-seven ronin: Ōishi Yoshio and others avenge two-year-prior death of their lord by killing Kira Yoshinaka.
1704	Ogata Kōrin paints a portrait of Nakamura Kuranosuke. Genroku era ends.
1705	Itō Jinsai (b. 1627) dies in Kyoto.
1707	Mt. Fuji erupts.
1709	Tokugawa Tsunatoyo (1662–1712), eldest son of Tsunashige, lord of the Kōfu domain and grandson of third shogun Iemitsu, becomes sixth shogun, Ienobu. In November and December, Arai Hakuseki interviews Italian Jesuit Giovanni Batista Sidotti, who had sneaked into the country. Kaibara Ekiken publishes *Japanese Herbal* (*Yamato honzō*).
1711	Fifth Korean embassy offers congratulations on succession of Shogun Ienobu. Arai Hakuseki reforms ritual protocols.
1714	Kaibara Ekiken (b. 1630) dies.
1716	Ogata Kōrin (b. 1658) dies in Kyoto. Tokugawa Yoshimune (1684–1751), lord of the Kii domain, becomes eighth shogun; promotes Kyōhō Reforms and loosens restrictions on Western learning.
1719	Sixth Korean embassy offers congratulations on Yoshimune's succession.
1728	Ogyū Sorai (b. 1666) dies in Edo.
1748	Ieshige, ninth shogun, receives seventh Korean embassy.
1751	Yosa Buson moves to Kyoto.

1763   Hiraga Gennai publishes *Classification of Various Materials* (*Butsurui hinshitsu*) in Edo; four months later, publishes his first *gesaku* novels: *Rootless Weeds* (*Nenashigusa*) and *The Tale of Dashing Shidōken* (*Fūryū shidōken den*).

1764   Ieharu, tenth shogun, receives eighth Korean embassy.

1765   Suzuki Harunobu creates *nishiki-e*, polychrome woodblock prints.

1768   First edition of *Record of Heian Notables* (*Heian jimbutsu-shi*) published.

1770   Buson assumes pen name of his former teacher, Yahantei. Itō Jakuchū begins series of hanging scrolls entitled *Colorful Realm of Living Beings* (*Dōshoku sai-e*).

1771   Sugita Gempaku, Maeno Ryōtaku, and Nakagawa Jun'an attend human dissection at execution ground in Senjū Kotsugahara and decide to translate Dutch book of anatomy *Ontleedkundige Tafelen*. Buson and Taiga collaborate on landscape series based on Chinese poems *Ten Conveniences and Ten Pleasures* (*Jūben jūgi*). Hungarian officer Maurice Benyovsky (a.k.a. Hambengorō) escapes from Kamchatka prison, makes his way to Amami-Ōshima, and falsely reports to Dutch in Nagasaki that Russia plans to invade Ezochi (Hokkaido).

1772   Tanuma Okitsugu (1719–1788) promoted from acting senior counselor to senior counselor.

1774   Sugita Gempaku, Nakagawa Jun'an, Katsuragawa Hoshū, and others publish their translation from Dutch, *A New Book of Anatomy* (*Kaitai shinsho*). Odano Naotake provides anatomical sketches.

1775   Swedish naturalist Carl Thunberg (1743–1828) arrives in Japan and becomes head surgeon at Dutch trading post; following spring, visits the shogun's court in Edo.

1776   Ike no Taiga (b. 1723) dies in Kyoto. Ueda Akinari publishes *Tales of Spring Rain* (*Ugetsu monogatari*). Hiraga Gennai invents *erekiteru* (static electricity generator). United States Declaration of Independence adopted on July 4.

1777   Buson publishes collection *Midnight Melodies* (*Yahanraku*) containing long poems "Spring Breeze on the Kema Embankment" (*Shumpū batei kyoku*) and "Yodo River Songs" (*Dengaka*).

1779   Hiraga Gennai (b. 1728) dies in Edo prison.

1781   Kan Chazan opens a private academy in Kannabe, Bingo province.

1783   Mt. Asama erupts, crops fail, famine spreads. Buson (b. 1713) dies in Kyoto.

1787   Matsudaira Sadanobu (1758–1829) becomes senior counselor.

1789	French Revolution.
1790	Kansei Edict forbids teaching of any ideology but Neo-Confucianism of Zhu Xi at Shōheikō academy.
1791	Hayashi Shihei publishes *Defense of a Maritime Nation* (*Kaikoku heidan*) in Sendai.
1792	Matsudaira Sadanobu destroys Hayashi's printing blocks and sentences him to house arrest. Russian emissary Adam Kirillovich Laxman lands at Nemuro in Hokkaido seeking to open trade, accompanied by former castaway Daikokuya Kōdayū.
1797	Shōheikō academy, run by Hayashi family, is renamed Shōhei-zaka Gakumonjo and brought under central control.
1798	Motoori Norinaga writes *Kojikiden*, a commentary on *Kojiki* (712).
1800	Itō Jakuchū (b. 1716) dies in Kyoto.
1804	Russian fleet carrying minister plenipotentiary Nikolai Petrovich Rezanov arrives in Nagasaki seeking to open trade. Napoleon Bonaparte becomes emperor of France.
1805	Russians depart in failure. Admiral Nelson's British fleet defeats Franco-Spanish fleet at Trafalgar. Napoleon's planned invasion of Britain fails.
1808	British frigate HMS *Phaeton* enters Nagasaki Harbor, seeking to take over the Dutch factory as the Netherlands have become French territory.
1811	Ninth and final Korean embassy arrives in Tsushima.
1812	Napoleon's army invades Russia and is defeated. Two years later, Napoleon abdicates.
1815	Napoleon is defeated at Waterloo and exiled to the island of Saint Helena, where he dies in 1821.
1817	Sugita Gempaku (b. 1732) dies.
1819	Britain occupies Singapore.
1821	Inō Tadataka's *Maps of Japan's Coastal Area* (*Dai Nihon enkai yochi zenzu*) presented to shogunate.
1825	Shogunate issues Edict to Repel Foreign Vessels.
1827	Kan Chazan (b. 1748) dies. Rai San'yō presents *Unofficial History of Japan* (*Nihon gaishi*) to Matsudaira Sadanobu.
1832	Rai San'yō (b. 1780) dies in Kyoto.

1833	Great Tempō Famine begins.
1837	Ōshio Heihachirō leads attack on wealthy Osaka merchants (Ōshio Rebellion) and ends up committing suicide.
1839	Watanabe Kazan sentenced to house arrest, Takano Chōei to life imprisonment in crackdown known as Suppression of the Barbarian Studies Group (*bansha no goku*). Friction between Qing dynasty and Britain over opium imports increases in Canton. Viceroy Lin Zexu halts opium trade. Opium War heats up.
1841	Watanabe Kazan (b. 1793) commits suicide at home in Tahara. Britain occupies Hong Kong.
1842	Treaty of Nanking opens Canton, Shanghai, Fuzhou, and other Chinese cities to trade.
1853	United States Commodore Matthew Perry's East India Squadron arrives in Uraga, seeking to open trade. Expedition of Russian Admiral Ycvfimiy Putyatin arrives in Nagasaki.
1854	Convention of Kanagawa signed with the United States, shogunate's first treaty with any Western power.
1855	Institute for Study of Barbarian Books (Bansho Shirabesho) established in Edo, Naval Training Center (Kaigun Denshūsho) in Nagasaki.
1856	Kōbusho military academy (later Gunkan Sōrenjo) established in Tsukiji, Edo.
1858	Treaty of Amity and Commerce signed with the United States in July. Umeda Umpin, former retainer of Obama domain, captured; Ansei Purge begins. Treaties of amity and commerce signed with Britain, the Netherlands, and Russia in August.
1860	Japanese warship *Kanrin Maru* crosses Pacific Ocean, to San Francisco and back. Shogunate's embassy to the United States sets sail from Edo Bay aboard a United States Navy ship; travels by Panama Railway to Washington, D.C. to ratify Treaty of Friendship, Commerce, and Navigation; returns by way of Atlantic and Indian Oceans. (Other embassies follow: to Europe in 1862; to France in 1864, 1865, and 1867; and to Russia in 1866. Shogunate sends students to the Netherlands in 1862, to Russia in 1865, and to Britain in 1866.) Ii Naosuke assassinated outside Sakurada Gate of Edo Castle.
1861	Kazu-no-miya, daughter of Emperor Ninkō, journeys to Edo to wed Shogun Iemochi.
1863	Sanjō Sanetomi and other court nobles siding with "Expel the Barbarians" faction expelled from Kyoto.

1864   Extremists from Chōshū domain try to seize control of Kyoto Imperial Palace, are stopped by Satsuma and Aizu forces (Kimmon Rebellion or Hamaguri Gate Incident).

1866   Satsuma-Chōshū Alliance is formed. At year's end, Tokugawa Yoshinobu becomes fifteenth and final Tokugawa shogun.

1867   Yoshinobu announces return of power to the emperor. At year's end, Meiji Emperor issues formal edict declaring restoration of imperial rule.

1868   Battle of Toba-Fushimi at first of new year marks beginning of Boshin War. Charter Oath establishes basic policies of new government. Era name changes to Meiji.

1869   Emperor goes to Tokyo and convenes Great Council of State (Daijō-kan), making Tokyo the new capital. Enomoto Takeaki's anti-government forces surrender in Hakodate, ending Boshin War.

1871   Domain system is abolished. Iwakura Embassy to the United States and Europe sets sail from Yokohama, to return in 1873. Fifty or so mission members are joined by over fifty male and female students.

INDEX

Photographed by Haga Mitsuru

About the Author

Born in Yamagata in 1931, Haga Tōru earned his B.A. and doctorate in literature from the University of Tokyo. A professor emeritus at the University of Tokyo and the International Research Center for Japanese Studies, he was also visiting researcher at Princeton University, Woodrow Wilson International Center for Scholars fellow, president of Kyoto University of the Arts, the director of both the Okazaki Mindscape Museum and Shizuoka Prefectural Museum of Art, and a member of the Japan Academy. He died in 2020.

Haga's many distinguished publications include: *Watanabe Kazan, yasashii tabibito* (Watanabe Kazan, Gentle Traveler), *Yosa Buson no chiisana sekai* (The Small World of Yosa Buson), *Shi no kuni, shijin no kuni* (Land of Songs, Land of Bards), and *Hiraga Gennai* (Hiraga Gennai).

About the Translator

Juliet Winters Carpenter is a professor emerita of English at Doshisha Women's College of Liberal Arts. She received the Japan-US Friendship Commission Prize for the Translation of Japanese Literature in 1980 for *Secret Rendezvous* by Abe Kōbō and again in 2014 for *A True Novel* by Mizumura Minae. Carpenter's other recent translations include *An I-Novel* by Mizumura Minae, *At the End of the Matinee.* by Hirano Keiichirō, and *The Kidai Shōran Scroll* by Ozawa Hiromu and Kobayashi Tadashi. After more than 45 years in Japan, she and her husband now live on Whidbey Island in Washington state.

〈英文版〉文明としての徳川日本　一六〇三―一八五三年
Pax Tokugawana: The Cultural Flowering of Japan, 1603–1853

2021年3月27日　第1刷発行

著　者　　芳賀　徹
訳　者　　ジュリエット・ウィンターズ・カーペンター
発行所　　一般財団法人 出版文化産業振興財団
　　　　　〒101-0051 東京都千代田区神田神保町2-2-30
　　　　　電話　03-5211-7283
　　　　　ホームページ　https://www.jpic.or.jp/

印刷・製本所　　公和印刷株式会社

定価はカバーに表示してあります。